THE COOK'S GARDEN

THE COOK'S GARDEN
Lynda Brown

A Jill Norman Book

CENTURY
London   Sydney   Auckland   Johannesburg

First published in 1990 by Random Century Group,
20 Vauxhall Bridge Road, London SW1V 2SA

Random Century Group (Australia) Pty Ltd,
20 Alfred Street, Milsons Point, Sydney, New South Wales 2061, Australia

Random Century Group New Zealand Ltd,
PO Box 40–086, Glenfield, Auckland 10, New Zealand

Random Century Group South Africa (Pty) Ltd,
PO Box 337, Bergvlei, 2012 South Africa

British Library Cataloguing in Publication Data
Brown, Lynda
    The cook's garden.
    1. Gardens. Vegetables. Cultivation. Manuals   2. Food:
Vegetable dishes. Recipes
    I. Title
    635

ISBN 0–7126–3821–0

Illustrations by Tracey Joanne Ramsdale
Design by Judy Linard
Typeset by Speedset Ltd, Ellesmere Port
Printed and bound in Great Britain by
Butler and Tanner, London and Frome

For Rick,
with fond memories of gardens enjoyed and meals shared

Contents

Acknowledgements and sources 11
Introduction 13
Spring 25
Summer 69
Autumn 153
Winter 219
Bibliography 245
Index 251

Until you have done so yourself, you can have no conception what a different thing a vegetable is from your own garden as compared to that bought from a shop. And what a different thing a freshly-dug or picked vegetable is from one that has been kept. You readers with kitchen gardens are lucky people if you like your food.

Ambrose Heath, *From Garden to Kitchen*, 1937

No occupation is so delightful to me as the culture of the earth, and no culture comparable to that of the garden. Such a variety of subjects, some one always coming to perfection, the failure of one thing repaired by the success of another, and instead of one harvest a continued one through the year. Under a total want of demand except for our family table, I am still devoted to the garden. But though an old man, I am but a young gardener.

Thomas Jefferson, 1811

Acknowledgements and Sources

Many authors and publishers have kindly allowed me to print various recipes and extracts; they are clearly set out in the book; my sincere thanks to all. Likewise to the *Daily Telegraph* and *Times* newspapers where some of the recipes were first printed. I should also like to thank the staff at Skipton library who have conscientiously responded to a flood of requests over the past two years with great cheerfulness and patience. Particular thanks also to the library at Rothamsted Experimental Station, Harpenden, for generously supplying me with photocopies of rare pamphlets not easily accessible; to the staff at the Royal Botanic Gardens, Kew, and the National Vegetable Research Station, who both gave me considerable assistance with my queries; also to Harold McGee.

To Alan Davidson I owe a general debt and heartfelt gratitude for time and talk freely given; for allowing me access to the vegetable section of his yet unpublished *Oxford Companion to Food*, particular thanks.

Lastly, I should like to pay tribute to the two people without whom this book would not have borne fruit. First, and most importantly, my husband, Rick, a gardener of considerable talent. It is his good gardening sense which has made this book possible; and secondly, my editor, Jill Norman, whose knowledge and gentle thoroughness shines throughout: I count myself doubly blessed.

A select bibliography is included at the back of the book. Here I wish to acknowledge those books I have found especially useful and rewarding. The first is Jane Grigson's *Vegetable Book*. During the three years I have spent writing this book, it has never left my side and has been a constant companion in the kitchen for many years more. There is no better vegetable cookery book. Another book I have drawn on greatly is Joy Larkcom's *The Salad Garden*. Again, it is without peer for those who are interested in growing a range of salad plants. As a source of ideas for vegetable cookery generally, I would also refer you to those books written by Colin Spencer, and to both Madhur Jaffrey's *Eastern Vegetarian Cooking* and Julie Sahni's *Classic Indian Vegetarian Cooking*. In a different vein, but for anyone who shares a scientific curiosity about food, Harold McGee's excellent book, *On Food and Cooking*, is an invaluable addition to any cookery library.

On the historical side, two books are to be particularly recommended. The first is *The Gardener's Dictionary*, by Phillip Miller, first published in 1731. A fascimile of the 1754 edition, the one I have, is available through specialist booksellers or can be borrowed from public libraries. Philip Miller was one of our great gardeners who became head gardener of the Chelsea Physic Garden in 1722, remaining there until a year before his death at the age of 80 in 1770. His book became a standard reference work for many generations.

The second is *The Encyclopaedia of Gardening*, first published in 1821 by another eminent horticulturist, J. C. Loudon. This became a successor to Philip Miller's book. It too is available from specialist booksellers or through public libraries. J. C. Loudon was a man of indefatigable energies who travelled, worked and wrote tirelessly, despite enduring great physical hardships towards the end of his life. He was a great cottage gardener as well as plantsman, and published the first gardening magazine. Both books are absorbing for their historical interest and contain a wealth of information still relevant today.

Finally, *The Vegetable Garden* by M. M. Vilmorin-Andrieux, published in English in 1859, and available in facsimile, contains comprehensive descriptions of old varieties in addition to much useful information on growing vegetables. Of contemporary books, the account of the last great kitchen garden to be to cultivated in England until 1986 at Cottesbrooke in Northants, *Cottesbrooke, an English Kitchen Garden*, by Susan Campbell, is also to be thoroughly recommmended.

Introduction

If I had to give advice to a new kitchen garden enthusiast, I should make three simple points. The first is not to be too ambitious. Gardening takes a lifetime to learn. It is far better to grow some of your own vegetables and enjoy your efforts, than to attempt self-sufficiency and fail. The second is to grow as wide a variety of produce as you reasonably can, especially the kind of things – unusual salad plants, herbs, different kinds of peas and beans, seakale – which are easily grown but not readily found in the shops. The third is to learn patience. A gardener needs to be an optimist: enjoy your successes and write off your failures.

There is no doubt that healthy well-grown garden vegetables have a sweetness, freshness and flavour that cannot be matched by those you buy. This is fact not fantasy. Home-grown produce offers the yardstick by which you can judge the true worth of a vegetable. There is no doubt also that growing your own produce is tremendously satisfying. For cooks, this is especially so. But perhaps most significant is the reassuring knowledge that what you grow is wholesome. Concern over chemical residues and modern horticultural practices is something shared by all of us who care about what we eat. Looked at from this perspective a kitchen garden, however modest, is becoming less of a luxury and more of a necessity.

It is important to share the pleasure of home-grown vegetables with others, because the more people are encouraged to grow even a little patch of herbs, the greater the collective appreciation of good vegetable taste will be. In time I hope this will lead to a demand for better quality vegetables in our shops. I remember visiting a small walled town in the Pays Basque, and marvelling at rows of leeks, onions, tomatoes and beans crammed into the smallest backyards, or raised in pots on balconies and overflowing into alleyways. Although I cannot prove it, I have a suspicion that one of the reasons the French and Italians are so knowledgeable and particular about buying vegetables is that most households still grow something for themselves, or have neighbours and friends who pass on a few tomatoes, the odd cabbage or bunch of radishes, thus keeping the link between kitchen and garden alive. Is it too idealistic to wish the same for everyone, country and city dweller alike?

All our gardens have been cooks' gardens, every nook and cranny filled with edible things of one kind or another. Historically, most kitchen gardens have been out of sight, fruit and vegetables considered a poor second to flowers and lawn. The 19th-century agriculturist William Cobbett is the only person I have read who thought otherwise and could see beauty in the kitchen garden. I agree with him. Visually, I find the kitchen garden immensely satisfying. I could never imagine any other kind of garden, nor would I want one.

This way of life is not always idyllic or convenient. Growing good vegetables takes experience and time. Eating from the garden also imposes its own discipline, meals shaped not by weekly visits to the supermarket but by what the garden has to offer. By and large, vegetables are enjoyed for a brief period only, following natural patterns rather than those dictated by supply and demand or what happens to be convenient – yet, 15 years later, I find myself still as enthusiastic. Nothing has helped me to appreciate food more.

Vegetables from the garden have a special place in our affections and appreciation of food. In writing this book I wanted to share the experience we have gained and the pleasure our kitchen gardens have brought. But I must confess another reason – it often puzzles me why so many gardeners do not cook, and so many cooks do not garden. A gardener will lavish consummate care on his vegetable plot, yet shed responsibility at the kitchen door. Similarly, there are many devoted and enthusiastic cooks who have no idea of how vegetables are grown and therefore little idea of when they are at their best, nor any knowledge of that special relationship which binds cook and garden together. This book is about forging that link. If, as a result of reading it, but one more gardener takes up cooking, and one more cook takes to gardening, I shall be content.

The book is arranged according to the four seasons, spring, summer, autumn and winter. This is conventional and convenient, but in some senses arbitrary.

For modern cooks, cushioned by supermarkets, freezers and food flown in from all corners of the world, seasons have lost much of their meaning. Though there may be much talk of cooking in season, and it is fashionable to do so, to a large extent the term has become academic. A woman I know was bemoaning the fact that she couldn't get the strawberries she wanted for Christmas – it has come to that. What is fresh these days may bear little resemblance to a plant's natural growth cycle, or to what is appropriate for the time of the year.

For the gardener, the opposite applies. When you grow your own food, your thoughts and meals become intertwined completely with the seasons. But the general assumption that the seasons fall neatly into four quarters, apportioning themselves three months apiece, is rarely borne out by reality. The vegetable harvest is dependent on the vagaries of regional weather, and on what is happening to the crops in your garden. For a cook-gardener, seasons are very personal. It is this individuality which makes the kitchen garden so appealing for the cook, for it both enriches and simplifies your approach to food. More than anything, to be in harmony with your food supply is something I have come to value greatly. It is the foundation of this book, and I hope I can convey something of its measure.

The balance between a gardening book and a cookery book is not easily achieved. Throughout, I have tried to give the kind of information which I think relevant to someone interested in getting the best from their home-grown produce. For this reason, growing details have been kept to a minimum, concentrating on those factors which in our experience make for success and which a gardener should look out for.

Inevitably a work of this kind cannot hope to be comprehensive. This has meant some hard decisions, for it was not possible to include all the vegetables and edible plants I would have liked. Omissions are governed also by what we grow at home, based on personal preferences, locality and soil. Gardeners anxious to find out about globe artichokes, sweetcorn or pumpkins will regrettably therefore need to consult other writers.

The majority of our gardening life has been spent in the north of England where winters are long, springs generally late, wet and cold, summers brief, and autumns often glorious. It is to this pattern we have had to adapt and plan. Gardeners living in sunnier or warmer parts of the country will obviously find our sowing and cropping dates later than theirs. They may also find some of our scheduling puzzling. For example, our broad beans arrive late, during early August. It is not that one *cannot* grow broad beans earlier than August in the north, but this is the pattern that suits us best, and which therefore I have recorded.

When it comes to selecting varieties for your own garden, the picture is rarely clear. A gardener needs to balance several factors, for how well a particular variety performs depends as much on growth conditions as on its inherent genetic qualities; and how well it grows may determine to a considerable extent its final flavour. This is why the same variety grown in one garden may well taste better than that grown in another. The only true test of a variety's worth is how it performs for you. So I have been sparing with recommendations. If a variety has been particularly successful for us, or is clearly, as in the case of Sweet 100 cherry tomatoes for example, an outstanding variety by any standards, I have included it. For general advice, I recommend you consult books by the gardening author Joy Larkcom, whose opinions are always reliable.

Gardening is a constant learning process. Each year throws up something new, forcing you to change your ideas, or modify how you grow and view a particular vegetable. Be prepared for this in your own ventures – and bear with us if sometimes your own experience differs from ours.

GROWING VEGETABLES

We grow our crops organically. No one seriously interested in eating good food would spray their crops with chemicals out of choice, or subject them to an impoverished soil. The premium that organic vegetables now command in the shops, and scientific studies which show that plants raised organically can have greater nutritional values, should provide an added impetus to new gardeners who have decided that growing their own food is best.

The extent of the commitment to an organic approach each gardener makes depends on individual philosophy and circumstances. For example, our current garden is plagued with slugs, for which as yet there is no reliable truly organic remedy. Those we have tried, including efforts to entice hedgehogs into the garden (which is not as easy as it sounds, even for rural folk), have failed. We are thus faced with the fact that if we did not use slug pellets, we would have very little food. It is an unpalatable compromise, one which causes me much personal disquiet, but in our present circumstances we feel it is necessary.

Growing organically is not difficult, and it makes sound gardening sense. Many books have now been written on the subject, some of which you will find listed in the bibliography. In addition, there is an organic gardener's magazine, and a National Centre for Organic Gardening at Ryton near Coventry. The organic gardeners' association, HDRA, of which Prince Charles is now patron, enjoys a membership of over 15,000. It has many local groups throughout the country, and offers its members help and advice. I have been a member for as long as we have gardened, and have found it invaluable. It publishes a quarterly newsletter and operates a mail order business for seeds and sundry supplies. Their address can be found at the end of the book.

For the last 10 years we have gardened using the deep bed method of cultivation. Anyone who watches 'Gardener's World' on BBC Television will need no introduction to this system. Essentially, it is a method of intensive cultivation. Instead of growing vegetables in long conventional flat rows, they are grown in wide, deeply dug beds usually measuring 4ft (1.2m) across by 12ft (4.8m) in length. A newly dug bed looks somewhat like a primitive burial mound. Digging raises the beds above the surrounding surface level, so they are slightly higher in the centre and slope down towards the sides. Paths, a minimum of 18in (45cm) wide, are left alongside and between the beds for access.

The initial labour involved is considerable. Each bed is first marked out to the required dimensions using rope. The whole area is then double-dug. Starting at one end, the soil is lifted from the first spit (a spade's depth) and set aside. This gives you a trench a spade's width. The soil in the bottom of the trench is dug and loosened. Organic matter is then mixed into the bottom spit, backfilling with fresh soil taken from the adjacent spit which then becomes the next trench. Working systematically down the bed, the exercise is repeated, incorporating organic matter into the bottom spit of every trench, the last being filled with soil set aside from the first trench. The bed is then finally raked to form a smooth mound and is ready for cultivation.

Once prepared, the bed is not disturbed. It is essential not to walk on it or work it in any way which causes the soil to compact. All planting etc. is done from either side. The depth of digging and absence of soil compaction allow better drainage and a freer root run. Because of this, crops can be grown much more closely together and still thrive. The close spacing means that weeding is considerably reduced and general maintenance cut to a minimum. Assuming you have access to, or can buy, reasonable quantities of organic matter, for small gardens there is no better way to grow your vegetables. The system is sensible, productive, and can be tailored to fit each family's gardening needs or energies. Anyone thinking of taking up kitchen gardening for the first time would be well advised to consider cultivation by this method.

The finished beds are also pleasing to the eye, especially if you can surround the perimeter with tiles or wooden planks to help them keep their shape. During the course of the year, the beds settle and sink. Once a year, usually at the start of the new season, it becomes necessary to re-define them. Once a deep bed has been made, one school of thought dictates that it is never re-dug, organic matter being replenished by laying well rotted manure or compost on the surface. Unless the soil is in tip-top condition, this is not always satisfactory, and many gardeners, including ourselves, prefer to dig the bed every year until the soil is in good heart, thereafter re-digging every three to four years as part of the normal gardening cycle, incorporating more organic matter with each digging. Remember that the function of organic matter is primarily to develop soil structure, rather than to provide plant nutrients. Because cropping is intensive, regular feeding with balanced fertilisers such as blood, fish and bone meal is essential in addition to manuring.

One aid to growing that we have found invaluable is a new material, Agryl P17, used by Jersey potato growers. This resembles a flimsy shroud and can be cut to whatever length you require. It acts like a floating cloche but allows air and moisture through. Because it is so light, it can remain as a protective covering, if necessary, until the crops are mature. Nothing brings on crops more, or protects them better from the weather and insect pests. You will find several references to it throughout the book. Ask for it in garden centres. Alternatively, it can by obtained by mail order from HDRA seed supplies (see p. 249).

Finally, because crops are grown much closer together, spacings between the plants are much less than those given in conventional rows. These are the spacings I have used throughout, and it is important to remember this when reading the entries, and increase the spacings if growing using conventional methods.

Recognising when a vegetable is in its prime is a skill every cook gardener must develop. It is not difficult, no more than common sense observation, but it is surprising how little attention is given to it. The best way is to try a few samples as the crop develops and grows, noting their physical characteristics and keeping a brief record of how they taste. A small notebook for scribbling down a few brief comments is all that is necessary and will prove invaluable over the years.

Every vegetable or fruit has its moment, that time when it reaches perfection and is bursting with health and flavour. Exactly when this peak is reached varies from one vegetable to the next, changes from year to year and is dependent on all sorts of factors – soil, variety, seasonal variation and sowing times. Immaturity should not be confused with youth and tenderness. The common fallacy that a perfect vegetable is one which is in its infancy is responsible for 'those table tots', as one writer drily named them, which have become part of restaurant eating in the last few years. The tiny peas we all adore are an exception to the rule exemplified by the baby carrot, which has little flavour to speak of.

The state of perfection does not last long. Every gardener knows that the sweetest pea is the one plucked from the plant and eaten there and then. This is no idle fancy. Peas and sweetcorn can lose up to 40 per cent of their sugar content in six hours at room temperature. At the other end of the scale are vegetables bred to stand, such as winter hardy brassicas. Here, if the weather is with you, a cabbage may remain in good condition for several weeks. Thereafter, as with all vegetables, a kind of creeping senility sets in. Almost as if by sixth sense, this is when slugs, insects and moulds move in. In addition, plants suffer progressive damage from their own enzymes, bruising and weathering and so on. Eventually, something which was wonderful to eat is fit only for compost. If the first rule of harvesting is to try and pick vegetables when they are in their prime, the second is that whatever the vegetable, once it begins to show signs of age, you should pick it and store it inside rather than let it deteriorate further.

In an ideal world, vegetables should be harvested just before you need them. In practice, much depends on circumstances. For most of the time, I prefer to get the picking and preliminary cleaning well out of the way before I come to prepare a meal. In inclement weather and over the winter often the practical solution is to gather in a few days' supply when you can. During periods of severe frost, it is almost impossible to collect anything, and anything you do will invariably suffer damage in the process (try prising a leek out of frozen soil and you'll soon see what I mean). Once you have got them inside, remember a kitchen is rarely the best place to keep vegetables of any kind in good condition. Because there are only two in my household, for most of the time I find I have enough room in the refrigerator for short-term storage needs. A cellar or larder or anywhere cool and airy is satisfactory.

Gluts will occur. My first experience of these was in Berkshire. This was the first and only large garden we have ever owned. Fuelled by inexperience and enthusiasm, we turned the garden into one gigantic fruit and vegetable patch, hopelessly out of all proportion to what two people could reasonably consume. Come summer, the crops began to pour in. I bought a freezer, then another. I blanched and processed and dried and bottled and juiced my way through countless gluts. By the end of our first season, I was worn out, my enthusiasm for vegetables reaching an all time low.

Since then, we have endeavoured to grow what we want in the quantities we need. This is not an easy equation to achieve, for it is impossible to predetermine what will succeed or fail, but it is the best policy to follow if you want to derive maximum enjoyment from your garden. Occasionally a surplus can be welcome, but despite what you may read in most kitchen garden books, the majority have little culinary appeal.

COOKING VEGETABLES

Vegetable cookery is not a precise art or science. So much depends on the feel of a dish and on personal taste. You will find too that seasons provide their own stimulus. Some of the dishes I have enjoyed most have been put together from vegetables which come in from the garden collectively and which naturally suggest their own partners or combinations. To be sensitive to this rather than starting from a specific recipe is one of the great joys of kitchen garden vegetable cookery. I have thus included a lot of ideas not tied down to precise quantities, as well as conventional recipes which you can follow or adapt as you like.

If I have a criticism of vegetable cookery and cookery books it is the tendency for over-complication. Home-grown vegetables provide pleasure when cooked plainly and simply, and the majority of recipes in this book are very simple and require little in the way of extra ingredients or lengthy preparation. Many can be cooked in a matter of minutes.

When you grow your own vegetables, cooking them well assumes paramount importance. Apart from the traditional British habit of boiling vegetables to death (which no cook with any sensitivity would think of doing these days), there is little to choose between any of the methods in general use; it is for the cook to decide which is best. What is important is to cook vegetables to their proper state of doneness, by which I mean neither half-cooked, nor overcooked. The modern trend for briefly cooked vegetables is commendable, but should not be taken too literally. A hard squeaky French bean, for example, is nothing like as enjoyable as one which is genuinely al dente.

Whichever way you cook your vegetables, there will be a significant loss of nutrients compared to their raw state. For this reason alone, the value of eating vegetables raw cannot be overemphasised. Raw food brings freshness to the table and is an excellent sharpener of appetites. Increasingly, authors point to the life-giving and healing qualities of raw food and the important role it can and should play in our diet. This is particularly so with home-grown vegetables, which by virtue of their freshness contain higher levels of vitamins and are unlikely to contain chemical residues.

When you cut vegetables, the cells are crushed, causing the cell contents to mingle together, and the cut surfaces are exposed to air. Both actions have a considerable detrimental effect on some nutrients, especially vitamin C. Naturally, the smaller you cut the vegetable, the greater the damage. It is sensible therefore, when preparing vegetables, to delay cutting them as long as possible, preferably until just before you cook them. If you need to cut or shred beforehand, keep the vegetables in a box in the fridge, which will slow down the degenerative processes. By the same reasoning, to maximise the nutritional content, the more whole or larger pieces the better, though this will be offset to some extent by longer cooking times.

Whether or not to peel vegetables is a vexed question. Generally speaking, there is a greater concentration of nutrients under the skin. The skin also provides a protective barrier which is useful for starchy vegetables with thick skins, which need lengthy cooking, such as potatoes.

Most vegetables I have tried, peeled and unpeeled, show little or no difference in their flavour. Nutritionally, much will depend on the method and care taken in cooking. Garden vegetables are often blemished or damaged. No matter how thoroughly you wash or scrub them, it is often necessary and sometimes preferable to peel them first. Shop-bought vegetables I peel as a matter of course as a precaution against sprays and chemicals they might contain.

How thickly or thinly vegetables are cut affects their appearance, taste, and, in some cases cooking qualities. This is not appreciated enough, particularly when it comes to slicing onions finely so that they melt into a sauce, chopping herbs into fine speckles, or slicing and shredding vegetables for salads. Too often a salad is ruined because the vegetables have not been cut into appropriately sized pieces. A finely grated carrot is sweeter, more pleasing in texture, and far juicier than one which is coarsely grated. And finely shredded cabbage makes the only decent coleslaw I know.

Blanching is the method of cooking vegetables in a large volume of water (or sometimes steam) for the shortest possible time. In industrial preparation of vegetables it is used extensively to pre-cook vegetables before they are frozen. This arrests enzyme activity, which would cause spoilage and hence shorten their useful storage life. Blanching is also employed to shrink and soften vegetables prior to canning and sterilising. Restaurants commonly pre-cook vegetables by blanching, then briefly reheat them to order over a steamer or in a microwave, or finish in a sauce. When done well, this gives the appearance, taste and texture of freshly cooked vegetables. In domestic kitchens, blanching is used mainly for conditioning vegetables prior to freezing, or to make strong tasting vegetables milder.

For certain vegetables, notably legumes, spinach and other leafy greens such as spinach beet or Swiss chard, blanching is an excellent method of cooking in its own right. That this is not generally recognised is due, I suspect, to modern conditioning against large volumes of water, but when the cooking times are short, i.e. 1–2 minutes, blanching compares very favourably. There is also the additional advantage that the large volume of water employed dilutes the plant's acids, thus minimising their destructive effect on the vegetable's nutrients.

To ensure success, the proportion of boiling water to vegetables must be great enough to enable the water to come back to a rolling boil within 1 minute – preferably less – of adding them. Put the lid on (which will speed things up), removing it as soon as the water boils again. Do not cook for a second longer than is necessary. Scoop the vegetables out, finish them off and serve.

You will often read that in order to keep green vegetables green after blanching, they should be plunged into cold water to set the colour and arrest the cooking process. This is not necessary. As long as the vegetables are blanched briefly, so that the chemical reactions which change the green chlorophyll to a dull greyish green or yellow do not take place, they need no refreshing. Simply spread them out on kitchen paper and they will retain their bright green colour. Secondly, to keep cooked vegetables bright green, do not cover them. Covering vegetables allows volatile acids to condense back on to them and dulls the colour.

Steaming has become popular in recent years, earning for itself wide acceptance as the method par excellence for cooking vegetables. It is said to conserve most of the nutrients and flavour, primarily because leaching losses are reduced to a mimimum. Steaming devices range from a sieve set over a saucepan and collapsible aluminium 'flower' steamers which expand to fit pans of most sizes, to bamboo steamers and more recently purpose-built steamers arranged in tiers. If you are going to steam vegetables in any quantity, a purpose-built steamer would be advisable.

As with blanching, to be successful, steaming needs to be carried out with care. The vegetables must not crowd each other and must be of equal size to ensure even cooking. The water in the bottom pan should not touch the steamer and should be boiling briskly. The lid on the steamer should fit tightly. All these factors help to ensure that there is a minimum loss of moisture and the vegetables steam quickly.

Though steaming has many enthusiasts, the claim that it is *best* is open to qualification. The quantity of vegetables you can cook in one go without investing in a purpose-built steamer limits the attraction of this method for me. Nor do I find that steamed vegetables taste better, and I must confess also to more than my fair share of burnt pans. More importantly, the minimum amount of water used means a greater concentration of potentially destructive plant acids which can condense onto the surface of the vegetables. Steaming takes two to three times longer than fast methods of cooking vegetables. This, too, affects the amount of nutrients lost.

Conservative methods of cooking employ a very little additional moisture, as the name implies, be it water or fat.
1 *With water*. This is essentially a halfway house between blanching and steaming. Vegetables are cooked briskly in a small amount of water in a covered pan for the shortest time until ready, removing the lid of the pan three-quarters of the way through. It is the method I find most convenient. Choose an appropriate sized pan for the quantity of vegetables, which ideally should form a single layer. Cooking times vary from 1–2 minutes to 2–5 minutes. If the water looks like drying up too soon, add a little more. Usually there will only be a small amount of liquid left at the end of cooking.

As a regular way of cooking vegetables, this method has much to commend it. It is quick, convenient, adaptable, and suitable for most vegetables. It does not require such critical timing as blanching, but yet allows the cook to get the vegetables *à point* every time. Nutritionally it combines the advantages of steaming and blanching and avoids the worst excesses of either.
2 *In fat*. The vegetables are first coated in a little of the chosen fat, then cooked gently in a covered pan until tender with no additional moisture, yielding a small amount of delicious juices at the end. As anyone who has cooked potatoes by this method (referred to in old cookery books as

'stoving') is aware, it produces a richly flavoured result. It is, however, tricky to get right, and only works successfully if you have a heavy based pan with a tightly fitting lid and a heat supply sensitive enough to give minimum heat. The heat builds up considerably within the pan and the vegetables can quickly catch and burn. A heat diffuser is a great advantage, and a worthwhile precaution if your heat supply is in any way erratic. For this reason it is vital to choose the right sized pan for the quantity of vegetables, and for the vegetables to be of even size. If you are at all unsure, a couple of tablespoons of water can be added during the cooking, though this does produce a slightly different result.

Most vegetables can profitably be cooked by this method. Nutritionally, the coating of fat helps protect the vegetables, and there is less loss of volatile suubstances and vitamins through leaching. This is offset to a certain extent by the length of time it takes to cook the vegetables, the gentler heat employed and the greater concentration of plant acids present.

Braising is an extension of conservative cooking in fat, the main difference being that vegetables are cooked for long periods of time with other aromatics and some additional liquid, resulting in a very flavourful dish. Garlic, spices, herbs, bacon, finely chopped onion and carrots are often the ingredients of a braise; stock, wine, tomato sauce often the liquid employed. It is especially suitable for vegetables such as fennel, celery, chicory, peppers, onions and leeks, and some root vegetables such as carrot and salsify which respond well to long, slow cooking.

Sautéing is simply frying in fat. It is similar in some respects to stir-frying, but is more leisurely. The quantity of fat used is not large and the pieces are kept moving around so that they brown and cook evenly over a moderate heat. You need a good pan. A few tablespoons of liquid and other aromatic additions are often added towards the end to produce a quickly made savoury sauce. It is a useful method for finishing root vegetables, or for cooking softer vegetables such as courgettes and mushrooms.

Stir-frying is another method which has become very popular in recent years. A Chinese cookery book I have offers the following definition: 'Stir-frying consists of cooking foods which have been cut into thin slices, or into shreds, in a few tablespoons of oil in a frying pan over a high heat, stirring and turning all the time.'

When you have prepared the vegetables, heat the pan, then add the oil, followed by your chosen aromatics – ginger, garlic, chilli, shredded spring onions. Stir-fry for 30 seconds, then add the vegetables (those taking longer to cook can be added first). Stir-fry for 1–3 minutes. Add the sauce ingredients, usually a combination of soy, sugar, sherry, cornflour and other

Chinese condiments such as hoisin and chilli sauce. Stir to coat, cook a minute or so longer, and serve.

A rapid and sensitive heat source and a large pan that conducts the heat quickly are essential. A frying pan, provided the volume of vegetables is not too great, is reasonable, but a proper wok will do the job much more effectively, as success depends on all the vegetables coming into contact with the heat – otherwise they end up steamed rather than stir-fried. The correct cutting of the vegetables is very important. The aim is to expose the largest surface area (particularly with hard vegetables such as carrots), and this is achieved by slanting and cutting diagonally or into thin strips. In China, stir-frying has been perfected to an art form. Anyone seriously interested in this method of cooking should consult a good book such as Yan-Kit's *Classic Chinese Cookbook*.

Once you have grasped the basics, any competent cook can soon master a respectable stir-fry. For the cook-gardener, it is a useful method, for it enables you to produce any number of delicious vegetable dishes quickly and simply from whatever is available at the time. You do not have to stick rigidly to Chinese flavourings.

Nutritionally, the great advantage is both the speed with which vegetables are cooked and the high heat employed. The preliminary coating in fat helps to protect the vegetables and leaching losses are minimal, as any moisture is incorporated into the final dish. But cutting vegetables so finely results in maximum exposure to air and hence degradation of nutrients by oxidation; also the lack of moisture means a greater concentration of plant acids, which causes further nutrient loss.

Measurements
Measurements are given in both British Imperial and Metric. To save repetition, a knob of butter is about a third of an ounce (10g), a good knob, half an ounce (15g); a little olive oil is the smallest amount you need to cover the base of the pan you are using, generally a tablespoon.

All recipes are designed for four
people unless otherwise stated.

SPRING

March, April, May

Every gardener looks forward to spring. This is the time when the new year's hopes are sown, and anticipation of good things to come runs high. It is a complex season, a season of contrasts that taxes a gardener's patience more than any other; a wholly frustrating period, a matter of waiting for the weather, worries over late frosts, deliberations over sowing times, and the rush to get everything done in time. A northern gardener feels this keenly. Work in our garden rarely begins before March. Even then, as the first batches of seeds are put under the propagator, and we observe the annual ritual of shrouding the beds in protective polythene, gardening seems untimely and unnatural.

The first job is to prepare the beds as they become vacant, and to mulch the fruit with a thick layer of protective manure. If possible, a month or so before the beds are prepared, they are covered over with polythene sheeting to keep off the worst of the rain and help make the soil manageable. Once the beds have been dug, the polythene is put back in place until conditions are suitable for sowing.

From April to the end of May, sowing seeds is a regular preoccupation. Sowing seeds is the most basic and fundamental operation of all gardening. How important it is to do this well I learnt to my cost in the spring of 1988 when I found myself temporarily in sole charge of the garden and nothing germinated anything like as well as it should. Everything must be done to ensure the seeds are given the best possible start, otherwise germination will be sporadic. Sometimes you can make good by filling in the gaps, but this is rarely satisfactory. In small gardens, working on tight cropping schedules, to lose a row can have severe consequences. Sometimes the whole crop can be lost and it often means another year's wait before you can try again.

As a general rule, do not be tempted to sow when the soil cannot be worked to produce a tilth, for results will be patchy. Depth of sowing is not as critical as evenness of sowing, otherwise, again, patchy germination results. Don't commit your hard work to memory. Stick the label in the centre of the bed, clearly marked with name and date.

Spring is traditionally the leanest time in the garden. Spring greens, sprouting broccolis, spinach beet and kale form the mainstay. Better crops you could not wish for on cold blustery days. Usually there are still overwintered chicories and small salad plants like lamb's lettuce and claytonia. Spring also brings a few coveted delicacies. The first of the overwintered lettuces, rhubarb, fresh new herbs – sorrel, chives, mint and chervil – and the greatest delicacy of them all, our own native seakale. How many greengrocers will sell you a bunch of that in May?

HERBS

A few fresh herbs, available as you want them, are an essential part of any kitchen garden. Although there is something intrinsically appealing about having an orderly collection of herbs, they are accommodating plants and can be fitted in here and there where space allows. The majority have no special requirements and are easy to grow, often thriving in poor soils. You do not need to grow a large number of herbs. A modest selection of those you like and use most frequently spread throughout the year will be of more lasting value than a garden full of those you use but now and then. With over 200 herbs to choose from, everyone should be able to find a pleasing selection with no difficulty at all.

For ordinary domestic purposes, herbs should be picked fresh. How well they keep depends on how delicate the leaves are. Wrap them gently in kitchen paper – this absorbs the excess moisture – and keep in a sealed box or plastic bag in the refrigerator. Most herbs will keep in good condition up to a week this way. Check them regularly, discarding any with yellowing leaves.

The modern way of preserving herbs is to freeze them. This is useful if you have a surplus of herbs you are particularly fond of. Pick the herbs while the leaves are young and tender, when their aromatic qualities are at their best. As summer progresses and the plants flower, the leaves toughen, the plant goes to seed and the flavour of many becomes duller and harsher. Some, like basil, become arid and unpleasant. Chop them first – a food processor makes light work of this if you are preparing any quantity – and then freeze in boxes. A small supply of whole leaves or small sprigs of tarragon and basil for flavouring soups and sauces such as béarnaise is also useful. Wrap them in clingfilm, and then freeze in boxes in the usual way.

Not all herbs freeze well. Sorrel, mint and coriander lose their pungency more quickly than others, and seem to retain their aromatic qualities for only a couple of months once in the freezer. By contrast, basil, dill and tarragon freeze exceptionally successfully. Once thawed, all herbs become mushy. In this respect, their usefulness is limited.

Fresh-drying is a useful method for preserving a small quantity of herbs which you are going to use fairly quickly, and it works particularly well for mint, oregano and parsley. Strip the herbs from their stems, chop finely, and spread them out to dry for a few hours on a wooden board or working surface. Keep in the fridge and use as required.

Using fresh herbs in the kitchen is a matter of common sense, arrived at by a process of trial and error. It is a mistake to think that herbs will automatically improve a dish. As you become more familiar with their individual qualities, so you learn which marry with fish or meat, which are especially suited to salads and vegetables, which other ingredients they complement, and, most importantly, when to leave well alone. A few herb vinegars are a must, as are one or two herb jellies.

Garden herbs have real depth of flavour, especially compared to those you can now buy in shops which often seem to lack aroma and character. The pungency of a herb depends on the volatile nature of its essential oils. In some herbs – rosemary, thyme and sage, for example – these are relatively stable and will withstand long cooking. Others – dill, basil, chives, mint, chervil, and to some extent French tarragon and parsley – are more fragile, and more usually added at the end. Remember that the strength of individual herbs varies considerably. Whereas you can be lavish with parsley, one or two sage leaves are usually ample as a flavouring. To take the trouble to remove the stalks and chop the leaves finely seems to me a basic and necessary step which easily repays the small amount of effort involved.

As far as the kitchen is concerned, herbs fall into three groups, each complementing their appropriate season. Whereas autumn and winter herbs are pungent, summer herbs delicate and aromatic, spring herbs have clean, lively tastes, astringent rather than aromatic, refreshing rather than pungent. After the drabness of winter, they mark the beginning of a new year.

Chervil

According to one interpretation, the Latin name for chervil means 'leaves of joy'. John Evelyn was particularly fond of it: 'Chervill is handsom and proper for the edging of Kitchin Garden beds', he wrote in his notes to his gardener at Sayes Court in 1687. Like mint, it should be grown in a shady place where it often survives through the winter. In hot conditions it quickly runs to seed. As it generally seeds itself, further sowings are likely to be unnecessary. Chervil will also grow successfully in a pot on the windowsill.

Chervil is frequently and erroneously spoken of in the same breath as parsley. In fact, the two make poor substitutes for each other. Chervil is by far the more assertive of the two, more akin to a mild form of anise or fennel, or even tarragon. In 1822 Dr William Kitchener, who claimed to be the first to recommend chervil in an English cookery book, wrote: 'Its flavour is a strong concentration of the combined taste of parsley and fennel, but more aromatic and agreeable than either; and is so excellent in a sauce with boiled poultry or fish, I cannot account for it being so little known in the English kitchen.' Its most common use is in *fines herbes*, a combination of parsley, tarragon, chives and chervil, being the most famous example. It has a natural affinity for eggs, fish, poultry, carrots and potato soup. It is rarely, if ever, cooked but added to soups and sauces at the last moment.

A few sprigs of chervil make an admirable addition to winter and spring salads. Separate the tiny lacy leaves painstakingly into individual fronds or *pluches* and scatter among the green salad. It gives the salad a tinge of anise.

Cheese of the seven herbs

This is an old Cumberland recipe, from Eleanor Sinclair Rohde's *Culinary and Salad Herbs*, published in 1940.

'To four ounces of grated cheese allow two tablespoons of thick cream, three tablespoons of sherry, and two level tablespoons of the following herbs in mixture: finely chopped parsley, sage, thyme, tarragon, chives, chervil, and winter savoury, also seasoning to taste. Put all the ingredients in a double saucepan and stir over a very gentle heat till the mixture is creamy and pale green in colour. Whilst still warm, fill up small pots with the cheese and use when cold.'

The cheese has an attractive speckled appearance. Use a mild crumbly cheese such as Lancashire or Wensleydale. If you do not have all seven of the herbs do no worry unduly. Include as many as you can, and always chervil.

Chervil pancakes

These pancakes can be cut up in strips to serve in clear soups, spread with cream or curd cheese and served with a fresh tomato sauce, or filled with chicken and avocado to make a light lunch or first course.

3oz (90g) plain flour (or use half fine
wholewheat and half white flour)
1 egg
5 fl oz (150ml) milk

pinch salt
2 heaped tbsp finely chopped chervil
knob of butter for frying

Make the pancake batter in the usual way, beating well. Allow to stand for an hour, beat again and stir in the chervil. Make 8 thin pancakes and use as described above.

Chervil chiffonade

For fish, poultry, or game: swill out the cooking juices with cream, removing any fat first. Boil down a little, add a chiffonade (finely shredded leaves) of chervil and the sauce is ready. Check the seasoning and serve. This comes from an American newsletter, *The Art of Eating*, by Edward Behr.

Chives

In sheltered parts, chives first begin to appear in late January. One or two clumps are sufficient and will need dividing every three or four years. They prefer a rich, moist soil and require regular feeding with a high nitrogen fertiliser or organic matter – yellowing leaves and leaf tips are sure signs of deprivation.

Chives should be cut young for the kitchen; later on the stalks coarsen and are not nearly so pleasant. This is why spring chives are always the best, though regular cutting helps to ensure a succession of young growth. They are said to be the most delicate member of the onion tribe, though an onion hater will find them just as indigestible. The pretty purple flowers taste of chives and should not be wasted. Chop them, teasing out each tiny speck of flower to use in salads, or as a garnish.

Giant chives are, as might be expected, a larger form of garden chives. Chinese chives, also known as garlic chives, are a different species. These form clumps but have flat rather than round bladed leaves. They look more like spring onions, and you can use them in the same way, but remember they have a garlic flavour.

Celeriac and chive soup

Chives can be employed as a last-minute addition to a number of soups where an onion flavour is required. This is a simple one, which can be eaten hot or cold.

8oz (225g) celeriac, chopped
1 large clove of garlic

1 pt (600ml) milk
big bunch of chives, finely chopped

Simmer the celeriac, garlic and milk until cooked. Blend in a food processor with half the chives for a good 5 minutes until the soup takes on a delicate green. Dilute with extra water if necessary and either serve hot or ice cold in small soup cups, stirring in the rest of the chives just before serving. Serves 4–6.

Courgette and cucumber salad with chives and sesame seeds

Prepare a bowl of matchstick slices of cucumber and courgette in roughly equal quantities. Toss in sour cream or thick yoghurt (or a mixture of the two). Sprinkle generously with lightly toasted sesame seeds, sparingly with chopped chives, and serve.

Mint and chive omelette

This is one of the nicest springtime omelettes.

Chop a good quantity of mint and chives together. Make the omelette in the usual way, keeping it moist and runny. Strew the herbs down the centre, fold and serve.

Variations: add small dice of goat's cheese, about 1 oz (30g) per person, to the eggs in the pan. The cheese should just soften. Delicious.

Trout baked with vermouth and cream

This recipe, slightly adapted, comes from Nicola Fletcher's *Game for All*, published in 1987.

4 trout, or other white fish fillets
2 fat cloves garlic, chopped
2–3 tbsp chives or dill, finely chopped

pinch of salt
5 fl oz (150ml) dry white vermouth
5 fl oz (150ml) whipping cream

Ask your fishmonger to clean the trout and remove the gills and backbone (or buy filleted trout). Lay the fish in an ovenproof dish which will just hold them snugly, and distribute the garlic around the fish and down the sides. Scatter over the herbs, season lightly and pour over the vermouth and cream.

Cover tightly with foil and bake in the oven, 190°C/375°F/gas mark 5 for 20–25 minutes or until just done. Carefully transfer the fish to hot plates and keep warm. Pour the sauce into a blender and blend until smooth. Transfer to a wide pan, boil down until it thickens slightly. Pour around the fish, decorate with fresh herbs and serve with rice.

Stir-fried chives

No matter how fond you are of chives, sooner or later you will have a surplus. Remedy: use them in stir-fries with meat, fish or vegetables. They need hardly any cooking, the blades wilting down to bright green strands.

Mint

Everybody knows and has mint, yet it remains as undervalued as it was 20 years ago, when Elizabeth David celebrated it in her *Summer Cooking*. It is one of the few herbs used for culinary purposes which may be found growing wild. I have often come across it walking in the Dales by running water and in wet places. Another kind of mint I have recently been introduced to is pennyroyal, a marvellously astringent herb with tiny leaves and prostrate habit, much used in traditional herbal medicine. Its country names include lurk-in-the-ditch and pudding grass, a reference, perhaps, to the herb puddings they used to make. The friend who introduced it to me swears by it for clearing colds (pennyroyal tea is a well known old-fashioned remedy), and says it makes a delicious flavouring for dumplings.

Common garden spearmint and the milder furry-leaved apple or Bowles' mint serve most purposes, and are the two I prefer. Suffolk Herbs now offer Moroccan mint which I hope will make invigorating mint teas. All require moist shady positions and need containing sooner or later. Mints are greedy feeders. Ideally the soil should be fed with a top dressing of manure and the bed replenished ever three or four years, though no one seems to bother. For winter use, pot up a root and bring inside.

Herb pestos

The original – and best – pesto is made with basil, but American cooks make pestos with tender leaves of all kinds of fresh herbs. Use the standard formula given below, adjusting the herb or herbs according to strength and succulence.

1oz (30g) fresh herb, finely chopped
½oz (15g) each pine kernels or
    walnuts (or use 1oz or 30g of either)

½oz (15g) finely grated parmesan or
    pecorino
1 crushed clove of garlic
2–3 tbsp good fruity olive oil

Combine everything in a blender or food processor, adding enough oil to make a smoothish paste. Keep under oil in the fridge for 1–2 weeks, using it to add to soups and sauces.

Chilled cucumber and mint pesto soup

6oz (180g) cucumber, peeled, de-
    seeded and roughly chopped
5 fl oz (150ml) creamy yoghurt
1 strip cucumber rind
1–2 tbsp mint pesto (see page 31)

To finish
mineral water plus cream/creamy
    milk/sour cream
2–3 tsp rice vinegar
extra mint pesto
3–4 tbsp cucumber, peeled, de-seeded
    and diced

Blend the cucumber, yoghurt, strip of cucumber rind and pesto with enough mineral water to give a thickish base. Add cream/milk/sour cream to taste, diluting further if necessary with more water. Add the rice vinegar plus extra pesto to taste. Chill thoroughly. Ladle into soup cups, stir in the tiny dice of cucumber and serve.

Mushrooms with mint and anchovy dressing

Wash and dry your mushrooms and slice thinly. Pour over a dressing made from pounded anchovies, olive oil, finely chopped mint and a good quantity of lemon juice, all to taste. Leave for a little while for the flavours to infuse. Set in a ring of watercress and serve at room temperature.

Moroccan mint tea

The problem with mint is its voracity. Fragrant cooling mint teas are the answer. The best variety to use is spearmint. Elisabeth Luard, in her book *The Princess and the Pheasant* published in 1987, has an excellent recipe for what has become my favourite summer drink. Sugar can be optional.

'You will need a thick glass tumbler for each person, plus 4–5 sprigs of mint. Wash the mint. Put at least 1 heaped teaspoon of sugar in each tumbler – Arabs like their sweet things twice as sweet. Now there are several options open to you: either make a pot of weak tea, leaving it to stand for 2–3 minutes only and then pour the tea over the mint leaves in each glass. Or add a few leaves of green tea and a long spoon to each glass, then pour boiling water over the leaves. Or make it with no tea, just the mint and, if you like, a slice of lemon. Deliciously refreshing.'

Mint and currant jelly sauce

This is from *Cantaloup to Cabbage*, by Mrs Philip Martineau, published in 1929.

Moisten finely chopped mint with a little wine vinegar, just enough to make it wet. Warm some redcurrant jelly so that it is soft but not liquid. Beat in the mint and serve. Try it also as a dressing for hot beetroot.

Sorrel

Sorrel is the sharpest and liveliest of spring herbs. Every garden should have a patch, for it will grow on any scrap of spare ground. In mild winters it can come through in January, and is usually the first herb to show its presence in my own garden. Its lemony astringency was much valued in the 16th and 17th centuries for mixing with other salad plants, and is better now than when the leaves have had chance to grow large and coarse.

There are several varieties, but the French sorrel is the cook's kind. The familiar large-leaved variety grows to about 12in (30cm). The leaves soon coarsen and need to be kept well picked. For salads, the small buckler-leaved variety (*Rumex scutatus*) is better. This is a sprawling ground cover plant with pretty arrow-shaped leaves. The young leaves in particular are mild and most attractive in misticanza salads. All sorrel has an infuriating habit of running to seed as summer progresses, and needs to be chopped back regularly.

The unadulterated acidity of sorrel is not appreciated by everybody, but this is easily mollified with the addition of a little butter, cream or mayonnaise, or a pinch of sugar. Its natural partners are eggs, fish, veal and potatoes. A few leaves do wonders for early spring salads, and nothing is nicer in spring soups and sauces.

Sorrel cooks very quickly, wilting down to virtually nothing in the pan. Its bright green colour turns instantaneously sludgy – a function of its oxalic acid content. To preserve its freshness and colour, chop it to a purée, removing the central midrib first, and add it to the dish at the last moment.

Sorrel does not freeze well; a better solution for preserving it is the sorrel purée described on p. 34.

Sorrel and yoghurt or buttermilk soup

One of the simplest of the many good sorrel soups.

½ pt (300ml) yoghurt, preferably homemade, or buttermilk
½ pt (300ml) mineral water

good handful young sorrel leaves, midribs removed
cream, chopped chives or mint to garnish

Mix the yoghurt and mineral water. Chop, and then pound the sorrel to a purée with a little of the liquid. Add to the base, stopping when the taste seems right. Serve well chilled, embellished with a swirl of cream and the tiniest amount of finely chopped chives or mint.

Salmon trout with mushroom and sorrel purée in a filo case

Mushrooms and sorrel have an affinity I like, the softness of the one ameliorating the sharpness of the other. This can be adapted for smaller quantities of fish by making individual parcels and serving as a first course, or for a large tail piece.

A little cream mixed with some thick yoghurt, warmed through gently in a double boiler and served in a jug makes as good a sauce as anything, and compliments the dish nicely.

4 thick salmon trout steaks	2–3 tbsp cream
at least 4oz (120g) sorrel, midribs removed	½oz (15g) melted butter mixed with 2 tsp olive oil for brushing
1oz (30g) butter	4 sheets filo pastry
4oz (120g) finely chopped mushrooms	

Skin and bone the salmon trout, and set aside. Chop the sorrel coarsely and gently soften in 2 tbsp water in a covered pan for 2–3 minutes until it melts into a purée. Press out the moisture, beat in the butter and set aside. Meanwhile sweat the mushrooms in a small knob of butter, turning up the heat at the end to evaporate any moisture. Mix in the sorrel, adding enough cream to form a soft mixture.

Brush a baking sheet or dish with a little of the butter and oil. Divide the filling and spread on top of each steak. Wrap each in a sheet of filo pastry, making a neat parcel. Brush the top and sides and seal the edges with the rest of the butter and oil. Transfer to the baking sheet and bake in a hot oven, 200°C/400°F/gas mark 6, for 10 minutes. Turn off the oven and leave for another 5 minutes. Serve.

Sorrel purée

An admirable idea from *Leaves from our Tuscan Kitchen*, by Janet Ross and Michael Waterfield:

'The most practical way of using sorrel is to make it into a buttery purée which will keep in a glass jar in the refrigerator. This can then be used for a soup, a fish sauce, an omelette, mixed in with some young peas, or chopped cooked potatoes and cream.

'Wash the sorrel carefully and put it into a pan with a little boiling water, season lightly and cover. Uncover and stir now and then until the sorrel is soft and a brownish colour (only three to four minutes). Drain and mix with melted butter. Keep in the refrigerator until needed.'

The purée keeps very well for 2–3 weeks. The recipe can be streamlined somewhat. Remove the midribs first. Cook the sorrel with 1 tbsp water, beat to a purée and beat in the butter while hot (no need to melt the butter first). The proportions I use are ⅓–½ butter to the cooked weight of sorrel; the seasoning is unnecessary.

A quick sorrel sauce

Take some of the purée above, mix with ricotta cheese and let down with cooking water or creamy milk. Use for homemade pasta. For a more substantial dish, add a few fresh prawns, or chunks of lightly cooked salmon.

Green sauce

Green sauce is part of our national heritage, an ancient relish to enliven the meat course, made with green herbs (especially sorrel), vinegar and sugar. Like many ancient foods it survived longer in the north. Jennifer Stead, in issue 3 of *Petit Propos Culinaire*, writes that in the 19th century the sauce was so popular as an accompaniment for roast meat, especially veal, that a special large lead mustard ball stood at the ready in its own box in the dining-room or kitchen to pulverise the sorrel. (The dangers of lead were clearly not realised.)

The sauce was made with either wild sorrel, 'saar grass' picked from the fields, or from a specially cultivated plot in the corner of the garden. It was much enjoyed as a sweet sharp relish (like mint sauce is today), or as 'wet salad' that other northern accompaniment to Yorkshire pudding and roast beef. Northerners will stress malt vinegar is essential to achieve the necessary searing bite; be cautious here, the taste for malt vinegar is an acquired one.

2 large handfuls sorrel, midribs *removed*	*sugar* *malt or cider vinegar*

Chop the sorrel and then pulverise to a dark green paste with 1 tbsp sugar in a pestle and mortar (no need to poison yourself with the lead ball). Stir in vinegar to taste, correcting the acidity with extra sugar. The sauce should be both sweet and sharp and it will need more sugar than you imagine. A little chopped mint, stirred in at the end is also good. Use with roast veal or cold meats and salad.

VEGETABLES

Purple and white sprouting broccoli

The sprouting broccolis are the finest of the cabbage tribe. The winter kind are the white and purple sprouting broccolis and came originally from the Levant, Cyprus or Crete, spreading to Italy first then across the rest of Europe sometime in the 17th century.

They are large handsome plants developing a small central head which is picked first, followed by a profusion of tender sideshoots. Like all spring green vegetables, nature has wisely invested them with a good supply of vitamins, particularly those of group B and vitamin A. The white kind matures earlier by two weeks or so and has lighter coloured leaves with a smoother edge, but the purple kind in our experience is far more prolific. In flavour, there is little to choose between the two.

The gardener most associated with sprouting broccolis and who did much to encourage their introduction into England was Stephen Switzer, a Hampshire man, self-educated, who took to landscaping and writing books, and was for a time a seedsman of some note in Westminster. He is perhaps best remembered for his pamphlet on foreign kitchen vegetables written in 1729. 'In my humble opinion,' he declared, referring to broccoli, 'next to the true asparagus, [it is] the best boiled winter salad we have . . . and is in season at such a time, when nothing else equal to it, can be got.' The shoots, he instructs, should be gathered while young, the bigness of a man's little finger: 'and then it is, I think, an excellent dish, at least much better than any other kind of sprouts.'

I agree. Sprouting broccolis are very fine indeed, more delectable to my mind than the calabrese which has become so popular of late. They are an excellent crop to follow early potatoes, and straightforward plants to grow, though they are not completely hardy and may fail in severe winters. Sow in early June (no earlier or the plants may become too large), planting out about six weeks later, 15in (37.5cm) apart. Stake them firmly, as with brussel sprouts.

Sprouting broccoli tends to come in one main flush, particularly after the first spell of mild weather. Cut the shoots while young and very tender, removing all but the tenderest leaves, and, ideally, pick not long before you cook. If you need to keep them, wrap them loosely in a plastic bag and keep somewhere cool. To stagger the crop, you can leave the heads on the plant for up to two weeks before they show signs of running to seed and they will still make excellent eating.

Do not be in too much of a rush to cut away the stalk. The tender parts can be eaten with pleasure. Press your thumb into the stalk; if it goes in easily, the

stalk is tender enough to eat (this is a good tip, incidentally, for all stemmy vegetables). The rest of the stalk, peeled to remove the outer tougher skin, can be chopped and used in soups and stir-fries.

Broccoli should never be boiled. Rinse quickly and lay the sprigs in a single layer in a large covered pan with ½ in (1.25cm) boiling water. Cook hard in the usual way for as little as 1–2 minutes, depending on size. Timing is absolutely critical, as even slight overcooking diminishes them considerably. Drain very well and serve on a piping hot dish – this will soak up any remaining moisture and prevent the broccoli from cooling too quickly.

The best way to savour the shoots is on their own as a separate vegetable course, or dunked in a newly laid soft-boiled egg. Or have them as a salad, warm or cold (never chilled), dressed with olive oil or walnut oil and a few drops of lemon juice. Alternatively, finish in some of the ways suggested below.

Quantities are difficult to gauge. 1lb (450g) broccoli should feed four people generously as a vegetable or side dish; at home we easily manage 12oz (340g) cooked broccoli as a first course between two.

Broccoli, potatoes and eggs

A springtime treat: make individual borders of creamy mashed potato. Sit a poached or fried egg in the centre. Carefully lay cooked broccoli spears around the outside, pointing inwards, and eat. Bliss.

Broccoli, pine kernels and raisins

This is the Italian way and cannot be bettered. Briefly toss a handful of pine kernels and half that amount of raisins in olive oil or butter until the pine kernels have browned and the raisins have plumped. Scatter them over freshly cooked broccoli shoots and serve immediately. Fried breadcrumbs can also be added.

As a variation, add 1–2 beaten eggs to the pan with the pine kernels and raisins. When set, break into small pieces, pulling the omelette apart with a fork. Cook until brown on both sides. Scatter over the broccoli spears as before, moistening with a few extra drops of olive or nut oil.

Broccoli with golden sauce

Olive oil and broccoli are excellent partners. This is an olive oil version of hollandaise – in effect hot mayonnaise, but made slightly differently.

2–3 fl oz (60–90ml) mild olive oil, or half butter, half olive oil
1 crushed clove of garlic
1 large fresh egg yolk

salt
about 2 fl oz (60ml) hot water
few drops lemon juice or white wine vinegar

Gently heat the oil and butter if using, in your smallest pan with the garlic. Put the egg yolk into a small bowl over simmering water and beat with a pinch of salt and few drops of lemon juice or vinegar. Carefully pour on the heated oil mixture, beating thoroughly, a little at a time. Add enough water, again gradually, to give a thick pouring consistency. Check the seasoning, remove the garlic, and serve in a small jug or bowl. The sauce can be made in advance and kept warm in a bain-marie with a lid on top to prevent a skin from forming, or left to cool and reheated later, again covered to prevent a skin from forming. If it becomes too thick, add a little more water. Sufficient for 2–3.

Anyone who makes egg emulsion sauces regularly knows that the amount of oil or butter you can add is variable. The idea is to balance the ingredients to your taste. The other thing to remember is to make sure the sauce is sufficiently hot for the thickening action of the egg to take place.

Broccoli salads

Cooked vegetables, particularly the soft-textured green kind, have been enjoyed as salads since Roman times. It is important to serve them at room temperature, or even straight from the pan, dressed, and to the table. Eating them with your fingers adds to the pleasure.

Broccoli with walnuts and black olives

Roughly chop 1–2 tbsp walnuts and mix with a little walnut oil and the finely chopped flesh of a few black olives. Mix with freshly cooked and chopped broccoli, season with a few drops of basalmic vinegar and serve warm.

Broccoli and roasted red pepper salad

Arrange a plate of salad leaves, including some chicories and endives if you can. On top, lay some lightly cooked broccoli spears. Spoon over strips of red pepper, which you have previously prepared by roasting under the grill in the usual way until blistered, removing the skins, slicing into little strips and storing under olive oil. Dress with some of the same olive oil, scatter generously with rinsed capers, and finish with a squeeze of lemon juice.

Broccoli and pasta

Many a meal can be made with broccoli and pasta, either as a simple supper dish or as a salad, combining the two with chopped tomatoes, mushrooms, red peppers, fried breadcrumbs, and flavourings such as anchovies, olives, garlic, and sharp, salty cheeses. A dressing of good olive oil, which may be plain or heated through first with a dried chilli in the Roman style, is essential.

Broccoli and pasta salad

8oz (225g) wholewheat pasta shells or
  shapes
6–8oz (180–225g) broccoli, freshly
  cooked and chopped small

1–2 ripe tomatoes, chopped
4–6 stoned olives, chopped
1–2oz (30–60g) feta cheese
olive oil, lemon or lime juice

Cook the pasta, keeping it al dente, and mix in all the other ingredients except the feta cheese. Lubricate with a little olive oil, season with lemon or lime juice and lay the feta cheese, cut into thin small slivers on top. Serve at room temperature. To give the salad a nice bite, heat a tablespoon of the olive oil with a dried chilli before mixing with the salad. Serves 4–6.

Broccoli carbonara

8oz (225g) wholewheat pasta shells
8oz (225g) broccoli
2oz (60g) lean ham, diced

3 eggs, beaten
parmesan cheese

The essence of any successful carbonara is speed and very hot serving plates. The eggs should never curdle but cook sufficiently to thicken and form a sauce. In practice, this is more difficult than it sounds – a little judicious re-heating helps, so long as you keep the heat very gentle and remove immediately the eggs begin to thicken.

    Put the pasta on to cook and have the plates warming in the oven. Time the broccoli to be ready with the pasta – 2–3 minutes rapid cooking should be enough; keep both al dente. Chop the broccoli into bite-sized pieces, drain the pasta thoroughly and return both to the pan. Quickly stir in the ham and the eggs, shaking and stirring over a very low heat until the eggs show signs of thickening. Serve immediately, handing round parmesan separately. Serves 2–3.

Radishes

Radishes are members of the *Cruciferae* family, which includes the brassicas, cresses and horseradish. Their wild ancestor is a type of charlock. Writings on the walls of tombs in the Egyptian pyramids show that radishes have been eaten for millennia. Early radishes were large, the kind that are grown as winter radishes today, and were either black or white. They were probably introduced into Britain by the Romans and continued to be grown constantly throughout the following centuries.

    Daintier forms of radish emerged some time in the 16th century. The herbalist Gerard records four types and comments that some are long and white, others long and black, and yet others round or pear-shaped. Note no red form yet, though there is a hint. The small garden radish, he writes, is long and white 'except a little that sheweth itself above the ground of a

reddish colour'. By the 18th century small forms were common, and the red radish, when it finally arrived, quickly established itself as our favourite.

Radishes were made for nibbling, on their own, or with butter and salt, or if you were poor, as Gerard records, with bread and salt alone. In the 16th century they were eaten as a digestive when the stomach was 'slack or irksome with meat', or as a refresher between courses, or to stimulate the appetite. They did many other things as well: good for pimples, the noise in your ears, swellings in the throat, woman's milk, or to 'send down the termes and worms in the belly'.

As far as I can tell, there is little to choose between the varieties, certainly as far as flavour goes, though you will find a difference of colour and crispness. My own affection remains staunchly with the plump round Cherry Belle rather than the long-legged French Breakfast kind.

A recent addition to seed catalogues is a variety of radish called München Bier, grown specifically for its pods. (As far as I am aware, any radish can produce pods if left to grow and seed itself, but this variety is especially recommended.) Eventually, long thin light green pods form, which are crisp, succulent and mildly peppery. They should be eaten young, scattered over salads, or sliced, and well before the pepperiness becomes mustard hot. They can also be sliced and stir-fried and in former times were pickled.

However, a word of caution. Be sure and grow radishes destined for pods in an odd corner in ground you are not likely to need for some time. The plants are unruly and grow amazingly large; note, too, that it takes a good four months for the pods to form.

The best radishes are those of spring and early summer; sow lots, and pick them in bunches, like lovers' posies. Wash, trim, leaving a tuft of stalk, and present them in a small white dish, or dotted over salads. Nothing grows so easily. If the weather is cool and moist, they grow quickly and are mild and succulent whatever their size. As summer progresses, even young ones become unbearably hot.

Radishes picked straight from the garden, as they should be, need no crisping in water. If you need to store them, prepare them first and keep in sealed plastic boxes in the refrigerator. The colour dulls and they lose something of their fresh earthy crispness. In this case, plunge them for a while in cold water to freshen them.

When you tire of nibbling radishes, or when there are only a few, use them sliced thinly and make little salads with oranges and other fruits, or with cucumber or fennel, mixed with a sweet mustardy vinaigrette.

Radishes can be cooked, though I do not see the advantage with the spring and summer kind.

Rhubarb

Before rhubarb became a garden plant in the mid-18th century, it had been a medical plant, for some 4,000 years. The roots were valued for their purgative powers, and were first brought to Europe from China and Russia in the Middle Ages.

Garden varieties were less efficacious as a drug but the stems were palatable enough to be put into pies, and came early in the year before gooseberries ripened. However, it was not very highly thought of until the early 19th century, when it was discovered that forcing turned ordinary rhubarb into a delicacy. This resulted in the rapid development of countless new varieties of garden rhubarb, both for forced and natural cultivation. Almost a hundred of these still survive in the national Rhubarb Collection at the Northern Horticultural Society at Harlow Car in Harrogate, yet hardly any are available commercially today.

It does not surprise me that rhubarb has a dowdy image in the kitchen. Most common garden rhubarb has little to commend it. It is tough, stringy, and often unbearably tart. As the Victorians discovered, forced rhubarb is immeasurably better. What I suspect few gardeners realise, is that rhubarb can be forced easily at home. Any variety of rhubarb can be forced but those specially bred for the purpose are better. These are divided into early, mid and late, each maturing at approximately monthly intervals apart. By taking account of this, you can spread the season out over two or three months. The flavour of rhubarb can vary considerably. Timperley Early, discovered as a sport in a Cheshire rhubarb field in the 1920s, is one of the most popular forcing varieties. It is still the earliest maturing variety of rhubarb, but though commendable in every other respect, lacks the finesse and flavour of some of the later maturing varieties. Seek out one of the few specialist suppliers like Chris Bowers, of Whispering Trees Nursery, Norfolk, and ask their advice. The Rhubarb Research Station at Cawood in Yorkshire has also bred some very creditable rhubarbs, such as Cawood Castle, specifically for garden cultivation rather than forcing.

To do well rhubarb must have a rich soil, and will require liberal applications of muck or other organic matter every year. Whether you grow rhubarb for forcing or not, the procedure is the same. Begin by potting up root cuttings early in the year, choosing those with a good eye. Grow them on under cover, planting them out in June, making sure you give them ample room, spacing the plants 2–3ft (60–90cm) apart. Leave the plants to grow on two years before forcing.

Rhubarb forced naturally in the garden often has greater depth of flavour than commercially forced rhubarb which is dug up and forced under heat, but it comes later, around late March and through April. Strictly speaking, by not applying heat you are blanching rather than forcing. Victorian chimney pots make superb blanching pots. They soak up the warmth from the sun, providing a sheltered micro-climate in which the rhubarb grows quickly. Otherwise, an upturned dustbin, weighted down on top, covered with a black polythene bag to ensure total exclusion of light, placed over the crowns or young plants, is perfectly satisfactory. Inspect diligently for slugs; these ruin the stalks. The stalks grow quickly, especially in mild weather. Check their progress every couple of days. Pull gently from the base, taking care not to break off the young secondary stalks cradled in the base which will produce further pickings.

It is false economy to let the stalks grow too large. Forced or not, they become tough and more acid, especially in cold weather when they are not growing as fast. Pick them young before the oxalic acid has time to assert itself too much. Reserve the best sticks for compotes, the thinner sprue going for general cooking, jams and so on. Avoid picking too much and thus exhausting the root. Commercial growers throw away the spent roots, but in the garden they need to gain strength for the following year.

Rhubarb can be forced as soon as the crowns start into growth, from January onwards, though there seems little to be gained until the weather has become noticeably milder. We generally wait until February or early March. Start forcing as soon as the crowns show signs of real growth.

Once picked, rhubarb quickly becomes floppy. This is of no consequence – unless reliving childhood pleasures of eating sticks of rhubarb dipped into sugar – but can be prevented to a certain extent by slicing off the leaves, and storing the stems wrapped in clingfilm or in a plastic bag in the refrigerator. Forced rhubarb needs merely to be wiped and chopped. The skin is generally tender and should be left on.

In British cookery, rhubarb is used almost wholly as a fruit, in desserts, cakes and puddings, and to make jam and chutneys. Botanically it is a vegetable, the leaf stalk being the part of the plant we eat. As with tomatoes, beans, aubergines and corn, we pay scant regard to botany in the kitchen, but it is useful to remember that the gentle tartness of forced rhubarb serves equally well in savoury dishes, especially with fish and fatty meat.

Forced rhubarb is more tender, requires far less sugar than ordinary garden rhubarb, and careful cooking if it is not to collapse. It keeps its beautiful pink colour when cooked.

Poached rhubarb

A bowl of perfectly poached rhubarb is no easy matter to get right. The simplest method I have found – which prooduces perfect results every time – is as follows. As a general guide, 1¼–1½lb (570–675g) prepared rhubarb will provide 4 good servings:

Make a light syrup by simmering 2oz (60g) of sugar per pint (600ml) of water for a few minutes. This can be plain or flavoured with vanilla, cinnamon, cardamom, citrus peel, ginger or scented leaves and flowers such as the lemon scented geranium or elderflower leaves. Add the rhubarb, wiped with damp kitchen paper and cut into lengths. Don't crowd the pan – the rhubarb sticks should remain in one layer. Cover, and bring gently back to the boil. Turn off the heat and leave to cool, by which time the rhubarb will be tender.

Much of the pinkness goes into the syrup. Boil some of this down to a sticky sauce and pour over the rhubarb – the juices from the rhubarb will dilute it sufficiently, resulting in a beautiful deep rosy pink liquid. The rest of the syrup can be used another time. If you can, allow to stand for 12–24 hours in a cool place or the refrigerator before serving.

Poached rhubarb keeps extremely well in the refrigerator. Keep it in an enclosed plastic box or cover the dish with cling film. It can be frozen successfully, though there is some loss of texture.

Rhubarb and grapefruit compote

A friend introduced me to rhubarb compote for breakfast, quite the nicest springtime purge I know.

*1 large grapefruit, scrubbed in hot
  water
2oz (60g) sugar*

*1 pt (600ml) water
1lb (450g) forced rhubarb cut into 2in
  (5cm) lengths*

Peel the rind thinly from half the grapefruit, cut into long spillikins and simmer with the sugar and water for a few minutes. Add the rhubarb, bring back to a gentle boil, cover, turn off the heat and cool. Transfer to a dish, draining well, and add the grapefruit segments, free of pith and peel. Boil the syrup down to a quarter of its volume, and pour over the compote. Serve cold.

Julienne of rhubarb

This is the simplest way to serve rhubarb with meat or fish: slice the rhubarb into matchstick pieces and toss in a little butter for 30–60 seconds. Sprinkle sparingly with sugar and serve in little mounds as a garnish. Other flavourings – ginger, chives, crushed cardamom – can be added. One stick should be sufficient for four.

Rhubarb and ginger sauce

If you have never tried rhubarb with fish, this sauce is the place to start.

8oz (225g) forced chopped rhubarb
½in (1.25cm) piece of fresh ginger,
    chopped
½ small onion, chopped

4 tbsp water
piece of orange rind
juice of 1 fresh orange

Put all the ingredients in a small pan, cover, and cook gently until the fruit and onion are quite soft. Sieve, pressing hard against the sides of the sieve, and sweeten marginally. The sauce should be smooth and of medium consistency. Serve with oily or white fish, or with rich meat such as duck.

Braised pork with rhubarb and honey

2lb (900g) shoulder of pork, tied in a
    piece
1 large onion, finely sliced
12oz (340g) forced rhubarb, chopped

1 tbsp honey
6–8 fl oz (180–240ml) white wine or
    dry cider
½oz (15g) butter

Seal the meat in a nonstick frying pan. Arrange the onion in the bottom of a casserole dish which will just take the meat comfortably in a single layer. Follow with the rhubarb, dribbling over the honey. Lay the meat on top. Deglaze the frying pan with the wine or cider and pour over the meat. Cover tightly, and cook in a very low oven 130–140°C/250–275°F/gas mark ½–1, for 2½–3 hours, until very tender.

Remove the meat to a serving dish. Fish out the vegetables with a slotted spoon and boil down the juices to about 5 fl oz (150ml). Enrich with the butter and recombine with the vegetables. Slice the meat and serve with the sauce poured round. Accompany with rice.

Note This dish easily adapts to pork chops or shoulder steaks. For a one pot dish, thinly sliced potatoes can be included, arranging them neatly over the meat. Cover tightly and cook slowly as before, allowing around 2 hours cooking time. The dish can be served as it is, or the meat and potatoes removed and the sauce thickened with potato flour slaked in water.

Rhubarb and cream sauce for white fish

Should you have some fish stock of quality, this is a simply made sauce to accompany any grilled or plainly cooked white fish. For 4 people, simmer about ½ pt (300ml) stock with a little vermouth until reduced by half or of a good flavour. Throw in a stick of pink forced rhubarb cut into orderly julienne strips. Simmer for a minute, then add cream to soften. Continue cooking for a few moments until the rhubarb is soft but not mushy. Now take the edge off the tartness with little sugar, 1–2 small teaspoons. Bind the juices very slightly with potato flour slaked in a spot of cream or water, arrange around the fish and serve. Do not be nervous about the addition of the sugar. It makes all the difference to the sauce.

Herring or mackerel stuffed with rhubarb

This recipe comes via the Irish section of Alan Davidson's *North Atlantic Seafood* and is from the Irish Sea Fisheries Board. It is one I frequently turn to, rhubarb and herring and mackerel being at the best around the same time. It works especially well with forced rhubarb. I have added allspice and have scaled down the original quantities.

4 large boned and filleted herrings, or
  4 mackerel
1 small onion, finely chopped
knob of butter for frying
4–6oz (120–180g) forced rhubarb,
  chopped
1 tbsp toasted breadcrumbs

10–12 allspice berries, lightly roasted
and ground in a mortar (or 1 generous
  tsp of ground allspice)
For the sauce
8oz (225g) chopped forced rhubarb
a little lemon or orange rind
1 tbsp each of water and sugar

Sweat the onion in a knob of butter in a covered pan until soft, add the chopped rhubarb and cook for 5 minutes until the rhubarb is soft but not mushy. Stir in the breadcrumbs and set aside.

Lay the fish skin side down, spread the stuffing evenly over the surface, then sprinkle each generously with allspice. Roll up from head to tail, secure with a cocktail stick and lay in a greased snug-fitting dish. Bake, uncovered, in a hot oven, 200°C/400°F/gas mark 6, for about 20 minutes or until done.

Meanwhile, simmer the sauce ingredients until the rhubarb is very soft, and blend to a smooth pink purée. The sauce needs to be sharp, but correct with a little more sugar if necessary. Hand the sauce round separately.

Rhubarb, hazelnut and cinnamon sponge

A light pudding.

1¼lb (570g) prepared forced rhubarb, cut into 2in (5cm) lengths
1 large egg and 1 egg white
1oz (30g) soft brown sugar, plus 2–3 tbsp for the rhubarb

1oz (30g) freshly ground hazelnuts
1oz (30g) wholewheat pastry flour
1 tsp cinnamon

Par-cook the rhubarb by poaching in syrup for 2–3 minutes. Drain very thoroughly and layer neatly in a deep pie dish. Sprinkle with 2–3 tbsp sugar and set aside.

Whisk the egg, egg white and ¾oz (20g) of the sugar in a bowl over simmering water for about 5 minutes until thick and mousse-like. Take off the heat, and gently fold in the dry ingredients, sifting them together first and keeping back 1 tbsp hazelnuts for the topping. Spoon over the rhubarb mixture. Sprinkle the top with the rest of the hazelnuts mixed with the remaining sugar and bake in a hot oven, 200°C/400°F/gas mark 6, for 15 minutes. Allow to cool a little before serving. Serves 3–4.

Seakale

Seakale is an enigma. It is one of the easiest plants to grow, long-lived, productive, and delicious. Great gardeners like Thomas Jefferson and Gilbert White have grown and praised it, yet I doubt whether more than a handful of people have it in their gardens today.

It's also our one true native delicacy, a seashore plant of dry shingly beaches, once common along much of the south and west coast. The transition from native wild plant to garden vegetable took place sometime early in the 18th century. The man who did most to popularise it and to bring it to the attention of the greater gardening public was William Curtis, founder and editor of the *Botanical Magazine*. He had been introduced to seakale by his friend and benefactor, the physician and philanthropist Dr John Coakley Lettsom, who had discovered it on holiday in Southampton and grown it in his own garden in London. Curtis was impressed, and eventually set aside seven acres next to his botanical garden and nursery at Brompton for its cultivation. Whenever he could, he encouraged clients and acquaintances to grow it and at the end of his life published a pamphlet on how to grow and use it to be included with every box of seed.

William Curtis did a good job. By the 19th century seakale had become popular with middle-class Victorians the length and breadth of the country. The quantities enjoyed were prodigious, some 200–300 plants considered an appropriate number for a large household, requiring 60–100 forcing pots and no doubt an army of gardeners to attend to the forcing.

A modern gardener can be content with half a dozen plants. Provided your soil is suitable – well drained and fertile – and a sunny spot can be found for it, nothing is less trouble. The most reliable method is to grow from root cuttings or thongs. These can be obtained from the family firm of A. R. Paske, Regal Lodge, Kentford, Newmarket, Suffolk, who have been growing seakale for 50 years. It is a perennial plant and should be given a bed of its own. 'The cuttings of the roots are as of the size of the ring finger,' explains William Curtis in his pamphlet. 'Cut them into pieces of about two inches in length, burying each in an upright position about three inches under ground. The middle of March will be a proper season for doing this.' Make the cuts up to 4in (10cm) in length, square at the top and slanting at the bottom. This is to ensure the roots are planted right way up, i.e. square side pointing upwards. The pieces of root seem small but grow into sizeable plants and should be planted 12in (30cm) apart,with at least 12in (30cm) between the rows. Apply a dressing of seaweed meal, water in dry weather and religiously remove any flower stems which appear. Feed it annually. After two years the first crop can be taken.

It occurs to me I had better describe what seakale is like. I do not think one could call seakale beautiful. Once blanched, it has long thin pale stems, which often twist, crowned with a tuft of yellow or sometimes pinky brown fronds. Its taste is often compared to asparagus, but this will not do at all. It has none of the seductiveness of asparagus, nor does it share its softness on the tongue. It tastes of itself, agreeably mild, and with a very slight hazel nuttiness or, depending on how you see it, a faint hint of cabbage.

To be palatable seakale needs to be blanched. Seakale forcing pots are a thing of the past, though one or two potters are now making them again. We use a Victorian chimney pot which serves for seakale and rhubarb, but any large pot or box will do. Paske's suggest covering the plants in January, though they can just as easily be left until they have started into growth. You will need to protect against slugs and exclude all light with either a tile or a black polythene bag pulled over the pot. Check the plants regularly. Old gardeners would pile dung around the pot to give it extra warmth and protection and bring the plants forward. Connoisseurs favoured blanching under leaves. If you live by the sea, you could do as your predecessors did and heap smooth shingle over.

Blanched outside, seakale is ready from late April. The season is short, no more than a month. The pale fleshy stalks are quite brittle and need to be picked with care. Cut – do not pull – near the base, taking care not to damage the crown. Leave sufficient stems to enable the plant to build up strength for the next year, taking away the blanching pot as soon as you are through. This is the lazy gardener's way. The usual practice in former times was to force seakale inside. Victorians utilised their vineries, mushroom, cucumber and melon houses to give a succession of seakale through the winter and spring, discarding the spent crowns afterwards. If you are interested in this, you will find an excellent and detailed modern account in Christopher Lloyd's book, *The Well Tempered Garden*.

Seakale should be picked fresh, it is not a vegetable which stores well, losing those nuances of flavour which contribute to its finely tuned delicacy. There is in addition a faint suggestion of cabbage rankness about old seakale, which turns it from a cherished vegetable into an ordinary one. Some authors believe, also, that the outer skin toughens when seakale is stored. Certainly I have noticed that on the odd occasion I have been able to buy seakale or have had it sent by post, it has been tougher than my own picked fresh from the garden, and, consequently, takes longer to cook.

The stalks should be washed gently under running water, rubbing away or cutting out any slimy bits the slugs may have had. Thinly pare the outer skin from the large stalks using a potato peeler. It is difficult to be precise about cooking seakale. Young thin stalks may take 4–5 minutes, fatter and older stalks may take up to three times as long. Cook it as you would asparagus, laying the stalks in a single layer in a large pan and cooking gently in a little water, until the point of the knife inserts easily into the centre, testing every couple of minutes. It should be served plain with a little melted butter or hollandaise. William Curtis liked it buttered on toast.

Seakale is also very good raw, which in many respects brings out its virtues better. Both young and fat stalks are crisp and juicy, more refreshing to my mind than either celery or cucumber. Pare off the outside skin if you want, though this should not be necessary for young, fresh seakale. Trim the ends, cut into batons and serve to accompany mild English farmhouse cheese, or cut and use in salads.

Seakale and hazelnut salad

This is a good way of making the most of tender young stalks of seakale; 6oz (180g) diced celery and 2oz (60g) diced apple makes a very different but equally respectable salad.

8oz (225g) young seakale stalks, wiped clean and tops removed
a mixture of young green salad leaves, (as many different kinds as possible), washed and diced
1oz (30g) lightly toasted hazelnuts, coarsely chopped

For the dressing
1 tsp Dijon mustard
1 tbsp hazelnut oil
3–4 tbsp single cream
2 tsp finely chopped chervil

If the seakale stems are fat, slice them down the middle before cutting crosswise into short lengths. Mix all the dressing ingredients to a smooth cream, and toss the seakale in the dressing. Arrange the salad leaves on 4 side plates, spoon the mixture in the centre of each, scatter over the hazelnuts and serve as a first course.

Seakale with cream sauce

Recipes for seakale are few and far between. Eleanor Sinclair Rohde, a keen seakale grower, was one of the few to offer suggestions on how to cook and serve seakale. This recipe comes from her book *Vegetable Cultivation and Cookery*, published in 1938. I have added a small amount of potato flour which saves the anxiety over the egg curdling and helps to bind the sauce.

12oz-1lb (340–450g) seakale, washed and trimmed
1 large egg yolk
2–3 fl oz (60–90ml) single cream

½ tsp potato flour
2–3 fl oz (60–90ml) cooking liquor (see method)
salt

If possible, choose seakale of even size. Cook in a scant 1in (2.5cm) water in a covered pan until soft, fishing out the stalks as they are done if of varied sizes. Drain and keep warm while you make the sauce.

Whisk the egg yolk, cream and potato flour in a bowl until frothy. Quickly boil down the cooking liquor to 2–3 fl oz (60–90ml). Pour on to the egg mixture, stirring constantly. Tip the lot back into the pan and, still stirring, heat the sauce gently until thick and very hot. Season lightly to taste with salt and pour over the waiting seakale. A little finely chopped tarragon or chervil can also be added.

Spinach beet

Spinach beet is the ancient form of beetroot. It has spinach type leaves and a spinachy flavour but no swollen root. Though the leaves differ in appearance, it is a very close relation to Swiss chard, but is far hardier.

Spinach beet is not a promising sounding vegetable. As you would expect, it lacks the delicacy and refinement of true spinach. It is nevertheless admirably useful for all manner of soups, stuffings, stir-fries, pâtés and terrines. It is best in autumn and spring. The weather is mild enough to encourage regular growth, and the leaves are tender and agreeably flavoured, respectable enough to serve as a vegetable in its own right. In winter, growth slows down to a minimum and the leaves become coarser in texture and flavour; cover with cloches, and this will improve matters somewhat.

It is an easy vegetable to grow, and a patch of ground should be found for it in every garden. Sow the seeds in August, thinning the plants to 6in (15cm) apart. Pick regularly, while the leaves are young and tender. Older leaves develop a slight bitterness and are not so good to eat; this bitter edge also seems to develop if the leaves are stored for more than a few days. Take the best leaves from each plant in turn. They need no preparation beyond a good wash and removing the central stalk.

Pot-roasted veal with spinach beet and saffron sauce

Saffron was used prodigiously throughout the Middle Ages. It was grown chiefly in the eastern counties – Walsingham in Norfolk and Saffron Walden in Essex were two famous centres – and fetched very high prices. It was an important medicinal plant and commercial production continued until the end of the 18th century.

Strangely British traditional use of saffron, save in saffron cake, has completely disappeared. Modern cooks know it through Indian, Spanish or Italian dishes. To appreciate its full aromatic qualities, it should not be used in too miserly a fashion. Packet saffron, as long as it is genuine, is easier to use than the dried stigmas. Here's a dish richly flavoured with saffron in the medieval style.

2lb (900g) silverside of veal, boned and rolled
For the stuffing
4oz (120g) spinach beet, midribs removed and washed
2 tbsp cooked rice
1 tbsp olive oil
1 clove garlic, chopped (optional)
1 dried fig
good grating of fresh nutmeg
½ packet of dried saffron

For the mirepoix
3in (7.5cm) stick each of carrot, celery and leek
½ small onion
knob of butter and little olive oil for frying
1 chopped tomato
1 glass white wine
remaining ½ packet of saffron
1–2 tsp potato flour slaked in water

Begin with the stuffing. Blanch the spinach beet for a couple of minutes, drain, squeeze out the moisture and chop finely. Mix with the rest of the stuffing ingredients and set aside.

Open out the veal and spread the stuffing over the meat, pressing it in firmly. Carefully roll up and tie with string. Choose a heavy casserole dish that will hold the joint snugly. In it, soften the carrot, celery, leek and onion in a knob of butter and little olive oil. Put the joint on top, tuck the tomato down the sides and cook uncovered in a very hot oven, 220°C/425°F/gas mark 7 for 15 minutes.

Pour over the wine, cover tightly with greaseproof paper and the lid, and continue to cook at 180°C/375°F/gas mark 4 for 1–1¼ hours. Remove and keep warm for half an hour. This allows the meat to settle and the delicious rich juices to flow out and help form the sauce. Transfer the meat to a serving dish.

Strain the sauce through a sieve, pushing through enough of the vegetables to give it body and texture. Add the rest of the saffron, check the seasoning and thicken to your liking with the potato flour slaked in water. The finished sauce should be quite sharp, and a vibrant golden orange. Either serve separately or carve the meat and spoon the sauce around.

Potatoes are not appropriate for these richly flavoured dishes. Pasta or rice is better, keeping other vegetables as a separate course.

Spring greens

Spring greens is a catch-all phrase to describe any early green brassica. All spring greens are high in vitamin C. They properly divide into the loose-hearted cabbages and the kales, but sprout tops, spinach beet, even garden nettles if you have them or can be bothered with them, are all admirable in their way.

True spring greens, collards, do not form a heart but remain flattish in appearance like a cabbage that has been squeezed gently from both sides. For the gardener, seeds appear to be difficult if not impossible to procure. Virtually every kind of seed available seems to develop a pointed heart as spring progresses. It then becomes a spring cabbage, which if needs be will last into June or July. In itself, this is no bad thing, but hardly the point. With some varieties, April, for example, if you cut the heart quite early leaving a good length of stalk, this encourages the side shoots to grow, and will give you greener greens. Harbinger is another excellent spring green.

Spring greens are an easy and satisfying vegetable to grow, a good crop to follow broad beans or peas. Sow the seed in mid-July and plant out sometime in August, spacing the plants 9in (23cm) apart. Cloches help to protect them from snow and rain during the worst of the weather. A boost of nitrogen scattered round them in spring acts as a tonic and encourages growth.

Spring greens are sturdy plants that can be left in the ground until required; picked fresh they are deliciously sweet. Cut them above the base, leaving enough of the stalk to enable regrowth of new leaves – much favoured by Pliny.

Bought spring greens need diligent picking over, but garden greens need very little preparation. Discard the very outer tough leaves, throwing them to the chickens. Rinse briefly, trim the stalks, and shred coarsely. There is no need to remove the midrib unless this seems a good idea, or the recipe calls for it.

Recipes habitually indicate that greens need lengthy boiling to be tolerably tender. Garden spring greens do not, and take no longer than ordinary cabbages, though their texture is more resilient. Blanching suits them very well – see the recipe opposite on page 53 for spring green and potato cake – the inner leaves requiring only 1–2 minutes and the outer tougher leaves 2–3 minutes. Otherwise, give them 4–5 minutes hard boil in a small amount of water in a covered pan, less for the tender inner leaves. Drain very well and chop before serving. The midribs make pleasant eating, chopped and used in soups or stir-fries.

A patch of spring greens brings much grateful pleasure, but do not expect too much from them. Their role is to invigorate. Hearty soups and bubble and squeak are more in their line than butter or cream. Think of them as a robust chard rather than a cabbage, and you will find them agreeably accommodating – skeptics should try the risotto or the sauce for pasta on page 54.

Tuscan bean soup with cabbage

Bean soups of all kinds are great restoratives. Few soups soothe in quite the same way. Use spring greens now; later on, use Swiss chard. The quantities are meant as a guideline – the ratio of beans to cabbage can be altered preferentially, but do not stint on the olive oil, which should be your gutsy best. It is prudent to cook a large batch of beans in one go, freezing the rest for more soups another time.

4oz (120g) uncooked haricot beans, soaked in water
6–8oz (180–225g) shredded spring greens

1–2 large cloves garlic, finely chopped
olive oil
salt

Cook the beans in ample fresh water until soft. Reserve a couple of tablespoons or so per person, and blend the rest with sufficient cooking liquor to produce a smooth, thick purée.

Meanwhile, cook the cabbage briskly in 1in (2.5cm) boiling water; keep it crisp. Thin down the soup with some of the cabbage liquor, adding extra water if necessary to give the desired consistency, thick or thin. In a separate pan, gently sweat the garlic in 1–2 tbsp olive oil. This is the 'odori' (in the version without the cabbage, you would add a handful of chopped parsely also). Tip in the soup, reserved beans and cabbage. Stir, cook for a few minutes only. Taste and add salt as necessary, pepper if you want. Ladle into shallow soup bowls and serve with a little flagon of olive oil; this is to be sprinkled on top and stirred into the soup as a final aromatic.

Spring green and potato cake

It is a pity that any kind of bubble and squeak is so often made with leftovers. Freshly prepared, it is as good a dish as you will find anywhere. Recipes allow a fair degree of latitude (Dr Kitchener favoured beef in his), though potato and cabbage are the constants. This is a bright green version made with spring cabbage. Fried onions, cooked first and then incorporated into the cabbage and potato mixture, can be added, as can garlic, spring onions or herbs such as parsley, dill or chives.

10–12oz (285–340g) spring greens, washed, trimmed and coarsely shredded
1¼ lb (570g) freshly cooked potatoes

2 tbsp fine oatmeal
1–2 tbsp fat – beef dripping, bacon fat, or failing that, lard

Begin by blanching the greens in a large pot of boiling water, in two batches if necessary. Cover, bring back to the boil (which should be almost immediately) and cook for 2–3 minutes. Fish out a piece to try it; it should be soft but firm. Drain into a colander with a soup bowl underneath to catch the drips and repeat with the next batch. Once done, squeeze out all the excess moisture from the greens and chop finely – a moments' work in a food processor.

Mash the potatoes, leaving a few lumps here and there to give the cake texture. Mix with the greens and oatmeal, seasoning if you wish. Melt half the fat in a heavy or nonstick frying pan and press in the mixture, smoothing it out to form a flat thick cake. Give it 10–15 minutes on a low heat until the underside is nicely crisp and brown. Turn over by inverting a plate on top and flipping the pan upside down. Add the rest of the fat, slip back the cake, and give it another 10 minutes. Serve cut into thick wedges from the pan. Marvellous with sausages, cold beef or fried eggs and bacon. Serves 3–4.

Crispy fried spring greens

This is the dish served in Chinese restaurants disguised as seaweed, served as a crisp appetiser with almonds sprinkled on top. It is an easy dish to prepare at home. It is excellent also scattered over a plain green undressed salad.

8oz (225g) spring greens, washed, dried and midribs removed
vegetable oil for frying
salt

soy sauce (optional)
¾–1oz (20–30g) skinned almonds, or 1 tbsp sesame seeds, toasted

Lay the prepared leaves on top of each other, roll tightly to form a fat cigar, and carefully shred crosswire into hair-like strands using a serrated knife. Lightly run your fingers through the strands to separate the coils. Using a deep fat frier or wok, deep fry in small batches in hot oil for barely a minute until the foam subsides and the strands become translucent. Drain very well, spreading the glistening crispy strands on kitchen paper. To serve, pile into a dish lined with paper, season with

salt, a few drops of soy if you like, and scatter over the almonds or sesame seeds.
Note It is advisable to cook a trial batch first. If the strands darken at the edges, the oil is too hot. The strands splutter ferociously as they hit the pan – this soon subsides and there is no need for concern, but do not attempt to fry too much in one go.

Spring green and walnut sauce for pasta

3oz (90g) prepared tender spring
  greens, washed and coarsely
  shredded
½-1 small onion, chopped

½oz (15g) walnuts
½oz (15g) brown bread, crusts
  removed
about 2½ fl oz (75ml) creamy milk

Blanch the spring greens and onion until soft – about 3–4 minutes in a large pan of water. Drain well, and blend with the other ingredients in a blender or food processor, using enough milk to form a smoothish paste. It should have a texture similar to pesto. The sauce can be used in one of two ways:
1 As a filling on its own or mixed with about half its weight of ricotta cheese for ravioli or cannelloni, keeping the paste stiff.
2 As a sauce for hot pasta. Reheat in a small pan, thinning with a little of the cooking water, mix with the pasta and serve with finely grated parmesan or pecorino cheese, or else a creamy cheddar of character. My husband favours olive oil and no cheese. Either way, much better than you think. Serves 2–3.

Spring green risotto

A mild, soothing risotto, good to accompany crisp grilled chicken or chicken in vinegar (p. 158).

6oz (180g) finely shredded spring
  greens, cut into 3–4in (7.5–10cm)
  lengths
3 tbsp fruity olive oil
1 small onion, finely sliced

8oz (225g) arborio rice
about 24 fl oz (720ml) well flavoured
  beef or chicken stock
parmesan or pecorino cheese to serve

Blanch the greens for 2 minutes in a large pan of boiling water. Drain thoroughly. Heat 1 tbsp olive oil in a heavy pan and soften the onion for a few minutes. Add the spring greens and stir in another tablespoon of oil. Cover, and cook over a very gentle heat for 15–20 minutes. Stir occasionally and add a splash of water towards the end to prevent sticking or burning.

Now make the risotto in the usual way: have the stock ready and hot on a low flame. Stir the rice into the greens and add a quarter of the stock. Cook gently, adding more stock as it becomes absorbed by the rice. Stir gently from time to time. After 20 minutes, check the rice. If it is almost cooked, add the last of the stock, turn off the heat, cover the pan and leave for 5 minutes. The risotto will continue to cook in its own steam. Check the seasoning, stir in the last tablespoon of olive oil and

serve immediately, handing round the cheese separately. Serves 2–4.
Note It is impossible to say precisely how much stock a risotto will absorb.
The finished risotto should be creamy rather than sloppy, and should just
spread a little on the plate.

Kale

The kales are among our most ancient vegetables, and closest to the original
cabbage. They are without doubt the earliest cultivated brassicas, stretching
back several thousand years. The name derives from the Greek, *kaulos*,
meaning stem, which gives a clue to its growth habit, a mass of leaves sitting
on top of a thick stem like a frilly mop-headed palm.

Modern kale is a thoroughly northern vegetable, lumbered with images of
poverty and toughness. The name given to northern kitchen gardens was
kail-yards, and poor people grew little else. The term has come to apply to
any cabbage with sprouting, curled or finely dented leaves which does not
form a solid heart. As such there are – or were – innumerable varieties, one to
every kitchen garden almost. Today, they come either plain or frilly. The
frilly sort are by far the most common, and are generally thought better,
though a gardening friend is most enthusiastic about the flat-leaved
asparagus kale.

Kale is a winter/spring crop. Depending on the season, it matures after
Christmas and lasts well into spring when the sideshoots develop. These are
similar to sprouting broccoli but smaller, and provide choice eating. A frost
sweetens kale and improves it considerably. Like all overwintered crops, it has a
long season of growth. It is sown in June and is a good crop to follow early
potatoes. Curly kale does not seem to like being transplanted and is better sown
in situ, where it is to mature. On a deep bed, there will be room for three plants,
approximately 15in (38cm) apart. Kale are very hardy plants, though not
infallibly so. Expect to lose some occasionally in very severe weather.

Pick kale fresh, young, and successively, choosing from the tender inner
leaves. Regular picking will help delay it running to seed and ensure a
continuous succession of new growth. When you pick, allow at least twice as
much as you think you'll need – it fills the basket quickly but wilts
considerably in the pan. If needs be, it will keep for a few days in a plastic bag
in the refrigerator. Depending on your passion for greens, allow 2–4 oz
(60–120g) per person uncooked weight. Kale is obligingly clean and
blemish-free. Cut away the midrib if it seems coarse, wash and shred and
cook as for other greens.

Curiously, people find little to say in favour of kale. 'A coarse sort of
thing,' declared William Cobbet in his book, *The English Gardener*, who
couldn't understand why anyone should bother with such an unappealing

vegetable. He should have tried the tender young sideshoots dressed with olive oil, and served warm as a salad, or fried with garlic, or used them in a thick nourishing bean soup on a cold spring day. Kale has a robust character all of its own. The texture is chewy and the taste is earthy, strong and puritanical. Nothing quite like it with the Sunday roast or sausage and mash. It is not a vegetable to be dressed up, but should rather be used as is appropriate to its history with simple things like eggs and potatoes and in thick, meaty pottages. Garlic suits it admirably.

Kale with beans, tomato and garlic

An unsophisticated dish, for unsophisticated tastes. Take your kale, shred it coarsely and blanch for 2 minutes. Drain and press out as much moisture as you can. Now fry a crushed and chopped clove of garlic in a little olive oil for 30 seconds. Add the kale, an equivalent quantity, more or less, of cooked beans, mashing them lightly with a fork, and a little chopped tomato. Toss for a couple of minutes, season and serve with extra olive oil handed separately. 4oz (120g) each of cooked kale and beans, plus one tomato will feed two generously.

Kale with anchovies

This recipe comes from *Forbidden Fruits and Forgotten Vegetables*, by George and Nancy Marcus.

1 lb(450g) kale, washed and coarsely   *4 fillets of anchovy, chopped*
   chopped   *juice of half a lemon*
3 tbsp olive oil   *salt and pepper*
1 clove of garlic

Blanch the kale until tender, and drain well. Heat the oil and sauté the garlic for a few minutes until the oil takes on its flavour, then remove it. Stir in the kale and anchovies, toss until hot. Finish with lemon juice and season. As with all kale dishes, cooked diced potatoes fill the dish out nicely.

Kale, steak, and aïoli

Walking is our favourite pastime, from which we arrive home tired, happy – and hungry. In summer, a barbecue rounds off the day perfectly. In winter, this is replaced sometimes by steak grilled on a grillomat on top of the stove. Done well, this makes an admirable substitute. To accompany grilled steak, I have never yet found anything better than aïoli, a few boiled potatoes and perhaps a green salad. In winter, kale makes up the trio. A splendid dish. Don't forget the walk first.

    This is how to cook the steak (sirloin is best), which should be well hung and at room temperature: rub it on both sides with olive oil. Get the grillomat very hot. Lay the steak on top, at an angle to the ridges. After a minute, or slightly less, turn through 90 degrees and cook for another 45–60 seconds.

Turn the steak over, lower the heat right down and continue to cook for a further 4–5 minutes, depending on thickness. By this time there will be clear beads of red juice covering the surface. Do not overcook; it should be pink throughout, slice a tiny piece from the end to check. Serve immediately on hot plates, or better, warmed wooden boards.

Nettles

A patch of stinging nettles is a good thing to have in the garden: good for compost, good for attracting butterflies, and a useful spring supplement at a time when greenstuff can be sparse. All nettles should be picked well away from polluted roadside verges.

Nettles were once blanched. 'No plant is better adapted for forcing,' writes J. C. Loudon in his *Encyclopaedia of Gardening*. The creeping roots were collected and planted in hot beds or potted up and transferred to the forcing house, producing early tender shoots to be used as kale or spinach. In *Food for Free*, Richard Mabey writes that after early June the leaves become coarse and bitter and decidedly laxative.

At one time nettles formed a regular part of the spring diet, valued as a blood purifier and general promoter of good health. The young leaves are said to be especially beneficial, rich in vitamins and valuable for increasing the haemoglobin in the blood. The Roman naturalist Pliny wrote: 'Nettles make a not unpleasant food, which many eat in the further devout belief that it will keep diseases away throughout the whole year.' In the Scottish Highlands, March was considered tonic time; nettle kail soup taken three times in the month would clear the complexion and ensure good health for the rest of the year.

Pick only young shoots 'when the sun is in the sign of Aries', said the Roman cookery writer Apicus. Using gloves and a pair of scissors, snip off the tender tips. Wash them first in several changes of water to dislodge all the dust and dirt – the tips have hardly any sting to speak of and with care can be handled quite comfortably – and then shake dry. Like this, they will keep for a few days wrapped in a plastic bag in the refrigerator. The sting disappears in cooking.

Nettles are traditionally employed in soups, either simmered along with other ingredients such as potatoes and onions, or chopped and thrown into the pot for the last few minutes of cooking. Either way, they make an excellent addition to spring soups and cheap lamb broths thickened with barley or dried pulses.

Another way to use them is as follows: strip the leaves from the stems (these are inevitably tough) and simmer for about 10 minutes in a large pan with a few tablespoons of water until softened but still bright dark green.

Squeeze out the moisture and chop finely either by hand or in a food processor. Return to the pan and cook over a low heat to dry off any remaining moisture. You now have a basic nettle purée which can be stored in the freezer or a covered container for a few days in the refrigerator.

Reheat with a lump of butter, or better, cremé fraîche, and use as a filling for omelettes. Mix into some creamy scrambled eggs served with toast. Purée until smooth and use as a base for poached eggs. Or use as a last-minute addition to soups or other greens.

Nettle and sorrel purée

A handful of shredded sorrel leaves gives a lively kick to the basic nettle mixture above. Simmer together until the sorrel has wilted, enrich with butter or cream and use with eggs or in small quantities as an accompaniment to chicken or veal.

Patina of nettles

Apicius was the celebrated Roman gourmet who finding he had spent all his riches on food, poisoned himself rather than face the prospect of life without excess. He wrote *The Art of Cooking*, the only cookbook to have survived from the Roman Period. It includes a recipe for patina of nettles, which is the earliest recipe for nettles I have found. The nettles are washed, dried, chopped, moistened with liquamen, a fermented fish paste, pounded with pepper and simmered with oil. Beaten eggs are added, and the mixture cooked as a frittata or flat omelette, served hot or cold with black pepper sprinkled over. A modern version, for the experimentally minded, can be made by stewing chopped blanched nettles in olive oil. For liquamen use anchovy essence or – nearer the mark – either the Indonesian fish paste, *terasi*, or a southeast Asian fish sauce – *nam pla* or *nuoc mam*. (For an illuminating essay on these sauces, see Alan Davidson, *A Kipper with My Tea*.) Not bad.

Young nettle and potato purée

This very fine purée is from Anton Mosimann's book *Cuisine Naturelle*. The amount of potato used seems small when you first read the recipe but is in fact exactly right. It may be frozen halfway through and finished off when required. This quantity serves 8.

8 oz(225g) young nettle tops, washed thoroughly and drained
1 small potato, peeled and diced small
3/4 pt (450ml) vegetable stock

3½oz (100g) fromage blanc
freshly grated nutmeg
salt and pepper

Put the potato in a large pan and stuff the nettles on top. Add the stock, cover, bring to the boil and simmer for 20 minutes. Drain, squeezing the nettles gently against the sides of the pan. Purée in a liquidiser or food processor until smooth. The purée emerges a deep sea-green and can be frozen at this stage. To finish, season vigorously to taste – don't skimp the nutmeg – and beat in the fromage blanc. This gives the purée an attractive speckly appearance.

The purée can be reheated and is delicious with poached eggs or as a filling for omelettes, with fish such as trout, to accompany roast veal or as a sauce for salsify. If you have no stock, use water. For a different taste, substitute fromage blanc with a milky fresh soft goat's cheese. Or blend it with an equal weight of ricotta and use to stuff ravioli or courgette flowers.

Nettle and Welsh onion soup

An excellent springtime soup. Welsh onions grow quickly in the spring and can be used lavishly at this time. If you have none, use spring onions.

1½ – 2oz (45–60g) tender nettle tops, well washed, and stripped from their stalks
5 fl oz (150ml) each of milk, and chicken stock or water
6–8 spring onions, green and white part, chopped
8oz (225g) potatoes, peeled and diced

To finish
about ½ pt (300ml) extra water, or milk and water mixed
1 heaped tbsp finely chopped spring onion
up to ½oz (15g) butter

Simmer the first four ingredients in a covered pan until the potatoes are soft, about 15 minutes. Either mash with a potato masher to a rough purée, or if you prefer, blend until smooth and speckly. Dilute with extra water, adding a little more milk if you like, and bring back to the boil. Stir in the chopped spring onion, enrich with butter to taste and serve.

SALADS

Growing salads has been a happy and fulfilling education. For a small modern garden they are ideal, neither difficult nor too demanding, and provide more variety in taste, colour and texture than ever I thought possible.

Perhaps what I have come to appreciate most is spring, autumn and winter salads based on chicories, endives and a wide range of easily grown salad plants which the Elizabethans, then later the Victorians, were so fond of. Indeed, the range of salad plants available to the gardener prepared to search them out is remarkable, and numbers over a hundred. In 1910 the Royal Horticultural Society conducted extensive salad trials at Wisley and counted 18 varieties of corn salad, 39 endive, 12 cresses, 6 mustards, 7 dandelions, 81 cabbage lettuce, 25 cos, 21 spinach and 55 varieties of radish. It seems extraordinary to me that today's range of salad plants, though increasing, is not as great as it was, and I cannot help thinking that the diet of the nation is poorer for it.

Historically, the undisputed master of salads is the diarist, horticulturist, and founder member of the Royal Society, John Evelyn. There is much we can learn today from his good sense and imaginative instructions. In his *Instructions for the Gardener at Sayes-Court, Deptford* (his home from 1653), written in 1687, he defines and sets out the salad year most clearly. A salad, he writes, is to be a mixture of any greenstuff, blanched and unblanched, which may be found in the kitchen garden at any given time during the year, depending on the season. He lists 35 plants – lettuces, chicories, corn salad, purslane, cresses, spinach, fennel, the seed leaves of radish, cress and turnips, and herbs such as sorrel, parsley, burnet, tarragon, and the flower buds of nasturtium. By the time his famous book on salads, *Acetaria*, was published in 1699, John Evelyn's list of plants had grown to well over 70.

His instructions are quite definite. Only tender, choice leaves are to be used, the proportions of each chosen with care to create a harmonious balance of textures and flavours. For spring and summer salads he recommends sowing lemon and orange seeds, 'for the young leaves are excellent, to mingle with the rest of ye salade', and the tender tops of vine tendrils or hops. The measure he uses is the pugil, or small handful, 'as much as you can take up with the tops of your fingers: 3 with ye thumb'. The salad leaves are to be washed, swung dry, cut with a silver knife and dressed just before serving, his preferred dressing being oil and vinegar (the best oil, from Lucca), to which the yolks of hard-boiled eggs are added, or lemon or orange, or sometimes Tewkesbury mustard.

As John Evelyn demonstrates, the range of salads you can make is limitless. Provided you have the enthusiasm, it is one of the easiest of arts to master. It is rather like being a painter: you should have a love of colour and

texture and an eye for balance and harmony. No matter whether you are restricted to a few colours and a single paintbrush, or are given a boxful of every shade and hue, you can always enjoy the challenge it presents. It is the same with salads; only to make a good salad you must enjoy eating them.

Salads and salad plants are spread throughout the book as they fit our pattern of gardening and eating. Many span two or three seasons and some salad plants can be grown all year round. To this extent, salad growing is more flexible than other crops. They shift with the weather, the vagaries of the season and the whim of the cook. Each time you make a salad it will be a little different from the one you made yesterday.

Salad dressings

A salad dressing should perform two functions. It should add to the salad, and it should be sympathetic, be it to complement or contrast with the natural flavours. It should not be an afterthought, nor should it dominate. Nor, necessarily, should you feel a salad *has* to have a dressing to make it palatable or interesting. A dressing spoils the delicious buttery quality of summer lettuces, for example, which are quite perfect on their own. Where there is a dressing, my own feeling is that there should be only enough to coat the leaves lightly, but this is a matter for personal preference.

There are almost as many salad dressings as there are salads. Seasoned oil and vinegar, the basic vinaigrette, has been in use since Roman times, and is the constant. By varying the kind of oil, vinegar and seasonings, it is possible to produce an enormous range of dressings. Nut oils such as walnut, hazelnut or light sesame seed; honey, herb and fruit vinegars; seasonings such as chopped tomato, mustard, olives, capers, gherkins, anchovies, hard-boiled egg, and fresh herbs are all commonplace additions, as is garlic, though I do not share the general enthusiasm for garlicky dressings. At its simplest, a salad dressed with a few drops of fruity olive oil, a sprinkling of salt, and a scattering of croûtons is hard to better.

For dressed green salads, prepare the dressing in a large roomy bowl, rest the leaves lightly on top and toss just before serving. If you use very little dressing, as is my custom, even the bottom leaves will not spoil through soaking. For larger quantities of dressing rest the leaves over crossed salad tossers, or keep the leaves in a separate bowl. More often than not, I prefer my leaves simply arranged on a plate with a little nut oil or olive oil dribbled over from a teaspoon before the salad is served. Extra ingredients to give the salad piquancy, colour, texture and savour, can then be arranged on top.

Mayonnaise forms the basis of the second group of dressings, designed for salads based on cooked or root vegetables. Again, the permutations are many – you can flavour mayonnaise to produce a sauce which is delicate (fresh herbs), fiery (as in rouille), pungent (with garlic), piquant (with anchovies, capers or horseradish), spicy (curry powder) and so on.

Too much dogma is attached to the making of mayonnaise. Which oil you use depends on what you want the mayonnaise for. Decent olive oil is mandatory for aïoli, wonderful for fish, and delicious with broad beans, but will often swamp many other salads where a lighter oil would be a better choice. I have long been accustomed to using a blend of oils for most of my mayonnaises, and usually add both lemon juice and vinegar as sharpeners. Mustard acts as an emulsifier and will help the oil and egg yolk to bind more easily. Egg white has the same effect and, as anyone who customarily makes whole egg mayonnaise in a blender is aware, makes for a blander taste.

Something you may not know is that you can use egg white to correct a mayonnaise that has curdled. Add some of the white to a little of the curdled mayonnaise, blend until smooth, then re-incorporate the rest of the curdled mayonnaise. The main reason mayonnaise curdles is that either the oil, the egg or the basin was not at room temperature to start with. In cold weather, warming the bowl or blender bowl first is an essential precaution.

On the whole, I find undiluted mayonnaise in salad dressings too cloying. It is both lighter and more digestible if diluted with a little hot water, by adding no more than a teaspoon at a time, or if mixed with plain yoghurt.

Miscellaneous dressings based on yoghurt, cream, sour cream, or buttermilk; aromatic dressings based on pounded spices mixed with oil or coconut milk; and oriental dressings based on soy sauce and sugar with ginger, sesame seed, garlic and spring onion, form the third important group of dressings. There is much room for improvisation here and I have included a few suggestions, but you will find many more in Indian and oriental cookery books and in some of the more inventive vegetarian cookbooks.

Spring is traditionally a lean time for salad stuff, though with a little foresight the garden can be made to furnish a variety of fresh greenery to brighten up the table. For early spring, March and April, there are four possibilities: overwintered lettuce, misticanza, chicories such as grumolo verde and radicchio which put on luxuriant regrowth at this time, and small salad plants such as corn salad and claytonia. A selection of these is described below.

Mix a few leaves of each supplemented with a little of the first showing of sorrel, snipped chives, or chervil, or a few tiny sprigs of parsley or rocket. Supplement this if you like with watercress. The result is both refreshing and sympathetic to the time of the year.

One point. There are people who swear by dandelions. I find them terribly bitter myself, even when blanched. We have tried on two or three occasions to grow an improved strain with larger leaves from France, thinking this would be the answer. It was not.

Cresses

Cresses have been used for centuries as seedling crops to add to salads, and are valued for their pepperiness. They were amongst the plants with medicinal benefits that Thomas Hill included in his *Gardener's Labyrinth*, published in 1577, and recommended for various ailments – toothache, headache, coughs, and so on. They have survived in our familiar mustard and cress, popularised by the Victorians, though bought punnets today often contain salad rape seedlings instead.

The mature leaves of ordinary garden cress, *Lepidium sativum*, resemble rocket or flat parsley, but are more finely divided. A small patch soon makes a dense green carpet. It is best sown when the weather is cool, in spring and autumn, and cut frequently while young and tender and the pepperiness is not yet too pronounced. In hot weather, it quickly runs to seed.

There are other cresses to be grown in the garden. Greek cress is a variety of the ordinary garden cress, identical in taste and flavour. Land cress, *Barbarea verna*, also known as American, Belle Isle, or winter cress, is a strongly peppery hardy biennial salad plant. It resembles the common garden edible weed, bitter cress; if you compare them, save for the diminutive size of the latter, the two are almost identical. The dark green leaves look and taste very much like cultivated watercress (*Nasturtium officinale*), but are hotter and can become unbearably so as summer progresses. It is best grown in damp shady corners and makes a useful edging plant, the leaves spreading out to form a rosette. Sow in early Spring, or late summer for autumn and winter use. Land cress is very hardy, though protecting the leaves with a cloche over winter improves the quality. Overwintered plants throw up buttercup yellow cruciferous flowers in spring. Nip out the shoots as you find them, whilst still small, to add to salads. To subdue the hotness, chop and use in soups as you would watercress, for example, in clear Chinese broths with noodles and perhaps a chopped tomato.

The leaves of salad rape are pleasant, akin to rocket in flavour but less peppery. You grow it like cress and use it in the same way, except it runs to seed more slowly and germinates at very low temperatures, making it ideal for late autumn or early spring. Botanically, it is closely related to swede and it has mustard-like leaves. It was formerly one of our most popular salad plants, mentioned constantly in gardening and cookery books from the 17th century onwards. Today it is widely grown as cattle feed and for its oil (which, incidentally, from a nutritional point of view, in some respects compares favourably to olive oil).

Lamb's lettuce or corn salad

This charming salad plant is the cultivated variety of the wild corn salad, once a common sight in our corn fields. The herbalist Gerard was the first to mention it, describing its use among the French and Dutch who had settled in England. It became popular at once. By the mid-19th century, several varieties were in cultivation, including variegated kinds with white marbling in their leaves and one with a bright yellow heart.

The puzzle with this admirable plant is why it is not to be found in every back garden, or why it should be so expensive to buy. Nothing is easier to grow. It is extremely hardy, forming a tight rosette of floppy tongue-shaped leaves which hug the ground. Their flavour – which develops as autumn progresses – is mild, slightly astringent with a pleasant soft succulence. You can cut them within 1in (2.5cm) of the base, or pick them off a few at a time – either way they will grow again.

Lamb's lettuce can be grown at any time of the year but is most useful in spring, autumn and winter. Sow the seed in late summer and early autumn for autumn and winter use, protecting the winter crop with cloches for finer, larger and softer leaves. They are slow growing in the early stages, so do not worry if they seem unpromising at first. In spring they rapidly make new growth before running to seed and will need constant cutting if they are not to become leggy and start to flower. (The plant is said to be so named because it is best in the lambing season.) An early spring sowing under cover will tide you over through the June gap until the summer lettuces arrive, the leaves at this time being especially large and luscious.

Its famous partnering is with beetroot but you will find it invaluable in any green salad. Wash the leaves carefully, paying particular attention to the underside which is often dirty from close contact with the soil, dry and store in the usual way. There is no need to chop them unless they are particularly large. Mix them with other salad leaves, tucking in the larger rosettes here and there, or scatter them over the top of a bowl of salad to show off their attractive shape.

Breton salad

Dress a mixture of cooked haricot beans, beetroot and lamb's lettuce with an olive oil vinaigrette. The exact proportions do not matter. Mix the beans and beetroot very lightly so as not to blur the colours too much, tucking in the leaves around the edge. Pour over the vinaigrette, and let the salad stand a little before serving.

Lamb's lettuce and beetroot salad

This is a well known salad which really cannot be bettered, though you can jazz it up, should you want, with a few caraway seeds fried in oil first to make them crisp, or with the addition of a very little diced cooked potato. The addition of chopped celery turns it into Salad Lorette.

Arrange the lamb's lettuce carefully on a white serving platter, to show off the colours to the best advantage. Arrange diced or sliced beetroot on top, with the cooked potato if using. Dress with olive oil, or even nicer, walnut oil, and a few drops of vinegar or lemon juice. Scatter the caraway seeds on top and serve. The cooked vegetables should be at room temperature. From the fridge they are not nearly so good, and will spoil the inherent warmth of the salad.

Claytonia

Claytonia is also called miner's lettuce, winter purslane, or spring beauty. It is another very hardy plant, not to be confused with the much fleshier leaved summer purslane, *Portulaca oleracea*. A more attractive plant one could not wish to find, though it seems to have gone largely unnoticed. Richard Mabey is one of the few authors I have found to offer any clue about its origin. It arrived here from America in the middle of the last century. We eat the leaves, though its starchy bulbils were much prized by North American Indians.

Its common name, spring beauty, suits it well. Tiny lime green diamond shaped leaves quickly envelop the stem to form an open fleshy cup bearing a spray of tiny pure white starry flowers. The leaves are rich in vitamins, mild in flavour and slightly fleshy. It is no trouble to grow and can be sown in any odd corner at any time. It is at its best spring and autumn. As winter approaches, the leaves toughen and lose some of their succulence, and are better covered with cloches.

Use the plants as a cut-and-come-again crop, snipping off a handful as you would chives to add to a mixed green salad; or arrange them around the edge of a side salad, spread out like a ballerina's skirt.

Spring lettuces

One of the major delights of spring are the first early lettuces. It is something that friends and visitors are surprised by, for they do not realise how tough a plant the lettuce is. Overwintered lettuces divide into three groups: those which are sown outside the previous August, protected with cloches and mature in March; those which are sown in seedtrays in October, kept inside during winter in a cold greenhouse, and planted out under a frame to mature in April: and those which are sown under heat in February, and planted out under cloches at the end of March to mature in May. In this way it is possible to have a variety of fresh lettuces throughout the spring.

There are many different varieties of spring lettuce to choose from. Match reliable ones like Winter Density with some of the lesser known old varieties like Bath Cos, and some of the modern lettuces specially bred for overwintering such as the excellent Cynthia or Amanda. Inevitably losses occur, but generally overwintered lettuces suffer far less from disease and mildew problems than those grown in summer. They are smaller than their summer counterparts, but equally delicious, some so clean and perfect they can be presented on the table as they are – rinse them briefly under the tap, shake dry and serve them whole on a white plate, pulling off the leaves in turn at the table. This is how to enjoy them while the novelty is still new. Afterwards, treat them as you do other salad leaves to make mixed green salads and spring misticanza.

In the last couple of years we have also grown some spring maturing lettuces in the greenhouse. What is interesting about these is not so much their flavour – they are bland by comparison to other home-grown lettuces – but their lovely soft, velvety texture. They grow exceedingly well and look most impressive. The other thing to note is not to cut them too early and to wait until the heart has really filled out, for it is only when they are properly mature that their flavour develops. Which accounts in part, I presume, for the total lack of flavour of a commercial lettuce.

The variety we have grown is Marmer. Seeds are sown early in November and overwintered in the greenhouse, before being transplanted in early spring into growbags. They need to be given under-soil heating (we use a heating cable), maturing in late April and early May.

Misticanza

Misticanza is the Italian name for wild salad. According to Roman gastronomes, misticanza should contain 21 different kinds of edible weeds, though today in England there are more likely to be predominantly young cultivated leaves – the kind of thing John Evelyn referred to as 'saladings'.

It is now possible to buy packets of misticanza from seed merchants. These are sadly disappointing, little more than a miserly collection of three or four lettuce varieties plus the odd chicory and endive. The seeds are broadcast and the leaves cut by the handful when they are 2in (5cm) high. However, they are too immature and grown too close together to have any real flavour or delicacy. A far more satisfactory way is to grow a patch of individual salad plants, and mix your own.

A true misticanza is a riot of flavour and colour, deliciously piquant and quite refreshing to eat. To be successful a good variety of leaves and herbs is essential. A few flowers or seed pods, added judiciously, aid the overall attractiveness of the salad: borage, chive, nasturtium and heartsease are the ones I would choose. Misticanza salads can be made at any time of the year, but are best in late spring and early summer.

Misticanza, tarragon, caper and orange salad

Make a dressing from freshly squeezed orange juice, walnut or olive oil and a little tarragon vinegar. Toss a selection of young salad leaves in the dressing, and arrange on individual plates. Now scatter over a generous quantity of fresh tarragon leaves stripped from their stalks, a few fresh orange slices, and 1–2 teaspoons of drained capers per person. At the last minute top with fried brown breadcrumbs and serve immediately before the breadcrumbs have time to go soggy.

Misticanza, beetroot and quail's egg salad, with frizzled caraway seed dressing

selection of young salad leaves
2oz (60g) cooked beetroot, cut into
   tiny neat dice
8 quail's eggs

For the dressing
2 tbsp hazelnut or walnut oil
½ tsp caraway seeds
2 tsp sherry vinegar
pinch salt

Arrange the misticanza on four plates. Divide the diced beetroot equally, scattering it over the top. Boil the quail's eggs for 1½ minutes; they should be soft. Plunge immediately into cold water, then shell carefully. If you prefer, these can be done in advance.

   Heat a teaspoon of the chosen oil in a small pan. Add the caraway seeds and fry for 30 seconds. Cool. Make the vinaigrette in the usual way adding the caraway seeds and their oil. Spoon over the salads, arrange the quail's eggs in the centre and serve as a first course.

See also recipes in autumn and winter salads.

Rocket

Rocket is a popular Mediterranean salad plant, one I have come to appreciate and grow very fond of. The Greeks – who nibbled on thyme and rocket while watching plays and listening to lectures – christened it *euzomom*, meaning good broth. It was once popular here; it was recorded as early as the 12th century and deserves to be better known again. Its taste is unique, both aromatic and peppery. Used in small quantities in green salads, adding a few tender leaves, whole or coarsely chopped, it imparts a zesty tang. In late summer and autumn, when the leaves are particularly mild and succulent, I use it in tomato and onion salads and eat it by the handful with sliced tomatoes and feta cheese.

Heat dissipates its pepperiness entirely. Some Italian recipes call for it to be blanched, then fried with onions and anchovies or garlic and hot peppers, the mixture served with pasta and grated cheese. I myself enjoy it chopped raw and stirred into cooked hot pasta, dressed with olive oil and served with raspings of parmesan or pecorino, or in a bean salad or with potatoes as a salad or soup.

Rocket looks rather like a young brassica plant with wavy-edged leaves. It is an easy plant to grow, sown either like mustard-and-cress on the window sill or broadcast thinly in a shady corner. Spring or late summer sowings are best; it needs cool conditions and quickly runs to seed when the weather is dry and hot. It grows quickly, and should be picked while the leaves are young, and before their flavour becomes disagreeably hot. Over winter the leaves toughen and are not so pleasant. It survives most frosts, but like all salad plants makes much better eating if protected with cloches.

Bean and rocket salad

Cook white beans (or chickpeas) in the usual way. Drain, and when cool, mix with a large handful of chopped rocket plus a little skinned and chopped tomato. Dress with olive oil, season with salt, a few drops of lemon juice and serve.

Gruyère and rocket omelette

Make an omelette in the usual way, adding tiny cubes of gruyère to the egg mixture. Just before folding, fill the centre with chopped rocket to which you have added a pinch of finely chopped tarragon. Serve immediately.

Insalata di rucola

An Umbrian salad of rocket dressed with vinaigrette made with basalmic vinegar and olive oil, mixed with slices of raw mushroom and topped with shavings of fresh parmigiano. The combination of rocket and raw mushrooms is excellent. Try it also with pasta.

SUMMER

June, July, August

Summers in Yorkshire are brief. By early June, things are well underway, and the garden has a look of bright expectancy, but it is not yet summer. The arrival of spinach in late June is the symbolic turning-point: thereafter, whatever the weather, summer has arrived.

Early summer is the most frustrating time. This is the traditional June gap, the in-between time when the new season's crops have yet to mature and overwintered stuff is past its best. It is doubly frustrating in northern parts of the country, where the days are beautifully long but the weather is still cold and progress often slow. Now one begins to understand the desire for choice early crops, and the effort and cosseting that owners of Victorian kitchen gardens expected from their gardeners to achieve this end. A Victorian housekeeper could hope for peas by the beginning of June, and would certainly expect young carrots and turnips, salads of every description, and an abundance of cauliflowers and asparagus. For our part, we direct our energies into early salad stuff, and are grateful that spring cabbages last well and make good eating.

It is often presumed that summer is the busiest time in the garden. This is not necessarily so. Once the crops are growing well, they need little attention. We ourselves do less in summer than one might imagine, just enough to keep on top of the main work of successional sowing, thinning and planting out of crops which will follow on in autumn and winter. Weeding – the persistent summer chore – is fitted in when we have time, though it is far less of a problem on deep beds where crops fit more tightly than among crops grown in conventional rows. It is also possible to leave the garden for a few days unattended. If the weather is very dry, it helps (and will be necessary for prolonged absences) to have a neighbour who will see to the watering, but otherwise the garden will come to no great harm.

As summer progresses, and the garden reaches peak production, the balance of work shifts from the gardener to the cook. It is no accident that this is the largest section of the book. Summer cooking is cooking for the moment. From the time you pull the first bunch of radishes, savour the first peas, are presented with your first bunch of basil, or experience the aroma of freshly harvested garlic, summer is a glorious period. Everything you ever could wish for is down the garden path. Enjoy it to its full.

SUMMER SALADS

Summer salads are very simple. A large bowl of crisp sweet lettuce appears on the table every day, and that's it. This pattern was formed early on in our gardening life when we grew our first lettuces in our garden in Kent. Since then our range of lettuces has increased considerably, but the pattern of eating them remains essentially the same, and I see no reason to change. A bowl of lettuce, a few succulent radishes, and later, the first cucumbers and tomatoes warm from the greenhouse are the most perfect summer food.

Chilling to my mind dulls the flavour of lettuce, so unless you need to store them, when you bring them in from the garden, keep them cool but do not refrigerate. Wrapping in clingfilm or newspaper helps to prevent loss of moisture, though a freshly cut lettuce will remain in perfect condition in a cool place for several hours. Another ploy you can use is to quickly swill the whole lettuce under the tap, shake well, and leave on the drainer until the time comes to prepare the salad.

Often it is more convenient to prepare lettuce beforehand. Either keep in the salad spinner with the lid on, or transfer to the salad bowl and cover with clingfilm. Cos lettuce does not sit happily in a salad bowl. Lay the leaves out instead on a large plate, overlapping them like a fan to show off their curvaceous form to best advantage.

Thinnings of summer lettuces make worthy misticanza. Mix them in a bowl, adding as wide a variety of fresh herbs as you can using whole young leaves stripped from the stalk. A pleasant and fragrant salad can also be made by mixing lettuce leaves – either the frilly salad bowl type or the butterhead varieties – with whole or coarsely torn basil leaves. Add croûtons fried in walnut oil and chopped hard boiled egg just before serving.

Endives are a recent addition to early summer salads. Summer grown endives are tender and far milder than those grown for autumn and winter; they are superb when blanched. They are prone to bolting. Sow succession-ally from March onwards and pick whilst young.

Summer endive, cucumber, and hazelnut salad

Coarsely shredded summer endive, peeled and diced cucumber, peeled, cored and diced apple, a few hazelnuts, and a little finely shredded apple mint. Toast the hazelnuts, rub off the skins and crush with a rolling pin. Lightly mix all the ingredients, with a seasoning of sea salt and a little hazelnut oil. Pile onto individual plates, decorate with borage flowers if you have some and serve as a first course.

FRESH HERBS IN SUMMER

Almost all herbs flourish in summer and reach their aromatic peak at this time, filling the garden with their fragrance and presenting the cook with almost too much choice. These are the ones I would choose above others.

Basil

In cool temperate climates such as ours, basil is a temperamental herb. It is best grown in a greenhouse, for it needs warmth and shelter to do well. In cold wet conditions it will sulk and rot.

Our own method is as follows: sow in pots, half peat, half perlite, in late spring. The young seedlings are prone to damping off. Keep them dry and do *not* overwater. Plant out when strong enough in small clumps of five or six, 9in (23cm) apart, pinching out the tops to encourage side shoots to develop when two pairs of proper leaves have formed. Basil is at its most fragile in these early stages.

Our basil is planted in front of the tomatoes. Once established, it grows well, and cut regularly, lasts through the summer. Pinch out the flowerheads as soon as they form. Feed with a nitrogen fertiliser, and gently shake the leaves dry after watering, preferably at lunchtime. As the season advances, check the plants and remove any leaves showing signs of botrytis.

Basil is the king of summer herbs. A lover's herb, the symbol of fidelity and fertility. In India, where it originates, it is a plant of sanctity and every good Hindu, it is said, is lain to rest with a basil leaf on his breast, his passport to paradise. Its attraction is addictive, at once both sweet and pungent with a potent clove-like aroma. Seed catalogues now offer several varieties, including the small-leaved Greek pot basil, (not impressive), purple ruffles, cinnamon and lemon basil. Each kind has its own character. Sniff a bowlful and you can detect the differences readily. For pesto and general use Genoese basil and the Neapolitan variety, foglia di lattuga, which both produce large succulent leaves, are easily the best.

Commercial herb growers now grow basil round the year, pulling the plants whole when young. The flavour, I find, is generally much milder and lacks that intensity which home-grown basil achieves. Towards the end of summer home-grown basil becomes progessively rank and the leaves lose their succulent quality. Watch out for this.

To ensure a continuous supply of basil, pick it regularly, taking a few sprigs from each plant, pinching them off just above the leaf joint. Should you have a surplus, turn it into pesto rather than let the plant go to seed.

The leaves are very delicate and bruise easily. Consequently, they do not store well, 3–4 days at the most. Keep them in the refrigerator, wrapping them gently first in kitchen paper, and store in a covered plastic box.

Basil may also be kept under olive oil, though this is more a way of flavouring the oil than preserving the basil. After a time, the leaves become unpleasantly slimy, turning blackish and jelly-like.

There is no mistaking the fragrance when fresh basil is around in the kitchen. Its natural partners are tomatoes and garlic, a marvellously versatile summer trio. Basil is also the herb for pasta and pizzas. It can also be turned into some very good soups, sauces and purées. Other combinations to try include crab, chicken, courgettes, avocados, and a surprising number of fruits.

I have no time for those who insist that basil should be torn to preserve its flavour, but one thing basil does not do well is chop finely. The fleshy leaves soon turn to pulp. This does not matter for soups or sauces, but for salads, either tear the leaves or shred them into slender strips, rolling up the leaves like a cigar then shredding crosswise with a sharp knife.

Basil custards

These are lovely. The custards should be just set and very creamy.

generous 1oz (30g) basil leaves,
stripped from their stalks
2 large eggs
6 fl oz (175ml) creamy milk
4 level tbsp thick plain creamy yoghurt

For the sauce
8oz (225g) very ripe tomatoes, skinned
small knob of butter
1 clove garlic, crushed

Begin by finely chopping, then pounding the basil to a homogenous paste in a pestle and mortar. Put eggs, milk, yoghurt and basil into a blender or food processor. Blend until absolutely smooth. Divide between 4 buttered ramekins or small moulds. Put in a pan with water to come halfway up their sides and bake at 160°C/325°F/gas mark 3, until the centre feels just firm to the touch, about 20 minutes; be prepared to experiment to achieve the right consistency.

Meanwhile chop the tomatoes and cook gently in the butter with the garlic for 5–7 minutes. Remove the garlic and blend. Let the custards cool a little, run a palette knife around the edge, then invert on to 4 hot plates, giving a gentle shake downwards. Spoon around the sauce and decorate with a leaf of basil. Serve as a first course.

Basil, tomato and anchovy relish

A winner. Combine 1 largish peeled and very ripe tomato, a handful of basil leaves and 1 anchovy with enough olive oil to make a thick sauce. Use as a dip for crudities, a sauce for grilled fish or to stir into cooked rice. Sufficient for 2–3.

Buttery basil purée

A rich aromatic purée to serve as a relish with fish, chicken or veal, or to stir into hot rice. It can be tricky to get it just right, without the mixture oiling. An easier solution, which turns it into more of a sauce, is to add yoghurt or cream to taste, beating this in after you have amalgamated basil and butter.

1 oz (30g) basil leaves   *½ oz (15g) melted butter*

Chop the basil in a food processor, scrape out, then pound to a paste. Melt the butter in a small pan until hot but not sizzling. Stir in the paste to form a rich, thick, dark green purée. Put in a small warmed bowl and serve. Sufficient for 2–3 servings.

Melon and basil soup

1 small very ripe melon
½ oz (15g) basil leaves, stripped from
    their stalks
½ tsp sugar

about 5–8 fl oz (150–240ml) mineral
    water
about ¼pt (150ml) Greek yoghurt, or
    plain yoghurt and cream mixed
2–4 tbsp sweet rich wine (optional)

Chop, then pound the basil to a sludgy paste with the sugar in a pestle and mortar. Process basil, melon flesh and any juice squeezed from the skins in a blender or processor until smooth, adding water and yoghurt until taste and consistency seem right. Chill thoroughly. Add the wine if using, just enough to sharpen slightly, and serve immediately in small soup cups.

Crab and courgette ramekins with basil mayonnaise sauce

8oz (225g) young courgettes, wiped
pinch of salt
6oz (180g) fresh white crabmeat
lemon juice

For the dressing
½oz (15g) basil leaves, chopped and
    pounded to a purée
2 tbsp mayonnaise
2 tbsp yoghurt

Grate the courgettes finely into a bowl. Mix with a pinch of salt and leave for 5–10 minutes. Gently squeeze out excess moisture with your hands. Mix very lightly with the crabmeat, adding lemon juice to taste. Take a quarter of the mixture and press into a ramekin. Loosen the sides with a palette knife and invert onto a plate. Make the others the same way.

Mixing the dressing ingredients to a smooth cream, adding a spot of hot water if too thick. Pour the dressing in a pool around each ramekin, decorate with a tiny basil leaf and serve. If you are using a whole crab, dress the brown meat in the usual way with a little mustard, lemon juice and enough breadcrumbs to stiffen slightly, heap on to 4 large basil leaves and serve on the same plate.

Chicken breasts stuffed with basil

This recipe is adapted from *A Table in Provence*, by Leslie Forbes, published in 1987.

For the purée
2 oz (60g) basil leaves   3–4 tbsp fruity olive oil

Stuff the basil leaves in a food processor and process until finely chopped. Add the oil and process again, scraping down the paste repeatedly until more or less smooth. Transfer to a small dish. Alternatively, chop finely by hand, then pound in a mortar, stirring in enough oil to give a smooth paste. This can be kept for a couple of weeks in the refrigerator and used for soups or sauces.

4 large chicken breasts, boned but not
    skinned
4 tbsp basil purée
olive oil
For the sauce
1 medium leek, mostly white, trimmed
    and finely sliced

5 fl oz (150ml) single cream
1 tsp potato flour slaked in a little milk
    or water
pinch of salt
1–2 tsp basil purée

Place the chicken breasts skin side down and make a deep slash to form a pocket running along the length of the breast. Fill each with a good tablespoon of purée and fold back the meat. Arrange skin side up in a shallow dish. Brush skin and top with olive oil. Grill under a hot grill, keeping the dish 5–6 in (13–15cm) away from the heat source, for 15–20 minutes, until the meat is cooked and the skin is brown and crisp.

Meanwhile simmer the leek and cream in a covered pan for 15 minutes. Purée until smooth in a blender or processor. Return to the pan and thicken with the potato flour, stirring until the sauce comes back to the boil. Thin down if necessary with a spot of water. Season lightly, stirring in the basil purée to taste. Distribute the sauce between 4 hot plates, and arrange a chicken breast to the side. Serve with pasta.

Bay

The difference between fresh bay leaves, your own freshly dried bay leaves, and dried bay leaves bought in packets is incomparable. Once you have had your own, no other kind will do. Only the sweet bay, *Laurus nobilis*, is edible; all others are poisonous.

The bay tree itself is evergreen, but not fully hardy – or rather the leaves do not survive freezing winters. It succeeds well in tubs, a practice the Elizabethans were fond of. It will grow in shade but loves full sunshine. Bring it inside or into the greenhouse in late autumn. The leaves can be picked all year round.

Bay leaves are an indispensable ingredient of bouquet garni, in soups, broths, marinades, fish stock, rollmops, poached fish, stews, casseroles and braised dishes. Try them with stuffed cabbage dishes, adding two or three to the braising liquid. Some cooks advocate using them when roasting chicken or duck. Custards and rice puddings, or poached fish in milk flavoured with fresh bay leaves are revelatory. Throw a few bay leaves onto the drying embers of the barbecue: also revelatory. 'They crake wonderfully,' observed the 16th-century physician and herbalist, William Turner; they are supposed to have excitant and narcotic properties. Slip one, also, into the rice storage jar.

Mrs Beeton's cheap blanc-mange

This recipe comes from Mrs Beeton's *Book of Household Management*, published in 1861. It is much better, to my mind, than packet blancmange ever could be. At that time isinglass, prepared from deer antlers, was employed as a setting agent. Gelatine is the modern equivalent, but is too gluey a flavour for these delicate confections. A better substitute is agar-agar, a colourless and tasteless dried seaweed preparation available from health food shops.

1 pt (600ml) creamy milk
2 fresh bay leaves
2 thin strips thinly pared scrubbed
  lemon rind

2 tbsp agar-agar flakes
2–4 tsp sugar

Put milk, bay and lemon rind into a saucepan, sprinkle over the agar-agar, stir and bring slowly to simmering point. Allow to infuse over the lowest heat for about 10 minutes, or until the milk is well flavoured.

Remove the bay leaves and lemon, and strain through a sieve, pressing hard to push through any remaining globules of agar. Sweeten to taste – but not too much; this is a grown-up taste and is better for being only slightly sweetened. Pour into attractive glasses or other small dessert dishes and leave to set. 'Garnish with preserves, bright jelly or a compote of fruit.'

Greek-style lamb kebabs

Eating outdoors when the weather allows, grilling food over a small barbecue, is one of our chief pleasures during summer. Meals always follow the same pattern: a selection of salads and crudités from the garden to eat while the charcoal burns down to a white ash, bruschetta, or maybe sausages from the local butcher, with steak or fish and aïoli, or these lamb kebabs to follow. The onion cooks to a delicious charred sweetness and the bay leaves give off their wonderful aroma. A refinement of late is to lay the kebabs on sprigs of fresh rosemary, which is even more aromatic.

1 lb (450g) trimmed and boned leg of lamb, cubed into 1in (2.5cm) pieces
1 onion, peeled, quartered and separated into layers
1–2 tbsp finely chopped fresh oregano (or, second best, 1–2 tsp dried rigani

plus a little chopped fresh mint if liked)
bay leaves, fresh if possible
olive oil
lemon juice

Put lamb, onion, and herbs in a bowl, moisten lightly with olive oil, add a few drops of lemon juice, mix well and leave for an hour or so.

Assemble the skewers as follows: start with a slice of onion and a bay leaf, then a cube of lamb, then another slice of onion and a bay leaf. Repeat along the length of the skewer, finishing with onion, making sure you don't crowd the skewer and keep everything evenly spaced. Grill over charcoal, turning occasionally, for approximately 15 minutes. Serve with rice.

Dill

Dill is an easy herb to grow, though it does best in a sunny well drained soil. Raise a few plants by sowing the seed in small pots inside in late spring, planting out after all danger of frost. In hot dry weather it rapidly runs to seed. As summer progresses, the plants can grow up to 3ft (1m) tall, and develop large umbelliferous flowerheads. If left, these can be harvested and are sweeter than the bought dill seeds.

Alternatively, sow the seeds direct, thinning the plants to 8in (20cm) apart. Successional sowing is often recommended, though unless you are likely to use a lot of dill, this is not necessary. Dill seeds have a long shelf life, and will germinate successfully after three years and longer.

The name dill is said to derive from the Norse, *dilla*, 'to lull', an allusion to the mildly soporific effect of the seeds. They have excellent carminative and digestive properties, and have been used as a medicine since early times, though the only medicinal use we seem to find for them is in gripe water.

In English cookery, dill is a neglected herb. It is popular in Scandinavia, Germany and central and eastern Europe, where it is variously used with meat, fish, vegetable (particularly beetroot and cucumber), and rice dishes, and with yoghurt, sour cream and buttermilk for dressings and sauces. Its other main use is in pickles, where it is said that it should be cut when flowers and seedheads are on the plant at the same time. The taste of the leaves is surprisingly positive and a little is usually all that is required. To my mind, it is far more delicate and pleasant than fennel. Generally speaking, it is added last as its aroma fades in cooking. It freezes well, which is to say it keeps its flavour well. Like all frozen herbs, the texture is ruined. A few of its feathery leaves torn up make a pleasant addition to misticanza salads and a delightful garnish.

Apple and dill borscht

A summer fruit soup based on the Russian borscht. The wine adds a richness to the soup but can be reduced or omitted, making up with extra apple juice instead.

10 oz (285g) peeled and finely grated
   beetroot
1 pt (600ml) apple juice
½ pt (300ml) red wine
large sprig of dill

1oz (30g) chopped mushrooms
   (optional)
juice of half a lemon
1 tbsp finely chopped dill

Simmer the first four ingredients, plus the mushrooms if using, for 15–20 minutes. Strain, gently pressing the debris against the sides of the sieve. The consommé should be crystal clear. Bring back to the boil, sharpen with lemon juice to taste and ladle into small soup cups. Scatter over chopped dill and serve. Alternatively, serve ice cold.

Prawns, ginger and dill canapés

This quantity makes enough for one; multiply as required.

1–1½oz (30–45g) best peeled prawns,
   rinsed and dried on kitchen paper
1–1½oz (30–45g) fromage frais
¼oz (7g) finely grated fresh ginger
chopped dill

Chop the prawns and mix gently with the fromage frais and ginger. Serve in pastry cases, as a filling for avocado or cooked artichoke hearts, or with slices of melon or tomato, sprinkling chopped dill liberally over the top.

Oregano

Oregano is the wild majoram, as distinct from the annual sweet marjoram or the perennial pot marjoram. It most closely resembles the Greek rigani sold in packets, but is sweeter in flavour, with an aromatic scent closer to thyme, indeed it contains the same powerful antiseptic, thymol. It is a small bushy perennial plant, ideal for a rockery or dry wall, covered in summer with mauve flowers much appreciated by bees. It can become leggy and will need chopping back sometime in summer. There are four forms. The kind I grow is the golden marjoram, with golden yellow-green leaves, *oregano vulgare aureum*. I find it indispensable for lamb, chicken, or pork cooked on the barbecue, and for pizzas. If you chop it, then leave it to dry out for a few hours, it makes an admirable substitute – and a fresher one – for rigani, to sprinkle over Greek salads and other Greek dishes.

Rolo

This rustic dish, full of savour, comes from *A Kitchen in Corfu* by James Chatto. I have made but one amendment, to omit the salt, finding feta cheese more than salty enough.

4–4¹⁄₄lb (2 kg) lean pork belly
1 small onion
3 cloves of garlic

2 tbsp each of parsley and coriander
1 tbsp each of rigani or chopped
* oregano and paprika mixed*
3¹⁄₂oz (100g) feta cheese

Trim the pork of any excess fat, score the skin deeply and cut in half down the middle. Finely chop the onion, garlic, parsley and coriander in a food processor if you have one. Mix with half the rigani or oregano and paprika and the feta cheese to form a paste.

Spread along the inside of one half of the meat. Place the other half, skin side uppermost, on top to form a sandwich. Sew up loosely. Rub the outside with the rest of the rigani and paprika. Set the joint on a trivet over a roasting pan and roast very gently in a cool oven, 140–150°C/275–300°F/gas mark 1–2, for 2¹⁄₂–3 hours. The meat must cook evenly and gently, so adjust the temperature accordingly.

When cooked the surface should be a beautiful crisp deep red brown and the meat tender and succulent. Let the meat rest a little, then cut the string and serve cut into thick slices. I generally serve rice, and you will need some salad to cut the greasiness of the pork.

Note You can cook this dish with the skin on or not; both ways are good. If you remove the skin (save it to enrich stews or to cook with beans), score the fat and rub the herb and paprika mixture well into the cuts.

79

Pot roast chicken with garlic and oregano

3¼–3½ lb (1.5kg) chicken	*large glass of white wine*
2 or more heads of fresh garlic	*a little butter*
bunch of oregano	

Wipe the chicken and put into a deep, heavy casserole with a well fitting lid. A Le Creuset casserole is ideal. Separate the cloves of garlic, but leave them unpeeled and distribute around and under the chicken. Stuff the oregano down the sides and pour over the wine. Cover very tightly (a piece of greaseproof paper between the lid and dish is better than foil and forms an excellent seal). Cook in a hot oven, 200°C/400°F/gas mark 6, for about 30 minutes. Turn down to 180°C/350°F/gas mark 4 and continue to cook until the chicken is done, 1¼–1½ hours. Take the dish out of the oven and leave the chicken to rest in the pot for 15 minutes.

Transfer the chicken to a serving dish. Set aside the garlic and discard the oregano. Mop up the fat and boil down the juices to concentrate their flavour. Reheat the garlic in the sauce, enrich with a small amount of butter to taste and serve in a sauceboat.

You will find that, despite the quantity of garlic, the garlic does not noticeably permeate the chicken but rather provides a delicious vegetable. Take as much as you want – the idea being to squeeze the pulp from the garlic and spread over the slices of chicken.

Tarragon

There are two types of tarragon, French and Russian, both perennial members of the artemisia family. French tarragon, a native of southern Europe, is the cook's kind. Check this when you buy it, or beg a root piece from a friend instead. It is not completely hardy and requires a dry sunny spot in poor or sandy soil to do well, but otherwise it is straightforward to grow. In colder areas it will need protection during the winter months. Protecting it with a piece of Agryl P17 (see p. 18) in early spring is also beneficial. Once established, tarragon grows into a sizeable bushy plant, the root ball reaching 2ft (60cm) across. Allow for this when you first plant it out.

The French gourmet Alexandre Dumas said that there is no good vinegar without tarragon. It is one of the great classic herbs. Without it there is no true béarnaise sauce or fines herbes. It is a powerful herb, one which should be used with respect. It is at its best during the early summer months into July, when the plant is making new growth (this is the time to make your tarragon vinegar). Later, the leaves become coarser and lose some of their intense spicy aroma. Classic combinations are egg, chicken, beef and tomato dishes, though these days you are likely to find tarragon paired with almost anything you can think of. The young leaves add a pungency to green salads.

Salmon with red wine, tarragon and redcurrants

The use of red wine in fish cookery is not common but with certain fish it can be very good and not at all out of place. This is a simple dish in the modern style. The sauce comes out a deep purply red, so choose your plates accordingly.

4 thick salmon steaks
½–1 oz (15–30g) unsalted butter, plus
    extra butter for frying
8–10 fl oz (240–300ml) red wine
2 large sprigs of tarragon

1–2 tsp redcurrant jelly
To finish
a few leaves of tarragon
4 small bunches of redcurrants

Smear the scrap of butter in a nonstick pan and seal the salmon steaks for 2–3 minutes on both sides over a highish heat. Turn down the heat, cover and cook for 2–3 minutes longer. Turn off the heat and let the fish relax for 4–5 minutes. Remove to hot plates and keep warm while you make the sauce.

Add the wine and tarragon to the pan juices and simmer until reduced by half. Stir in redcurrant jelly to taste. Be careful here, the sauce should be in no way sweet – add just enough to soften the astringency of the wine. Off the heat, swirl in dabs of butter, shaking the pan. The sauce will thicken and become glossy. Remove the tarragon and divide the sauce between the four plates, pouring it around the fish. Decorate with a tarragon leaf or two and a little spray of redcurrants. Serve immediately with plain rice to accompany.

Note This is a good sauce to make with noisettes of lamb. Follow the procedure above, keeping the lamb pink. This time, the sauce can be a little sweeter.

Barbecued salmon steaks with tarragon

Salmon steaks barbecue well. Cook them in a fish basket, pressing a few sprigs of tarragon well into the flesh on each side (this stops the tarragon from burning). Cook gently turning once, for 7–10 minutes.

Tarragon cocottes

For each person allow a tablespoon of thick cream and one very fresh egg. Butter individual ramekins and break an egg into each. Heat the cream with one or two large sprigs of tarragon and an equal quantity of water, or a little more, in a small pan. Allow to reduce down to a tablespoon per person, simmering gently. Press the tarragon leaves against the side of the pan and remove.

Pour the tarragon flavoured cream over the eggs. Decorate with a leaf or two of young tarragon leaves and cook very gently in a bain-marie (a frying pan half full of water with a lid is fine) until the whites are barely set and the yolks are very creamy, not more than 4–5 minutes. Serve immediately as a first course, and eat with small spoons. One of the best tarragon dishes.

Lentils with mint and tarragon

Use the brown or slate green Puy lentils for this dish, which makes a good summer side salad. Wash the lentils and simmer with a handful of tarragon and mint sprigs and some chopped spring onion until soft, 20–25 minutes. Drain and remove the herbs. Season with salt and mix in a generous quantity of finely chopped fresh mint and tarragon – no oil is required for this salad. Serve with quartered hard boiled eggs. A few cooked peas can also be added.

Gooseberry and tarragon sauce

Wild gooseberries were known to the Anglo-Saxons and have been planted in gardens since the Middle Ages. Their refreshing acidity was appreciated first in savoury dishes to stuff geese and as a sauce for pork, lamb, veal and roast duck, as well as for mackerel.

This is a very simply made sauce. Top and tail 8oz (225g) green gooseberries, and cook in a little water until soft. Drain, then beat with just sufficient sugar to dull the sharpness without making it sweet. Stir in 1–2 tsp chopped tarragon. This will make sufficient for 4 small servings. Serve with chicken or veal or mackerel.

In *Elinor Fettiplaces's Receipt Book*, Hilary Spurling gives a richer tasting gooseberry sauce cooked in wine and chicken broth, to serve with chicken. You can also stir butter or cream into the basic sauce above. If you prefer a smooth sauce, the cooked gooseberries can be sieved, allowing a few extra to bulk up the volume. Coriander and other aromatic herbs such as mint also marry well.

VEGETABLES

Asparagus

Asparagus is regarded as the ultimate vegetable. It is easy to see why. No other vegetable combines delicacy of taste with such soft, voluptuous texture. From the earliest beginnings this has always been so. No one, not even Cobbett, ever had anything but the fullest praise for it. It is a member of the lily family, and was first valued as a medicinal plant. Wild asparagus is found in many parts of southern Europe and in Poland and Russia, though is apparently now a rare plant in Britain.

It will come as no surprise that asparagus has to be earned. It requires commitment and a three-year wait for your first real crop. Begin by buying asparagus crowns in spring. One-year-old crowns are easier to establish, but two-year-olds are larger and more readily available. They need a well drained but rich soil. Plant the crowns 18in (45cm) apart in a shallow trench spreading the roots out well, ensuring the crown is about 4in (10cm) below

surface level. Apply a top dressing of well rotted organic material and general fertiliser. Protect the young shoots from slugs. Leave to grow for two years before taking your first crop and do not start seriously cutting until the third or fourth year. Once established, the bed will last several years. Be careful when hoeing to avoid damaging the crowns that lie close to the surface.

By the early 19th century more asparagus was grown in Britain than in any other country, over half of it in Evesham. I doubt if that is the case today. Imports from as far away as Peru have meant that asparagus is no longer the choicest crop of early summer. Available whenever we want, but without either flavour or freshness, asparagus has become one of life's diluted luxuries. I think this is sad. English asparagus is the finest asparagus there is. What greater luxury in life than to have your own?

The season for English asparagus is from early May to around the end of June. From our limited experience, once the shoots start to show through, they grow quickly, especially in warm weather. The shoots vary in size considerably; all make excellent eating. Nothing as delectable as asparagus should be cut before it is absolutely necessary. Cut them when they look in their prime, near the base, with a sharp knife. New shoots continue to grow, staggering the season over a few weeks. Cease cutting towards the end of June, to allow the plant to build up strength for the following year.

The classic way to prepare and cook asparagus is to pare away the bottom part of the stem, where it begins to get tough, and steam the spears in an asparagus basket. This allows the bottom half of the stalk to cook in water, whilst keeping the more delicate spear enveloped in steam. Though the logic of the method is perfectly clear, I can only presume it was designed in the days when all vegetables were cooked for far longer than we would find acceptable today, for I have found it completely unnecessary. The spears laid flat in a little water in a large shallow covered pan and boiled hard for a couple of minutes will give you perfectly cooked bright green nutty asparagus. Lift the lid off towards the end, testing halfway down the stalk; if it responds to the point of a knife, it is ready. If the asparagus will not fit, trim the spears accordingly.

Unless you are extremely fortunate, and have more asparagus than you know what to do with, use the bought kind in soups and quiches. Garden asparagus has a delicate richness with a sweetness reminiscent of tender young peas eaten straight from the vine. If it is fresh and tender, it will not need trimming. Occasionally, the bottom half of the stalk is tough, but this can be peeled away with your fingers as you eat. Serve on its own, with perhaps a jug of hollandaise or melted butter in the usual way. For a change, try this variation from an Australian chef, Stephanie Alexander.

Asparagus, new boiled eggs and savoury breadcrumbs

Take freshly cooked asparagus spears, and for each person, a softly boiled egg, and a ramekin of breadcrumbs fried in a little butter with a crushed clove of garlic, then mixed with some very finely chopped parsley. You could use tarragon and chervil also. Dunk the asparagus spears in the egg, then the savoury breadcrumbs, and eat.

Summer beetroots

Summer beetroots are for pulling young: about 1 ½in (4cm) wide is generally considered to be the best size for salads. Red, yellow and striped varieties are available, though remember the striped varieties lose their markings when cooked. The yellow varieties look attractive in salads and do not bleed.

Unless you have a fondness for young pickled beetroot, a couple of rows of summer beetroot should be ample. Sow the seeds 1in (2.5cm) apart, and thin to 2in (5cm). Beetroot has only one fault, the young plants are sensitive to cold, and if sown too early are prone to bolt. The answer for April sowings is to grow a bolt-resistant variety such as Boltardy. They take approximately 12 weeks to mature. Pull when ready rather than leaving to grow on, twisting off the tops and storing somewhere cool in brown paper bags. The young tops can be used in stuffings and pasta dishes, or blanched and dressed with oil and vinegar as a salad. The leaves from the yellow varieties are best. (For more about beetroot, see p. 163)

Summer beetroot and carrot salad

A salad of grated beetroot and carrot makes a colourful summer hors d'oeuvre to serve before the meat course. Bake or boil your summer beetroot until almost done. Peel and put through the julienne shredder. Arrange on individual plates with a mound of raw shredded carrot and a few salad leaves. Mash 1–2 hard-boiled eggs and carefully surround the beetroot, topping with fried breadcrumbs in the polonaise style. Decorate the carrot with a black olive and serve.

Harvard beetroots

Colin Spencer is one of our best vegetarian cookery writers and has a knack of coming up with the right recipe exactly when you need it. This is one from his *Guardian* column for summer beetroot, eaten either hot or cold. I have halved the quantities.

1lb (450g) baby beetroots, boiled and
   skinned
2½ fl oz (75ml) cider vinegar
1½ fl oz (40ml) raspberry vinegar
zest and juice of half a lemon

½ oz (15g) fresh ginger root, peeled
   and finely grated
1 small red chilli
1¼–1½ tbsp soft brown sugar

If serving the beetroots hot, keep warm while you make the sauce. Heat the two vinegars with the zest and lemon juice, ginger and chilli. Simmer for three minutes. Stir in the sugar and cook for another 2 minutes or until the sauce becomes syrupy. Pour over the beetroot, toss well. Leave for a couple of hours if serving cold and serve at room temperature. Either remove the chilli or warn people beforehand.

Blackcurrant beetroots

A particular favourite of mine. Take diced cooked beetroot. Make a sauce with 1–2 tbsp homemade blackcurrant jam heated through with the juice of about half a lemon – it should be sharply sweet. Pour over the beetroot. Serve in a fringe of yellow beetroot. Also good hot.

Broad beans

Until the introduction of French and runner beans from the New World in the 16th century, broad beans were the only beans we knew. Subsistence food, shovelled into Bronze Age and medieval peasants alike up to the end of the Middle Ages, they were one of our most important vegetables, boiled in pottages or ground and made into bread, cakes and biscuits. With the arrival of potatoes and the greater availability of wheat and other foods, though broad beans were still grown in vast quantities (but note by now fed to horses and exported to feed the negro slave colonies), they ceased to be a staple and we began to enjoy them fresh. Parson Woodforde, the Norfolk vicar who recorded his daily dinners in his diaries for over 40 years, ate his with ham, bacon, pig's chap, and roast chicken from June till September.

We have found broad beans often grow better without transplanting, thus avoiding any root disturbance. To get early broad beans, you need to grow winter-hardy varieties such as Aquadulce and sow in autumn, protecting the plants over winter. However, these are deemed not to have as good a flavour as the spring-sown varieties. Though the crop comes later, the easiest plan is to sow the seed direct in April or as soon as the soil is workable. Relon is a recommended new variety, and Green Windsor an old favourite and a reliable bean. Sow in double rows, each 6in (15cm) apart, allowing 18in (45cm) between each double row, drawing out a proper drill. Cover with cloches or Agryl P17 (see p. 18) to get them away. Pinch out the tops in July when they are in full flower or when blackfly threatens. The crop comes all at once, maturing in July and early August.

Watering around the base of the plants during flowering and while the pods are growing has been shown to result in a better set, greater yields, and to delay them going tough and starchy. (The same is true of peas.) Like peas, broad beans need staking – a framework of canes with strings running around the plants is sturdy enough.

Sometimes you will come across references to raw broad beans being poisonous. There is no need to be alarmed by this. Broad beans do contain a toxin, vicine, which can lead to a serious anaemic condition, favism, resulting from eating undercooked beans or inhaling the pollen. In the Middle Ages, when bread made from uncooked mashed dried beans was commonplace among the poor, it struck regularly. But the disease affects only some Mediterranean communities, who have a genetic sensitivity to the toxin. Everyone else can consume their raw beans with pleasure.

Broad beans can be picked at any stage. The tiny, velvety, down-covered pods, no bigger than your little finger at most, can be eaten raw and are considered a delicacy in Italy and France. The gardener in the family would not quite see it that way – a picking will make a sizeable hole in the crop – and may reasonably protest. But he or she will agree that the plants need thinning (if too many flowers have set, often some baby pods will not develop but wither of their own accord), especially if large pods with large beans are desired. Thin them almost as soon as the pods have formed and the peace will be saved. The little furry mouthfuls are mild and slightly nutty in flavour. Eaten on their own with a piece of sharp tasting cheese such as parmesan or feta and some olives, they make a tasty snack, pleasant to eat out of doors on a sunny day with a glass of chilled white wine.

Alas, this does not last long. Once the beans have started to form, the pods become progressively bitter. Baby beans are bitter too, and you now need to wait until they have fleshed out before they become sweet and tender.

As with peas, once the pods fill out you need to check regularly. It is very difficult to tell exactly when they are ready for harvesting: feel the pods – they should be bursting tight and have a little residual woolliness to the outside. Inside, the scar on the bean will still be white or green, not black. This is when they are at their best for eating. Beans in their prime do not 'hold' on the plant for long. As they get larger and stiffer the pods become progressively shiny and then tough. By now the beans will be floury in texture and more starchy in flavour.

Generally speaking, the crop matures over 1–2 weeks. The beans should be picked and used fresh. If you need to store them, keep them in their pods. Young broad beans are a great luxury, ranking with peas or asparagus. Blanching suits them very well, 2–3 minutes being generally sufficient. They are also very good sautéed in olive oil and cooked in their own juices, or finished in the Greek way with beaten egg and lemon juice added to the cooking liquid. Whether or not to remove the skins is a matter of personal taste. It is something I do not generally bother with.

The best broad beans need minimal treatment, but older beans respond equally well to long slow cooking, becoming deliciously smooth and soft, and imbibing the surrounding flavours most agreeably. Try the Spanish dish in this section, where pods and beans are turned into a flavoursome stew. The best pods on their own can be turned into passable purées.

The only thing mildly unpleasant about broad beans is shelling them, a messy business which stains fingers and fingernails black. They are a bulky crop; 3lb (1.5kg) pods give about 1lb (450g) beans.

Broad beans freeze outstandingly well. The flavour is incomparably better than that of bought beans, and will be almost as good as those you pick and eat fresh. Follow the directions for spinach on p. 137 and blanch for 1 minute. They may also be frozen unblanched, and will remain in good condition for six months or more. Once thawed the beans will require very little cooking, 2–3 minutes, and young beans may require none at all.

Broad bean salads

It is always worth cooking a few extra beans to serve in salads: discard the skin (here it does make a difference) and use with other vegetables such as cauliflower, potatoes, carrots or mushrooms. Team them with hard-boiled eggs and anchovies. Add to other bean salads, or scatter over the surface of green salads with chopped dill, or a dusting of summer savoury or hyssop.

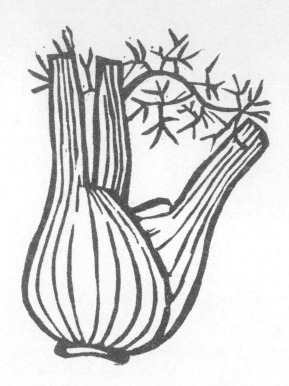

Broad bean, potato and fennel salad

Mix equal quantities of cooked broad beans and cooked, diced, new potatoes. Add a small amount of finely chopped raw fennel. Dress with olive oil and scatter thin slivers of anchovy on top.

Broad bean, bacon and mushroom salad

A winning combination from Jane Grigson. Mix equal quantities of raw sliced mushrooms and cooked broad beans with a mustard vinaigrette made with olive oil and a good pinch of sugar. Scatter over fried bacon dice, cooked in their own fat until well crisped, and finish with chopped chives and parsley (or mint) or other herbs to suit. Let the salad sit a little while before serving.

Broad bean, orange and rice salad

Cooked rice, broad beans and orange segments, free from pith and peel. Squeeze the juice from the debris of the orange and mix with the rice. Add a few plumped sultanas or raisins and a good sprinkling of freshly ground allspice. Gently mix in the broad beans and orange segments. Dribble over some thick creamy yoghurt, scatter with chopped dill and serve.

Broad beans the Apulian way

This is the way the Apulians cook their beans (broad beans are native to Apulia) as described by Patience Gray in *Honey from a Weed*, published in 1986:

Fresh broad beans 'When in April broad beans become just too large to eat raw, but are tender, the outer skin being green, they are thrown into hot oil in an earthenware pot (*la pignata*), in which a sliced *sprunzala* [onion shoot] is already simmering, and are cooked for a brief time with a little salt and a sprig or two of mint. A delicacy.'

Stewed broad beans 'When the beans are larger (older), husk them and pinch off their outer skins, no longer green but creamy white. Slice up a sweet white onion, put the slices in an earthenware pot (or enamelled pan) in a little olive oil, and, before they begin to brown, put in some strips neatly cut from a slice of prosciutto crudo (not paper thin), or, failing that, pancetta (salt belly of pork), both fat and lean, and brown them. Add the washed beans, salt and pepper, and some chopped mint, or coriander leaves or fronds of dill. If the beans seem to be drying up before they are tender, add a very little chicken stock. (A fresh green chilli pepper, seeded, is sometimes sliced and simmered in the oil with the sliced onion.)'

Broad beans with pasta

Broad beans and pasta is a dish we often enjoy during autumn and winter with homegrown frozen beans. Wholewheat pasta, shells or spirals are best. Allow equal quantities of each, 8oz (225g) for two as a main course. The frozen beans go into the pasta water at the end, and take only a couple of minutes to cook. Drain, and serve with a little jug of your best fruity olive oil and parmesan handed separately. Sometimes, leeks or mushrooms, softened first in olive oil will be added, or in autumn, Swiss chard, or other beet leaves, cooked with olive oil and garlic. Preparation time is minimal. Unbeatable with a glass of red wine.

In summer, broad beans and pasta make lovely salads. Add chopped tomato, olives, and a generous sprinkling of basil. Toss in olive oil with a squeeze of lemon juice to sharpen. A few cooked white beans can also be added to the salad.

Broad beans braised with ham, in the Spanish style

One of the very best broad bean stews, slightly adapted from Elisabeth Luard's *European Peasant Cookery*. You need tender podded beans for this dish, ones which prick easily with your finger nail and which slice with no resistance. It is worth making in large batches – it keeps in the fridge for a week and freezes well.

1 medium onion, chopped fairly finely
2 cloves garlic, chopped
2 tbsp olive oil
1–1¼ lb (450–570g) young broad beans in their pods, topped and tailed, and chopped into short lengths

2oz (60g) chorizo, diced
small bunch parsley chopped (1 heaped tbsp)
3–4 fl oz (90–120ml) sherry, plus 1 glass of water

Heat the oil in a stewpan and add the onion and garlic. Soften without colouring for a few minutes, then add the beans, sausage, and parsley. Cook for another minute or two, stirring everything around. Add the sherry and water, cover and simmer until the beans are tender – 40–45 minutes. The beans should be velvety soft and bluey-grey. Watch the water level towards the end, adding a little extra if necessary or boiling down if too much is left. Taste and correct the seasoning if necessary with a pinch of sugar. Salt and pepper should not be needed. Serve hot with garden potatoes, or warm or at room temperature as a salad with good bread.

Variation: add an equal quantity of shredded Swiss chard or beet leaves to the broad beans.

Rabbit with broad beans, basil and garlic sauce

Despite our traditional fondness for broad beans, English recipes show a marked lack of imagination when it comes to cooking them. Broad beans in white sauce. Broad beans with parsley sauce. Broad beans with no sauce. Broad beans with bacon. Sometimes you see them with duck or with rabbit and hopes begin to rise, only to fall again when you realise that the beans are not cooked with the meat, or made part of the dish but served plain. Nothing wrong with that, but broad beans have so much more to offer. Here's a rich, flavoursome dish where beans, meat and garlic blend into a harmonious whole. Use the back and hindquarters of two rabbits, neatly jointed, saving the forequarters for pâté or soup.

about 2lb (900g) rabbit, jointed	*1 large sprig of basil*
flour for coating	*12 fat cloves of garlic, peeled*
olive oil for frying	*4 fl oz (120ml) single cream and water*
1 shallot, finely sliced	*mixed*
12oz (340g) shelled broad beans	*fried breadcrumbs and extra shredded*
8 fl oz (240ml) white wine	*basil*

Lightly dust the rabbit pieces with flour and brown in a little olive oil in a heavy or preferably nonstick frying pan. Add the shallot, lower the heat and cook to soften. Add the beans, wine and basil, cover and simmer very gently until the rabbit is tender, about 25–35 minutes.

Meanwhile, prepare the garlic. Blanch the cloves in water to cover for 3–4 minutes in a small pan. Drain, just cover with the cream and water mixture and simmer for about 20 minutes until very soft. Mash or blend to a smooth purée.

Remove the rabbit to a serving dish and keep warm. The beans should be soft – cook a little longer if necessary. Discard the basil and then stir in the garlic purée to make a thick sauce. Check the seasoning and pour around the rabbit. Sprinkle with fresh basil and finish with a healthy scattering of fried crumbs over the rabbit pieces to provide a crisp contrast. Serve with pasta.

Calabrese

This beautiful dark green sprouting broccoli has suffered from over-exposure in recent years. Even in rural Yorkshire it can be found all year round, its fat heads tightly wrapped in clingfilm, offered for sale long past their best. It will crop successfully from a wide variety of sowing times, and will even stand mild frosts, but in the garden is perhaps at its most useful in July, from April sowing in seedtrays under glass. The plant first produces one large tight central head, which should be removed, and thereafter a continuing crop of smaller side shoots.

Because of its commercial popularity, there are several varieties to choose from. Many, however, are designed to produce one large head only – the kind you buy – and the crop of sideshoots is not impressive. Often, these are modern F1 hybrids bred in the first instance for commercial growers. For garden production, you may be better selecting traditional non-F1 hybrids or those which explicitly make a feature of sideshoot production. Note, too, that new varieties can be planted closer together: 9–12in (23–30cm) apart.

It is easy to tell when calabrese is ready. The heads are firm and tight and there is a vibrancy about their bluish-green colouring. They do not remain long in perfect condition on the plant, a few days at most. After this, the heads become more broken and you can begin to see the tiny flowers forming and opening. Check scrupulously for caterpillars which bury deep into the curds. The central head should always be cut first. Use a sharp knife, cutting just above where the side shoots are beginning to form.

Calabrese is high in vitamin C. Ideally, cut not long before you want to use it. If you need to keep it, wrap it in clingfilm and store in the fridge for 2–3 days at most. Trim off any large leaves and rinse the heads briefly. Though it spoils their looks, the largest heads are better cut into two or four, slicing from top to bottom. The stems should not be trimmed too vigorously. Unless the calabrese is old, they are as tender as the heads – check by inserting a knife into the stem first.

The benefit of garden calabrese lies more in its freshness than any advantage over flavour. It is easily spoiled by careless cooking. Though you can blanch calabrese, it requires split-second timing, and is apt to become watery. Steaming the heads takes around 5–7 minutes. My preferred way – and far the best – is the conservative method, laying them in a large covered pan with a little water and cooking hard for 2–4 minutes. Test them often, and whip them out as soon as the point of the knife will insert easily into the top part of the stem.

Calabrese has become one of the nation's favourite vegetables. Like French beans, it is ideal with almost anything. Keep your garden calabrese for the delicacy it is, and serve as a separate vegetable course, either hot or cold. If you have a surplus, I would put it with pasta, rather than turn it into quiches or soups where its delicate freshness is wasted, and where bought calabrese serves admirably.

Stewed calabrese

This recipe comes from Anna Del Conte's *Secrets from an Italian Kitchen*, and the long cooking changes the character of the calabrese completely. I made it constantly last year, using the smaller sideshoots or any calabrese which was just past its best.

Chop the stems, peeling them if coarse, and slice the calabrese if large. Blanch it for 2–3 minutes, draining well. Heat a little olive oil in a wideish pan (I use a nonstick pan). Add a dried chilli and five fat cloves of garlic. Cook for a couple of minutes, then discard the chilli. Add the calabrese, stir well, cover and cook very gently for 30–40 minutes. Check from time to time, stirring and scraping off any bits which may stick to the pan: 'By the end they become fairly mashed up, but they will taste delicious.' Serve, discarding the garlic first, and dribbling a little extra olive oil over. If you make it with fresh garlic, eat the garlic with pleasure, increasing the quantity if you want.

Summer carrots

Summer carrots are smaller, faster maturing and less hardy than main crop varieties, and come in various types ranging from long and thin to short and stubby or round. The one I should most like to try is a white carrot from France available from Suffolk Herbs. A novelty? Not so. In 1754 in his *Gardener's Dictionary*, Philip Miller praises white carrots as the sweetest for the table, though less popular than the orange type, which was valued for its colour.

Early carrots are tricky to grow well. They should be sown as soon as the ground is warm enough and the soil sufficiently workable to produce a fine tilth, and take 12–14 weeks to mature. For most gardens, this gives summer carrots from early July into August. We grow some under cover in a large glass frame to produce an earlier crop in June, as well as some in the open. Pelleted seeds are a modern improvement as long as the ground does not dry out. Sow them thinly, in rows 6in (15cm) apart, thinning the seedlings to 1in (2.5cm) apart. This is quite the most fiddly job in the garden and needs to be done with meticulous care. You must remove the thinnings, for they attract carrot fly, which is a major and persistent pest. It lays its eggs in late May and the grubs eat their way into the carrots and can ruin the crop (later sowings sometimes avoid this). The organic remedy is to build a physical barrier of some kind around the carrots such that the beast flies over the bed and goes elsewhere. Otherwise, be as sparing as possible with insecticides. Even one application minimises damage considerably.

Summer carrots never attain the full round flavour of the main crop varieties and you will need to watch how the flower develops. Don't let them get woody or too mature. To harvest, hold the tops firmly, and lever the carrots out gently. In heavy soils you may need to use a fork, easing it in gently by the side of the row. In good weather when the space is not needed for another crop, or in a slug-free garden, carrots can be pulled to order. However, this is not an inviolate rule. If you twist the tops off, pop them into brown paper bags and keep them in a cool place, carrots will keep perfectly satisfactorily for a couple of weeks with no loss of flavour.

Everybody loves a bunch of summer carrots from the garden. They are as fragrant as sweet peas, and fill the whole house with a warm earthy scent. The balance tips firmly in savouring summer carrots raw, either whole or diced into thick or thin fingers. Their sweetness and crunchy juiciness is unadulterated pleasure. The thin skins need only a gentle scrub under water with a soft brush. Cut away any blemishes, leave on a tiny tuft of green and arrange them neatly in a white dish, scatter over a salad, or cut them in half and stick them around the sides of a bowl of green salad, pointed end upwards. Thinnings make pretty additions to salads, and are useful in summer minestras, but have little flavour.

If you must cook them, do so briefly and simply. A pat of savoury butter is all the embellishment you are likely to need. Unless they have become woody, I personally think soup is wasted on summer carrots. Turn them into a healthy cocktail instead.

Carrot salad with olive oil

Put the carrots through the julienne shredder and pile into a bowl. Take about a third and moisten with olive oil seasoned with a pinch of salt. Replace on top of the salad, and decorate with black olives. Leave for a couple of hours for the sweetness of the carrots to mingle with the olive oil before serving.

Carrot salad with honey and orange flower dressing

12 oz (340g) carrots, washed and
   scrubbed, or peeled thinly
2 tsp honey
2 tbsp wine vinegar

scant ½ tsp orange flower water
1 tbsp mixed chopped herbs as
   available – dill, tarragon, chervil,
   salad burnet, chives, coriander

For this salad you need a food processor, or else slice the carrots into very thin matchstick shreds. Put the carrots through the julienne blade (not the grater). In a serving bowl, stir the honey and vinegar until dissolved, and add the orange flower water. Toss the carrots and herbs in the dressing. Leave to marinate for 1–2 hours in a cool place. Mix again just before serving. Serve with salad leaves before fish, or as part of a medley of summer salads. If you prefer a softer texture, cut the carrots into thin batons and blanch briefly for one minute in boiling water. Dress and leave to marinate as before. Serves 2–4.

Summer carrots with creamy garlic sauce

A beautiful dish, one of the few exceptions to the no-cook rule for summer carrots.

12–16 oz (340–450g) summer carrots,
   washed, scrubbed and cut into
   chunks or wedges
½ pt(300ml) chicken stock

garlic purée (see p. 108)
To finish
a little cream or creamy milk
chervil leaves for decoration

Simmer the carrots in the chicken stock until tender in a covered pan. Stir in enough garlic purée to make a binding sauce. Soften with cream or creamy milk to taste. Divide between four small hot dishes, decorate with a few tiny leaves of chervil and serve as a first course.
Note If the sauce is too liquid, bind with a half teaspoon of potato flour slaked in a little milk or water.

Courgettes

There are about a thousand species belonging to the *Cucurbitaceae* family, most of which are climbing plants from warm regions. Edible species include the melon and watermelon, gherkins, cucumbers, and chayote. Marrows, courgettes, summer squashes and many of the pumpkins are all members of the same species, *Cucurbita pepo*. All are similar in appearance and growth habit and can, to varying degrees, be grown successfully here.

Until the 1950s, courgettes or zucchini were unknown here, except to those who had travelled abroad or read Elizabeth David, who first stimulated our interest for these and other foreign vegetables such as aubergines and peppers. Since then their popularity has steadily risen;

indeed, we are swamped with courgettes almost to the exclusion of the English marrow. I find them overrated and less interesting to eat than many other vegetables. Yet a basket full of freshly picked courgettes bearing their yellow flowers will gladden the heart of any cook, even mine. Why we cannot buy them in this state, except at exorbitant prices, is a shameful indictment of the interest commercial growers show for the culinary potential of their produce.

Courgettes are nothing more than gentrified marrow, bred to be small and dainty. Gardeners like them because they are easy and prolific. Three or four plants should be sufficient. All squashes are tender plants that must be well watered and grow best on rich well drained soil. A trench filled with well rotted muck is the ideal. Do not sow before late April, and do not rush to plant them out until the weather is mild enough, otherwise they will sit and sulk. If the weather is cold in late May/early June, re-pot the plants up and keep them growing on in the cold frame, delaying planting until mid-June if necessary. Raise the plants under glass in individual pots and plant out 18in (45cm) apart, keeping them covered with cloches until they are growing strongly. You will find them slow at first, but they quicken as temperatures start to rise. By the end of the summer they will need hacking back if they are not to take over the garden completely. They produce both male and female flowers, the latter easily recognised by the tiny fruitlet immediately behind the petals.

There are many varieties of courgettes, green, yellow, long and round, as well as the custard marrows, vegetable spaghetti and pitty pan squashes. Each year, seed catalogues offer more. Thus far, the difference in flavour of those we have tried seems marginal. Should you tire of courgettes, you could do as we have done and go back to conventional marrows. These are delicious when cooked properly and store beautifully. Picked young, the same size as courgettes, they are delicate and have a natural buttery quality courgettes seem often to lack.

It is imperative to keep cutting courgettes regularly – turn your back, and you have another marrow on your hands. There are those who say they should be picked before the flowers have been pollinated; I find they are best just after. Your middle finger, 3–4in (7.5–10cm) is the proper size, though anything up to 6–8in (15–20cm) makes good eating. Generally speaking, the larger they become, the less interesting and more watery the flavour; very tiny courgettes will not have had time to develop flavour and are slightly bitter. Slice them neatly at the base with a knife and lay them carefully in the picking basket, so as not to dislodge the flowers if you want to keep them on.

Like all sub-tropical plants, courgettes do not take kindly to chilling and will suffer injury if left in the refrigerator for some time, leading to loss of texture and eventually flavour. You can see this easily for yourself. The fruit becomes dull and rubbery in texture, and loses the creamy quality of a freshly picked specimen. If you need to store them, a cool larder is best. Wrap them loosely to allow air and moisture to circulate, either in newspaper or brown paper bags.

To prepare courgettes for the table, check for marks, wipe off any soil, trim off the stalk and cut away the brown patch which sometimes forms at the rounded end where the flower is attached. Do not peel them. Put them in a pan and cook them simply with little water or stew them gently with olive oil or butter. Either way, they do not need very long – 3–5 minutes. Or steam them or cook them with the flowers still attached, proof of their youth and freshness. An attractive way to present them is to cut them in the form of a cross, making two longitudinal cuts almost to the base. Steam or cook briefly, testing with the point of a knife, brush with melted butter and serve.

Courgettes are remarkably adaptable. Their essentially bland flavour and texture combines well with other vegetables. Once you have tired of them served plain, or as fritters or stuffed, try them raw in salads, in breads, and with grains and pulses.

It is often recommended to salt courgettes before you cook them to draw out some of the moisture. Except for use in baking, or for some salads where a soft texture is desirable, I do not find this necessary, though they will soak up less fat if left moist. Rinse them and pat them thoroughly dry before proceeding.

Courgette flower fritters

Courgette flowers are pretty, make convenient containers for delicate stuffings, but actually do not taste of very much. They harbour insects (scrutinise them thoroughly) and wilt rapidly once cut. The best idea I have found for courgette flower fritters comes from the Italian writer Lorenza De'Medici. You pick the flowers unopened. Brilliant.

Courgette salads

Raw courgettes are surprisingly nice. Cut them into thin batons and serve with other crudités. They can also be used chopped or sliced thinly with salads, the kind you make in large bowls with a variety of vegetables, nuts, rice and other grains. Colin Spencer gives another way: grate the courgette finely, sprinkle on a little salt, squeeze out the excess moisture, add finely chopped mint or basil, pack into moulds, turn out and serve.

Zucchini with mint vinaigrette

This is an Italian recipe, *zucchine alla scapece*, taken, slightly adapted, from *The Time Life Good Cook* series. It takes its name from the cooking method, *scapece*, most often associated with fish which are fried then marinated or pickled in vinegar and flavourings. The method is an ancient one, dating from Roman times, and the word *scapece* an Italianisation of the Spanish dish for pickled fish, *escabeche*. This version produces a sweet-sour salad which I prefer. Other versions leave out the sugar and include more vinegar. Marcella Hazan, in her book *Marcella's Italian Kitchen*, gives a hot unsweetened version with pasta you may like to try also.

Heat sufficient olive oil to cover the base of a smallish pan. Slice your courgettes into ¼in (6mm) rounds and fry over a brisk heat until both sides are a light golden brown. Do not let them burn. Drain and layer in a bowl, sprinkling each layer with a little caster sugar, vinegar, chopped mint, and slivers of garlic. Aim for a balance between sweet and sour; neither should predominate – and be generous with the chopped mint. Allow to marinate for a couple of hours (or longer). Serve at room temperature.

Courgettes and caraway seeds

Fry strips of courgettes in a little hot butter with 2–3 teaspoons of caraway seeds for a couple of minutes. The seeds release their aroma, and the courgettes become coated with deliciously crunch bits of caraway. Serve with pork chops.

Courgettes, tomatoes and tarragon

Take an equal quantity of courgettes and ripe tomatoes – 8–10 oz (225–285g) of each should be sufficient for four. Cut the courgettes into strips the size of thin chips. Peel and de-seed the tomatoes, and cut into strips also. Heat a knob of butter and a little olive oil in a pan. Add the courgettes and cook for 3–4 minutes until just wilted, moving them around so that they do not catch. Try one to see – they should be on the soft side of crisp. Add the tomatoes, plus 1–2 tablespoons of chopped tarragon. Shake until the tomatoes have warmed through and serve immediately.

Courgette and onion pizza or pissaladière

Makes 1 large, 2 medium, or 8 individual tarts

For the base
8oz (225g) *white unbleached flour, or*
   2oz (60g) wheatmeal
   bread flour and 6oz (180g) white
   flour
1 tsp *fermipan dried yeast*
½ tsp *salt*
1 tbsp *olive oil*
1 egg, *beaten*
about 3 fl oz (90ml) *tepid water*

For the filling
1lb (450g) *onions, peeled and thinly*
   sliced
2 tbsp *olive oil*
1 lb (450g) *courgettes, wiped and*
   grated
To finish
Strips of anchovy fillet, halved and
   stoned black olives; or, for the
   pizza, 3–4oz (90–120g) mozzarella
   cheese, plus a few halved stoned
   black olives

Start with the dough. Put all the dry ingredients into a warm, roomy bowl. Make a well in the centre, add the oil and egg and most of the water. Mix to a dough, adding extra water as necessary and knead until smooth. Either cover the bowl with a plate or wrap loosely in a large plastic bag and leave for 2–3 hours, until well risen and puffy. Longer will not harm – simply punch it back and let it rise again.

Meanwhile, prepare the filling. Gently sweat the onion in the olive oil in a covered pan until very soft and beginning to brown. This will take a good 25–35 minutes. Stir from time to time. Add the courgettes, mix well, and continue to cook until the mixture is soft and pulpy and there is no excess moisture, stirring often. If it suits, this can be prepared in advance and kept in the refrigerator in a closed box.

Knock the dough back and spread out on to greased pizza pans in the usual way, pulling, stretching and patting the dough gently into shape with your hands. The base should be as thin as you can make it and the outside rim a generous ½in (1.25cm) thick. If you are making individual tarts, which are particularly attractive, Yorkshire pudding tins are ideal. Spread the cooled filling fairly thickly over the dough. Leave for 10–15 minutes for the dough to prove.

You can finish these bread tarts in one of two ways. Either make a lattice work of anchovy fillets and olives as in the classic pissaladière. Bake in a hot oven, 200°C/ 400°F/gas mark 6 for about 20 minutes until the dough is cooked and well browned around the edges. Alternatively, leave the top plain, cook as before, but 5–7 minutes before the end, top with slices of mozzarella cheese and decorate with a few olives. Continue to cook until the cheese is bubbling and beginning to brown. Serve hot as a first course. Any leftover filling mixed with beaten eggs makes an excellent eggah. A couple of chopped tomatoes, or oregano or basil can also be added to the filling.

Skate with orange, caper and courgette sauce

Skate has sweet firm flesh and a natural gelatinous quality that yields rich juices when cooked. It is advisable to buy more than you think you need – the bone to flesh ratio is high – and to choose the thickest wings you can find.

4 large thick skate wings
juice of 2 fresh oranges and 1 fresh
*   lemon*
6–8oz (180–225g) courgettes, wiped

and cut into julienne strips
butter for frying
1 heaped tbsp capers, washed and
*   drained*

Arrange the skate in a buttered casserole dish (you may need to use two), overlapping the thick edge of one with the thin edge of another. Pour over the fruit juices. Dot with shavings of butter, cover with foil and bake in a hot oven, 200°C/400°F/gas mark 6, until the flesh just parts from the bone, about 15–20 minutes. Do not overcook. Turn off oven and leave the fish for a few minutes to relax and release more of their juices.

Transfer to four hot plates and keep warm while you quickly finish the sauce. Strain the juices into a wide pan. Boil down until syrupy and the flavour seems right. Meanwhile, toss the courgettes in a knob of butter in a nonstick pan over a high heat for 1–2 minutes until they begin to soften. Add to the reduced fish juices, stir in the capers, bubble up, and pour over the fish. Serve immediately with saffron rice.

Scarpaccia

Scarpaccia is a zucchini pie made without pastry from Camaiore in Tuscany. Different versions I have found of the recipe vary slightly in their proportions, but the basic ingredients – young courgettes, spring onions, parmesan and eggs – are always the same. It makes a lovely light vegetable dish and is one of my favourites, quick to assemble, best served tepid.

12oz– 1lb (340–450g) young
*   courgettes, preferably with flowers,*
*   finely chopped or finely sliced*
3 large spring onions, finely chopped
1 clove of garlic, chopped (optional)
4 tbsp finely grated parmesan cheese

For the batter
2 eggs
2oz (60g) brown or white flour
4 fl oz (120ml) milk and water mixed
3–4 tbsp olive oil

Mix the first four ingredients together. Beat the eggs, flour and milky water to make a thin batter. Add the vegetable mixture and mix well. Grease a large shallow ovenproof dish with 2 tbsp of the oil, tipping it round to cover the base evenly. Pour in the batter – it should be no more than ¾in (2cm) deep – and smooth out the top. If there is too much mixture, use two smaller dishes. Drizzle over the rest of the oil and bake in a very hot oven, 200°C/400°F/gas mark 6, for 30–35 minutes, until the pie is set, golden brown and risen slightly. Cool a little before serving. Any leftovers can be eaten cold.

Pasta with courgettes and fried breadcrumbs

Because courgettes cook so quickly and retain a nice bite, they make an ideal basis for pasta dishes. This is a simple example which can be easily varied by adding mushrooms, slices of leftover chicken, a few prawns, or some fried pine kernels.

8–10oz (225–285g) courgettes, wiped and cut into thin matchstick strips
1lb (450g) pasta, preferably wholewheat or homemade fresh pasta

3–4 tbsp brown breadcrumbs, fried in a little olive oil
freshly grated parmesan or pecorino cheese
olive oil

The whole dish only takes a couple of minutes, so have everything ready, including hot plates, and time the pasta to be ready with the courgettes. Heat 2–3 tbsp olive oil in a nonstick pan. Add the courgettes and cook briskly, turning them constantly, until just softened. You want them brown at the edges, so keep the heat high. Drain the pasta, mix with the courgettes, scatter over the breadcrumbs and serve immediately, before the breadcrumbs have a chance to soften. Pass round olive oil and cheese separately.

Cucumber

The growing of cucumbers has long been a peculiarly English passion. A great deal of effort went into their cultivation and in the 18th and 19th centuries a gardener's brief was to supply the house with a constant succession of cucumbers from April onwards. On occasion greater feats were accomplished, George I being presented with two fine specimens on New Year's day in 1721. The length, smoothness and absence of seeds in an English cucumber was an obsession. Cucumber glasses were regularly employed by commercial growers, 'As one good and straight cucumber,' commented one author, 'is worth nearly a dozen small and deformed ones.'

In recent years, cucumber development has come on apace. Tastes, too, are changing, and we no longer view the prickly skinned misshapen varieties found in every continental market with as much disdain, realising that their flavour is as good if not better than that of our smooth skinned supermarket kinds. Most significantly, the development of the Japanese and Burpee F1 hybrids has made growing cucumbers much easier. These are the kind we grow, and they are thoroughly to be recommended. They have something of the finesse of English hot house cucumbers, but like all ridge or outside cucumbers, are less fussy and thus easier to grow. Another relative newcomer is the crystal apple cucumber, first introduced in 1933 by an Australian grower in Sydney. The fruit is roundish, about the size of a lemon with a similar flavour to ridge cucumbers.

Cucumbers are not especially difficult, but are prone to disease. They also have a habit of coming in flushes, resulting in a deluge one week and nothing for the next. The skill, therefore, lies in keeping them healthy and cropping steadily. This is achieved by constant watering and feeding, and trying to ensure they do not develop botrytis by ventilating properly, spraying if necessary, and picking off all infected leaves as they appear.

Cucumbers cannot stand the cold and should not be sown too early. For growing under glass, sow mid to late April, two seeds to a pot, planting out 2 ft (60cm) apart once the roots have filled the pot. In our greenhouse this gives us Burpee cucumbers from around early July through to October. They need a rich soil or a growbag (we cut out the base to allow the roots to penetrate into the soil below and plant two in each bag). They must be kept growing continuously without check. Water sparingly when young and copiously, daily if you can manage it, once they are growing well, spraying the plants to create the right humid atmosphere.

Sow twice as many seeds as you need, selecting the best and throwing out any plants with misshapen leaves, as it is these which tend to develop virus disease. Grow them up a framework so that the cucumbers hang down like Chinese lanterns. If you live in warmer parts of the country, it is possible to grow ridge cucumbers and gherkin cucumbers outside.

Cucumbers need to be picked regularly. Let them grow as long as you want – for the Japanese and Burpee kind, 9–11in (23–28cm) is about right – but pick them before they get too fat, for then they are too full of seeds. Ideally, pick them just before you need them, still warm from the plant.

A cold cucumber is a lifeless, tasteless thing. Like all tropical plants they should be kept cool but not cold and are better stored out of the refrigerator on a shelf in the larder. There is no need to wrap them unless you feel you have to put them in the fridge. Then they should be wrapped in clingfilm and stored in the salad drawer.

Though often slow to start, the season for cucumbers continues well into autumn until the colder weather sets in. Ours often have a surge about September time. Towards the end of the season, they grow less quickly and are less succulent. By now you will have had your fill of Greek salads, but these later cucumbers still make excellent soups and pickles. If the weather turns particularly cold, bring in the remainder and keep inside.

Kitchen garden cucumbers are delicious. They have more flavour than bought cucumbers and are crisper. As you cut into them, they will burst with beads of juice. The skins of Japanese cucumbers are tougher than greenhouse kinds, and need peeling. Remove the seeds if they are disagreeably large.

Garden cucumbers are to be used in quantity rather than for decorative slices. Should you not require a whole one, cut from the flower end. Their first use is in salads, or cut into chunky thirst-quenching wedges to crunch on while the barbecue is cooking. They combine well with yoghurt, dill, shellfish, particularly crab, rice and tomatoes. We eat quantities of them in the Greek salad of tomatoes, feta cheese, olives and oregano that I gave in *Fresh Thoughts on Food*; it is still the finest way to eat a home-grown cucumber.

Cucumbers are also delightful cooked. Here, I think, it is better always to remove the seeds. As a vegetable to accompany fish, chicken or veal, they can be fashioned into small ovals with a potato peeler and cooked simply with a little butter. Or they can be stuffed or pickled in many different ways. For soups, include a little of the skin to help with the colour.

Unless you want floppy cucumber slices, or the recipe specifically demands it, it is not necessary to salt cucumbers before you use them.

Cucumber salads

Cucumbers make any number of salads. With home-grown cucumbers, or at least the kind we grow, I prefer to remove the seeds when using them diced in quantities. Sweet dressings based on flavoured vinegars or yoghurt/sour cream mixtures perked up with fresh herbs such as dill and mint, or spices such as ginger and chilli, are in the main better than oily mayonnaise dressings, which tend to fight with the clean cool taste of cucumber. Serve cucumber salads at room temperature.

Cucumber with strawberry vinaigrette

A variation of Salad Elona: slice cucumbers thinly and dress with strawberry vinegar puréed with 2–3 ripe strawberries and sugar to taste. Pour the dressing in a thin trail over the cucumber. Decorate with a thinly sliced strawberry in the middle.

Cucumber and feta cheese salad

Slice your cucumbers ¼in (6mm) thin and arrange in a dish. Chop some feta cheese into crumbly bits, mix with 2–3 tbsp fruity olive oil and spoon over the cucumber. Leave plain, or sprinkle with a little finely chopped mint, strewing stoned and quartered black olives over the whole.

Tomato and cucumber salad with mustard and spring onion vinaigrette

Arrange alternate layers of sliced ripe tomatoes and cucumber in a shallow dish, or on individual plates. Mix together 2 tsp each of Dijon mustard and a grain mustard, sugar and vinegar. Beat in 2 tbsp olive oil. Thin to a pouring consistency with a little hot water. Add a finely chopped spring onion, green and white, and spoon carefully in little blobs over the salad.

Cucumber, rice and mustard seed salad

Cucumbers came originally from India, and have been cultivated there for 4000 years. Their coolness is especially appreciated – as in raitas, for example – in accompaniment to spiced dishes, but there is no reason why Indian cucumber dishes cannot fit into our European pattern of eating. This dish is based on a recipe from Julie Sahni's book, *Classic Indian Vegetarian Cooking*. Quantities are not important – be as flexible as you want with the basic rice/cucumber/yoghurt mixture. Aim for a pleasing contrast between the hotness of chilli and coolness of the cucumber. I like the chewiness of brown rice for this dish, but basmati rice can be used equally successfully.

1 whole cucumber, peeled, de-seeded, and cut into small dice
2–4oz (60–120g) cooked rice, brown or white
1 tsp finely chopped fresh ginger
pinch of curry powder (optional)

2–4 tbsp thick yoghurt
1 fresh chilli, de-seeded and finely chopped
2 tsp ghee or vegetable oil
2 tsp mustard seeds

Mix the cucumber, rice, ginger and curry powder, if using, and bind with enough yoghurt to moisten without being sloppy. Fry the chilli in ghee or vegetable oil for a couple of minutes, add the mustard seeds and continue to fry until the seeds pop (putting the lid over the pan to stop them from jumping out and spattling everywhere). Pour over the salad. Mix, and leave for an hour or so before serving.

Cucumber, apple and melon soup

A cooling summer soup, simplicity itself to make.

1 small very ripe melon
1 whole cucumber, seeded and peeled, with 3–4 strips of peel reserved
about 1 pt (600ml) apple juice

1–1 ½ tbsp elderflower vinegar
1 tsp sugar (optional)
1–2 tsp finely chopped mint

Remove the flesh and squeeze out the juice from the melon. Blend with the cucumber, peel, and apple juice until smooth, using extra apple juice if necessary to achieve the right consistency. Add vinegar, sugar, mint to taste. Chill thoroughly. Pour into soup cups, decorate each with a tiny sprig of mint and serve. Serves 6–8.

Omelette Czarina

A good book to turn to for ideas on omelettes is the *Omelette Book* by Narcissa Chamberlain, published in 1956, from which these two ideas are taken. There is little point in recounting how to make an omelette: use fresh free-range eggs and make the omelette, in the words of one French gastronome, 'drooling-moist' in the centre.

Allow 2 tbsp peeled, de-seeded cucumber per person. Cook gently in a knob of butter for 4–5 minutes until just beginning to soften. Moisten with a little sour cream or thick creamy yoghurt, stir in some chopped tarragon and set aside. Working quickly, make a 2-egg omelette in the usual way. Spoon the cucumber filling down the centre, fold and serve immediately.

Omelette Montenegro

Prepare the cucumber as above, allowing 1 tbsp per person, and cook with an equal quantity of cooked ham cut into neat little strips. Add a little finely chopped parsley. Fill the omelette as before.

Brill with saffron and cucumber

Brill is a member of the turbot family, a less fine fish by general consensus, but a respectable fish of more manageable size. To feed four people you will need one large whole fish. Otherwise, go for fillets, which are less impressive but easier to serve. If you cannot buy brill, use plaice or lemon sole.

1 large whole brill, head and tail removed, or 4 fillets	*1 packet saffron*
1½ cucumbers	*1 large glass medium dry white wine*
flakes of butter	*2–4 fl oz (60–120ml) cream*

Peel and de-seed 1 cucumber. Slice downwards into 4 long segments, then cut across into lozenge shapes. Blanch for 3–4 minutes in boiling water, drain and reserve. Put the fish in a large buttered casserole, folding fillets to form neat parcels. Scatter round the cucumber. Dissolve the saffron in the wine and pour over the fish and cucumber. Dot with flakes of butter, cover with foil and bake at 190°C/375°F/gas mark 5 until just done; this will depend on the shape and thickness of the fish, round 20–30 minutes for whole fish and half that time for fillets. Look for the creamy curd which appears on top of fillets. For a whole fish, test with the point of a knife near the backbone.

While the fish is cooking, peel and whizz the rest of the cucumber in a blender, sieve and reserve. Carefully transfer the fish to a hot serving dish or hot plates as appropriate. Pour the cooking juices into a shallow pan and boil down to 3–4 tbsp. Add the cucumber juice, cook for a minute, then soften with cream to taste, adding an extra pinch of saffron if this seems a good idea. Pour around the fish and over the cucumber. Serve immediately with rice.

Quick salted dill cucumbers

It is impossible to imagine how many hours country housewives have spent pickling gluts of cucumbers. Early books are full of recipes and instructions, sometimes with dubious additions such as alum to improve the colour, yet the basic principle remains the same. Richard Bradley, in *The Country Housewife and Lady's*

Director, describes July as 'the principal season for pickling of cucumbers, for that fruit is now in the greatest perfection, as well for pickling them in imitation of Mango's, or as Girkins.'

The spices Mr Bradley recommends for this task – bay leaves, ginger, dill, garlic, mace, pepper, mustard, chilli – have not changed in more than 300 years. This recipe comes from Lesley Chamberlain's book, *The Food and Cooking of Russia*. The pickles will keep for a couple of weeks in the refrigerator, but are better for making fresh and in small quantities. Put them on the salad table, or chop into soups.

Make a brine in the proportion 1 tbsp salt to 1 pt (600ml) water. Wash and dry the cucumbers if necessary and cut into 3–4in (7.5–10cm) pieces. Quarter these and pack into clean glass jars. For small quantities, a jam jar is ideal. Add a few dill seeds or a sprig of dill and a clove of garlic. Bring the brine to the boil and pour over the cucumbers. Cover when cool and keep in the fridge. They will be ready to use in a couple of hours.

Freezer dill pickles

Americans are enthusiastic dill picklers, as are the Russians. The following recipe is based on one given in *Pickles and Relishes* by Andrea Chesman and produces a sweet pickle, good with cold meat salads. I have reduced the quantities, three quarts of cucumber pickle not being my idea of fun. This makes about 12oz (340g).

1½–2 cucumbers, scrubbed but not peeled
½ small onion, pared into paper thin slices
1–2 tbsp finely chopped green pepper (optional)
1–2 tsp salt

8 tbsp cider or wine vinegar
1 oz (30g) sugar
For the seasoning
good pinch of turmeric; or celery seed; or dill seed; or ½–1 tsp grain mustard

Slice the cucumber thinly and put in a bowl with the onion and green pepper if using. Sprinkle over the salt, mix well, and leave the vegetables for a couple of hours for the salt to draw out the moisture. Tip into a sieve, wash under running water and drain well. Mix the vinegar and sugar, stirring until the sugar has dissolved, and then add a good pinch of whatever spices you are using. Pour over the cucumber mixture and leave in the refrigerator overnight. Next day, transfer to freezer containers, label, and freeze.

These crunchy freezer pickles can be used immediately and keep well for several months. The sugar content can be altered to suit. By using different spices you can produce a whole range of pickles.

Garlic

The ancient Assyrians, Egyptians, Persians, Indians, and Chinese all grew and revered garlic. So did the Greeks. The Romans took it with them on their military conquests, and planted it wherever they went, thereby introducing it into northern Europe. It was among the plants that Emperor Charlemagne decreed his subjects should grow in the early 9th century. Medieval botanists and monks all grew it. In the 17th century it was grown as far north as York. Even Gilbert White grew it once – yet how many people think of planting garlic in their gardens today?

The problem, I guess, lies in the association garlic has with hot countries. We think of garlic as a Mediterranean plant, or Indian, or Mexican, or Spanish, but not one belonging to northern Europe. Only very recently have English growers in Cornwall and the Isle of Wight begun to experiment with garlic as a commercial crop. Few seem to realise garlic is one of the hardiest members of the onion family, and comes with a built-in armoury of antibacterial and antifungal properties to repel pests and diseases. This makes garlic potentially one of the easiest plants to grow.

Two things are critical. Though warmth speeds up maturation of the bulb, it is the lengthening of the days as spring turns into summer which induces the bulbs to form. Second, garlic is one of those plants which needs a period of cold during its early development, otherwise the bulbs may not form at all. Hence the correct time for planting garlic is autumn rather than spring. If you have tried and failed with garlic this may be the reason why.

Its requirements are similar to those of onions – a rich, well drained soil and a sunny position. Avoid very wet or windy spots. The individual cloves should be planted in late October or early November, 2–3 in (5–7.5cm) deep, 3in (7.5cm) apart, with 9in (23cm) between the rows. The roots develop first. As long as these get a good month's growth, all should be well. The shoots do not appear for several weeks or even months after planting. To ensure success, cover with cloches after planting and throughout the winter. This keeps off rain and snow and enables the garlic to get off to the best start once the weather warms up. Apart from the occasional weed, they need no further work until harvesting.

In California, garlic mania runs high. Commercial and amateur growers have the choice of several varieties of garlic to choose from to suit different climatic conditions, size and flavour. In this country named varieties have only recently begun to appear, and are available from some specialist seedsmen. These are worth trying to find. Unnamed greengrocer garlic sold at expensive prices from gardening centres is not. Bring a couple of the fattest bulbs you can find from holiday abroad (which surprisingly seems to work well), or choose the best you can find from the greengrocer. Thereafter, save your own, selecting the best bulbs each year for replanting the following autumn.

Fresh garlic is a treat. Home-grown bulbs are never as large as those you find in the Provence, but are equal in every other respect. They are in any event superior by far to most of those you are able to buy. Stored properly, they should last well into winter.

Garlic generally matures sometime in July. Wait until the tops are yellowing and beginning to die back and pull up a bulb to see. If the cloves are well formed and starting to separate, it is ready for harvesting. Otherwise, leave a little longer. Don't leave them too long in wet weather, as this can cause the bulbs to rot more quickly. Pull them up and get them under shelter to dry out as soon as you can.

To store garlic, it must be properly and thoroughly dried, right through to the centre, otherwise mould will develop. Begin by laying the garlic out for 1–2 weeks in a dry shady place. Do not bunch them together but spread out in rows, keeping each bulb separate. If you're drying them outside, bring them in as soon as wet weather threatens.

After this, clean the bulbs as you would onions (p. 121). Inspect the necks for any signs of rotting and set these bulbs aside to use first. Any damaged garlic should be set aside also. Braid the garlic or gather them into small bunches and tie at the neck. Once this has been done, go over them again, trimming off any unnecessary tops. Hang in a well ventilated place out of direct sunlight for another couple of weeks to complete the drying process.

How long garlic remains in good condition depends partly on the variety (some are inherently better keepers than others) and partly on where it is kept. A steamy kitchen is quite the worst place to store garlic for long keeping. It needs somewhere cool and dry; a well insulated shed or unheated back bedroom is ideal. Properly cured, garlic should stay in good condition until Christmas. After this, though it is still usable, deterioration quickens. By spring, any remaining bulbs will be sprouting. Plant them out in an odd corner – no need to be fussy. The fresh garlicky shoots are considered a delicacy in some countries, and can be used in salads, omelettes, soups and stir-fries.

Fresh 'wet' garlic has paper thin skin and a sweet garlicky fragrance. The cloves are plump, full of juice, and have yet to attain their full pungency – this comes with drying. Speaking personally, this is garlic at its best. Get out your cookery books and pestle and mortar and prepare the family for a two-week garlic festival: soups, purées, bruschetta, pesto, aïoli – all the dishes that point to high summer and the flavours of the Mediterranean are given added dimension made with fresh garlic. Garlic is also not sufficiently appreciated as a vegetable in its own right. Whereas one small clove of raw garlic will produce a dramatic effect (and play havoc with the digestion of those who cannot take its volatile compounds), long slow cooking of many cloves subdues garlic into a deliciously mellow vegetable, sweet, benign, and one of the best accompaniments for chicken or a simple roast of lamb. This mellowing effect can also be achieved by blanching the garlic first, then gently sautéing in butter or oil.

Garlic purée

I first gave this unctuous purée in *Fresh Thoughts on Food*, and I have yet to find a better one: take at least 2–3 heads of fresh garlic (and twice that amount of the ordinary greengrocer kind) and separate the cloves. Put into a pan with water to cover, bring to the boil and blanch for 4–5 minutes. Drain and slip off the skins – this is easy; slice off the base, and the cloves should pop out with a gentle squeeze. Repeat the blanching process another 3–4 times, using fresh water each time. At the end, the cloves should be as soft as butter – cook a little longer if not. Drain thoroughly and purée until absolutely smooth. Season lightly with salt to taste. Keep in a small glass jar under a thin film of olive oil, packing it tightly and making sure there are no air holes, and store in the refrigerator for up to two weeks.

This admirable purée can be used in several ways: as a base for soups or sauces, either on its own or let down with meat juices or cream to serve with meat, vegetables or poached eggs; to flavour vegetables purées; or mixed with a little olive oil, spread on dry baked bread and lightly grilled to serve with crudités or float in good fishy broths.

Tourin blanchi a l'ail et a l'oseille (blanched garlic and sorrel soup)

This wonderful soup comes from the Hotel Terrasses du Beauregard in the Dordogne. It translates well into English kitchens, though I have added an extra egg to achieve the correct degree of mellowness.

3½oz (100g) fresh peeled garlic cloves
generous 1lb (450g) onions, finely
  sliced and chopped
2 tbsp vegetable oil, or oil and butter
  mixed

1 tbsp flour
seasoning
1¾ pt (1 litre) water
6oz (180g) sorrel, stalks removed
2 eggs, separated

Put the garlic in a small pan, cover with water, and bring to the boil. Drain. Repeat the blanching twice more, using fresh water each time. Slice finely. Gently soften the onion and garlic in the fat in a covered pan for 15–20 minutes, stirring frequently. Stir in the flour, season lightly, add water and simmer for 45 minutes. You can cool and reheat later at this point if you like.

Cook the sorrel in a separate pan until wilted. Bring the soup to the boil and add the sorrel. Lightly break up the egg whites with a fork, and stir into the soup, stirring round to form thin threads. Off the heat, beat in the egg yolks. Serve immediately in hot soup plates. Follow the custom of *faire chabrot* to finish the soup: swill the last few spoonfuls of soup with a little wine and drink. Serves 6.

Apple and garlic sauce

This is based on an idea from an American book, *The Official Garlic Lovers' Handbook*. The flavours are surprisingly complementary.

2 large cooking apples, peeled and
  cored
lemon juice

4 cloves of garlic
butter
sugar

Cook the apples to a pulp with a couple of tablespoons of water and a good squeeze of lemon juice. Meanwhile, cook the garlic separately with water to cover until soft. If you want a milder flavour, blanch the garlic first, then cook in fresh water. Mash the two together with butter, seasoning with sugar to taste – begin with a teaspoon and add more to give the right balance; it should be only slightly sweet. Excellent with pork.

Cod baked with olive oil, garlic and potatoes

4 thick cod steaks or fillets
12oz–1lb (340–450g) onions, finely
  sliced
olive oil

2¼lb (1kg) waxy potatoes
8 large cloves of garlic
8 black olives, stoned and quartered

Sweat the onion in a little olive oil in a heavy covered pan, over the gentlest of heat until soft, golden and much reduced. Take care over this, half the success of the dish depends on it: stir from time to time and allow 30–40 minutes. Boil the potatoes until just cooked. Cut into thickish slices. Blanch the garlic for 3–4 minutes (these can be popped into the potato water), peel, and slice into halves or quarters.

The rest of the dish is assembly. Choose a shallow ovenproof dish which will just take the fish snugly in a single layer and brush bottom and sides with olive oil. Arrange a thick layer of potatoes on the bottom, surmount with a third of the onion mixture and lay the fish on top. Tuck in the rest of the potatoes down the sides of the dish, slipping in a few slivers of garlic here and there. Top the fish with the remaining onions, dot with olives and the rest of the garlic. Dribble over 2–3 tbsp olive oil. Bake in a hot oven, 200C/400F/gas mark 6, for about 30 minutes until the fish is done.

The exact timing requires good judgment. What you're after is the fish nicely but not overcooked, and the onions beginning to brown at the edges in an appetising way – be prepared to juggle with the oven or shelf settings towards the end. Serve with a plain green salad, a jug of your best olive oil to add to the dish at the table and some good bread. One of the best recipes in the book.

New potatoes and garlic pearls

1½–2lb (675–900g) small, even sized
  new potatoes
2 tbsp olive oil or olive oil and butter
  mixed

about 16–24 large cloves of garlic,
  peeled

Scrub or scrape the potatoes. Choose a large shallow ovenproof dish which will take the potatoes and garlic in a single layer. Heat the oil, or oil and butter, add the potatoes and garlic, shaking them around to coat in the fat. Pour in enough boiling water to come ½in (1.25cm) up the sides. Transfer to a hot oven, 200°C/400°F/gas mark 6, and cook until done, 35–45 minutes, shaking the pan from time to time to turn the potatoes. As the dish cooks, the water evaporates, leaving the potatoes to acquire a lovely golden brown slightly crisp crust impregnated with the flavour of the garlic.
Note If the water looks like drying up too soon, add a little more.

Sweet and sour vinegared garlic pearls

Blanch peeled fresh garlic twice. Put in a pan with enough wine vinegar and water to just cover, using equal quantities of each. Add 2–3 tsp of sugar. Cook very gently, until the liquid has almost evaporated – 10 minutes or so. Stir the cloves around until they become coated with the caramelly juices – watch it doesn't catch. Serve with roast lamb or chicken.

Chicken breasts with garlic and sweet wine sauce

This recipe is based on one from Paula Wolfert's *The Cooking of Southwest France*. Don't be put off by the sugar or the quantity of garlic – both mellow completely to produce a very mild and savoury dish.

4 large chicken breasts, skinned and boned
small knob of butter for frying
For the sauce
1 medium carrot, 1 stick celery, 1 medium onion, all finely chopped
½ pt (300ml) medium sweet white wine
2 tsp sugar
generous 1¼ pt (750ml) well flavoured homemade chicken stock

bouquet garni – sprig of parsley, bay leaf, sprig of thyme
1–2 tsp potato flour slaked in a little water
2–4 tbsp cream
few drops of vinegar or lemon juice
For the garlic
32–40 large cloves of garlic
1½ tsp sugar
½oz (15g) butter

For the sauce, soften the carrot, celery and onion in a little rendered poultry fat (use the skin from the chicken) until light brown round the edges. Pour in the wine, add the sugar and reduce by two thirds. Add the chicken stock and bouquet garni, and simmer very gently, uncovered, for an hour. Mop up any fat with kitchen paper, remove the bay leaf and pass through a sieve, pushing through as much of the vegetables as you can – they help to thicken and flavour the sauce. If they do not go through easily, whizz with some of the stock for a few seconds in the processor and then sieve. If necessary, reduce the sauce a little more to concentrate the flavour. Set aside.

Cover the garlic cloves with water, bring to the boil and blanch for 3 minutes. Drain and peel off the skins. Transfer to a small dish, sprinkle over the sugar, dab with butter and cook uncovered in a very low oven, 130°C/250°F/gas mark ½, for 1½–2 hours until soft and golden. Shake from time to time. Reserve and keep warm.

Melt a knob of butter in a nonstick pan and quickly brown the chicken breasts on both sides. Reduce the heat and continue cooking until done, turning once or twice.

Arrange the garlic in little piles on four hot plates. Swill out the garlic pan with a little of the sauce, return to the rest of the sauce and bring to the boil. Thicken with the potato flour, add cream to taste and finish with a few drops of vinegar or lemon juice.

Arrange the chicken breasts on the plates. Pour round some of the sauce, serving any remaining in a sauce boat. Serve with rice and spinach.
Note The sauce and garlic can be prepared in advance if required. The method of cooking garlic cloves slowly with a sprinkling of sugar and dabs of butter can be used for other dishes or as a vegetable in its own right.

French beans

French beans are New World beans, discovered by the Spanish explorers who found them growing in the Americas in the early 16th century and brought them back to Europe. 'The fruits and cods of kidney beans' (we called them thus after the shape of their seeds), wrote the herbalist Gerard, 'boiled together before they be ripe, and buttered, and so eaten with their cods, are exceeding delicate meat, and do not ingender wind as the other pulses do'. Their collective diversity is enormous, stretching to several hundred different varieties. Even in Gerard's day, sorting them out was a headache. They may be green, yellow, spotted or purple. The seeds or beans range from the familiar white haricot to the pink speckled borlotti and Mexican black bean. Their habit may be dwarf or trailing. The climbing or pole bean varieties latterly introduced in seed catalogues are grown like the familiar runner bean (a different species, *Phaseolus coccineus*), supported by wigwam structures in the same way. The shape of the green bean may be round as in the haricots, flattened, as in varieties like Masterpiece, or broad like a ribbon as in some of the climbing beans.

All are varieties of *Phaseolus vulgaris*, or common bean. These had already been undergoing domestication for many thousands of years in South and Central America, the process continuing as they spread across the continents into Europe and beyond. Systematic breeding means that different varieties peak at different stages so that some are more suitable for drying, others best when young as haricot verts.

The surprise, or so I have found, is that there is little detectable difference in flavour between many of the French bean varieties. Some are slightly sweeter, others fleshier or crisper, but that is all. Generally speaking, of the dwarf varieties, those which grow long and straight with bright green cylindrical pods make better eating than those which are flattish in appearance. Beans that develop curled rather than straight pods (a cultural problem) are never as good and almost invariably tougher. Purple and speckly beans are attractive but lose their colour to a dull grey-green on cooking. If I could have just one French bean it would be the climbing bean, Garrafol Oro, from Suttons Seeds, a ribbon shaped bean, light green in colour, with an excellent sweet flavour. This is a good cropper, and the beans stay tender even when large.

It is more important to find varieties to suit your soil and conditions, than to worry about descriptions claiming superior flavour. Success is not always predictable, especially in cold summers or in the more northern parts of the country. French beans dislike cold intensely and will not grow well in temperatures below 50°F. Frost will kill them outright. Wait until early May, or later if the weather is cold, and sow the seed direct, taking out a V-shaped trough with a hand fork, spacing the rows at 9in (23cm), and thinning the plants to 6in (15cm) apart. The climbing varieties need 18in (45cm) apart to accommodate the wigwam. They prefer light, well drained soils but will succeed in a variety of situations. Cover with cloches or Agryl P17 (p. 18), keeping them well protected until mid-June. Water well in dry weather.

There is little point in successional sowing of French beans. By picking them regularly, the plants will keep producing new beans. For small gardens, a mixture of dwarf beans and trailing/pole/climbing beans, which mature about three weeks later, is to be recommended. If you have the room, leave some of your beans to develop their seeds. Even better, grow some specially for drying; a dish of creamy flageolets out of the garden is unsurpassable.

The beauty of French beans is that they are good to eat at any stage of development, except when they are very small and immature. A cook gardener can match the size of bean to the dish and need never worry if the beans have grown too large. Wait until the pods have rounded into adolescence before you begin to pick them, letting them grow to pencil thickness or slightly larger. One account I have read recommends picking for diameter first, rather than length, which is sound advice. Large, tough beans should be left to grow on and develop their seeds.

Sometimes the weight of crop demands more beans be picked than you can handle at a sitting. Pick them over, sorting out any damaged beans, and store in plastic bags in the refrigerator. Gluts are inevitable, especially with climbing beans. Though they have their enthusiasts, frozen beans do not have much appeal. A better way of preserving them is in the Greek style cooked with onion, tomatoes, garlic and olive oil. This and similar dishes freeze much better than the blanched or raw beans.

French beans are far more agreeable cooked than raw. Though they may be succulent enough, baby beans make disappointing eating with a flat, barely-bean flavour. To serve as a vegetable or in salads, the beans should be tender enough to prick the skin easily with your thumb. They require only to be topped and tailed. Blanch them in a large pot of water for 1–3 minutes depending on size, testing as you go. Do not have them too crunchy; the flavour is properly developed when they feel just slightly soft rather than squeak. There is no need to refresh them if you are serving them later as a salad or first course. The cooking times are so short, the beans retain their bright colour. The alternative method is to cook them in a little water in a covered pan, lifting the lid off after a couple of minutes, or to steam them. They can also be stir-fried, though I do not think this is as successful.

Older beans make splendid Mediterranean braises, as in the Greek recipe outlined above or the Spanish dish on p. 89. These form part of our daily eating in late summer and into autumn, either hot as a vegetable dish or, more often, cold as a simple salad eaten with pitta bread. Generally speaking, there is no need to remove the stringy fibre running down the back of the bean, but it is a good idea to check.

French beans can be finished in various ways. The simplest is to toss them in a little nut oil or add a pat of savoury or herb butter. Or you can finish them in the Chinese or Indian style by frying a few aromatics – ginger, mustard seeds, fresh and ground coriander, spring onions, bean curd – and then tossing the beans lightly in the mixture. A little diced celery or fennel or a few toasted and crushed nuts add a crunchy contrast and any combination of tomatoes and onions will work well.

French bean salads

French beans show their versatility best in salads, on their own or partnered with other summer vegetables and dried beans. More substantial salads, with hard-boiled eggs, chicken, tuna, or ham make excellent one course lunches.

French beans in sesame seed dressing

A most appetising way of eating young French beans. Blanch them for 2–3 minutes and toss in 1–2 tbsp light sesame seed oil. For each 8oz (225g) beans, allow 2 tsp sesame seeds, toasted until light brown, then briefly pounded with a pinch of sea salt in a pestle and mortar to release their aroma. Mix half lightly into the beans. Arrange on plates and scatter the rest of the sesame seeds on top.

French bean and aïoli salad

A good way of using up the remains of a bowl of aïoli prepared for another dish. Cook your French beans in a little water until just soft. Mix with roughly chopped tomatoes and diced potato, preferably freshly cooked (if not, make sure they are not fridge-cold). Thin down 2–3 tbsp aïoli with the cooking liquid from the beans. Pour over the vegetables, scatter generously with parsley and serve.

French beans niçoise

2 tbsp olive oil
1 leek, white part only, sliced
8oz (225g) chopped tomatoes
1 clove garlic, chopped
½ tsp sugar

12oz (340g) young French beans
a few stoned and quartered black
  olives
lemon juice

Melt the oil and soften the leek. Add the tomatoes, garlic and sugar, and cook for 10 minutes. Meanwhile, blanch the beans for 2–3 minutes. Add to the leek and tomato mixture with the olives and a good squeeze of lemon juice. Serve warm with bread as a first course. Serves 3–4.

French bean and red pepper salad

2 red peppers
1 tbsp olive oil
2 cloves garlic, finely chopped

1–2 tbsp finely chopped parsley
1lb (450g) young French beans
extra olive oil for serving

Grill and skin the peppers in the usual way (see p. 206). Slice into thin even strips. Heat the oil and add the garlic and parsley. Fry for a minute. Add the peppers and stew gently for 5–10 minutes. Meanwhile, cook the beans until just done. Tip the beans into the pan and stir to mix. Serve tepid as a first course with bread with a little more olive oil dribbled on top.

French beans and summer carrots in spicy almond dressing

Another sesame seed dressing, this time from David Scott's *Seasonal Salads*. The spice mixture, or *dukka*, can be stored in screw-top jars and used with potatoes, crudités or chickpeas, or stirred into yoghurt to make a quick savoury dip.

8oz (225g) slender French beans
8oz (225g) young summer carrots, cut
    into batons
For the dukka
3 tbsp sesame seeds
2 tbsp coriander seeds

1 tbsp cumin seeds
2 tbsp flaked almonds
salt and cayenne to taste

Lightly dry-roast the seeds over a moderate heat in a small heavy or cast iron pan. Move them around and don't let them burn but just colour to light brown. Cool, then grind to a paste in a coffee grinder. Toast the almonds in the same way. Mix everything together in a small bowl, adding salt and cayenne to taste.

Cook the beans and carrots until just tender. Mix with some of the paste and serve.

French bean and chicken salad

An all-in-one salad, based on salad niçoise. These quantities serve one person, and should be multiplied to suit.

3–4oz (90–120g) cooked chicken
washed lettuce leaves – a variety
 including the frilly edged La Lollo
½–1 hard-boiled egg
2oz (60g) cooked French beans
2–4oz (60–120g) cooked new
 potatoes, sliced

1–2 anchovy fillets, rinsed and split in
 half
a few stoned olives
vinaigrette
chopped tarragon and chervil

Cradle the lettuce leaves in a deep bowl or soup plate. Arrange everything else in layers, finishing with the chicken. Dribble over the vinaigrette, and scatter liberally with herbs. Pop a cherry tomato in the middle if you have one.
Variation Instead of olive oil, dress the salad with hazelnut oil and crushed hazelnuts. Scatter with finely chopped celery or fennel, chopped olives and parsley.

Green beans and potatoes à la Extremadura

A Spanish dish for large beans or the flat ribbon type such as Garrafol Oro, taken from *Spanish Cooking* by Elizabeth Cass. This quantity makes a large amount, but reheats well and can be frozen.

2 green peppers
2–3 tbsp olive oil
2¼lb (1kg) potatoes, peeled and
 coarsely sliced
2¼lb (1kg) flat ribbon beans, topped,
 tailed and diced

2 large tomatoes
1 large onion, chopped
5 cloves of garlic, chopped
2 tbsp chopped parsley,
bay leaf

Roast or grill the green peppers in the usual way (see p. 206), peel and cut into rings. Melt enough oil to cover the bottom of a deep pan, pile in all the ingredients. Cover tightly and simmer for an hour, stirring occasionally. Check the seasoning and serve.

A good variation, which makes a nice autumn lunch, is to divide the mixture into individual gratin dishes, break an egg into each, cover and cook until the egg is just set. For a spicier version, add a fresh chopped chilli and cook with the other ingredients.

Green beans and potatoes with coriander

A variation of the above recipe, but producing a very different flavour. Cook beans and potatoes as above with a sliced onion, crushed clove of garlic and large handful of chopped fresh coriander. Stir occasionally and watch the vegetables do not start to stick towards the end. This also reheats and freezes well.

Lettuce

Lettuce is a plant of great antiquity, grown by the ancient Egyptians and the Greeks, who praised its medicinal virtues. The Romans, who introduced it here, enjoyed it both raw and cooked; Pliny describes nine varieties including black, purple, red and 'crispa' lettuce. It was cultivated in China, where the thick fleshy stemmed celtuce was developed, and Emperor Charlemagne included it in his list of desirable kitchen garden plants, compiled around 800AD.

In more recent times, improved strains have played an important part in the emergence of lettuce as our principal salad plant. Primitive lettuces were loose headed, narrow leaved and coarse, probably bitter tasting. The Latin name, *lactuca*, indicates that they were valued for their milky latex. This is known to have a soporific effect, and was used as an opium substitute, according to one authority. John Parkinson went further: 'It abateth bodily lust. . .for Monkes, Nunnes and the like of people to eat, and use to keep them chaste'. (*Paradisi in Sole*, 1629). A tightly headed lettuce is sweeter and far more desirable. These made their debut in England sometime in the 16th century, and by the middle of the 18th lettuce had become firmly established with enough varieties to ensure year-round production for the growing band of enthusiasts. A hundred years later, J. C. Loudon was to remark: 'The varieties of lettuce are continually changing; hence those in fashion now [1833] are either different, or bear quite different names, from those which were most in demand when this Encyclopaedia was first composed in 1820.'

In a sense, this is still the situation today. Each year sees the introduction of new varieties of the four modern lettuce types – the ball-headed cabbage or butterhead type; the dense crisphead type; the upright cos; and the non-hearting loose-leaved salad bowl varieties which have seen a revival in recent years. Some of the modern varieties are very good, especially overwintered and early maturing lettuces, and should be considered along with older dependable varieties known for flavour.

For lettuces which mature later in summer, choose varieties such as Avon Defiance, which are resistant to mildew and lettuce root aphid. These are the two chief enemies of lettuce, and can cause a whole row to keel over and wither during August and September. An excellent early summer lettuce for June that is sown in pots in the greenhouse in March is Fortune. This is a well flavoured bolt-resistant cabbage lettuce which can form enormous solid heads. The frilly edged La Lollo, with its attractive red tinged leaves, and the richly coloured oak leaf lettuce, which grows equally well in summer as in autumn, remain my favourite loose-leaved types.

Each type of lettuce has differet virtues, and ideally you should grow all four. The cabbage type are the gentlest in flavour. At their best, these are the most buttery of lettuces, bearing no resemblance to the floppy tasteless things around in the shops. They are valuable early and late summer and are the best type for soups. Cos lettuces, by contrast, are meaty things, with bags of crunch. These have the most pronounced lettuce flavour and are often the sweetest. Well grown examples can be very large and require dedicated eating.

Crisphead lettuces are the juiciest and most succulent, their tight inner blanched crisp hearts keeping well. Loose leaved varieties add interest and colour. For small gardens or lazy gardeners, their attraction is their cut-and-come-again nature, enabling a few leaves to be picked at a time. But do not expect them to taste the same. They are coarser and sometimes have a slight bitterness. They mix well with other leaves but are not so attractive for summer eating on its own.

Summer lettuces should be sown successively from April through to the end of June, to harvest from July through to late September. They need a fertile soil to do well and are best sown either in situ, 12in (30cm) between rows, or in small pots where they can be transplanted without root disturbance, transplanted lettuces never performing as well. Thin the plants gradually to 9–12in (23–30cm) apart, depending on the type and form. Once they have grown to a good size, pick off any rotting leaves that collect around the base to help prevent mildew.

If you observe lettuces growing in the garden, you will find that different types stand better than others. Cos, for example, do not stand well. Whatever the type, weather is the determining factor. Wet weather produces

rotting, and dry weather bolting. Generally speaking, on reaching maturity, a good healthy lettuce with a firm heart and bright leaves remains at its peak for about a week. After this time, they become progressively prone to pests and the weather. When this happens, cut them, take off all of the damaged leaves, and store inside. Cut them cleanly with a knife at the base, leaving on some of the stalk. Trim away the outside leaves – the chickens will appreciate these – and bring into the kitchen straight away. If you need to leave them outside while picking other crops, do not leave them in the sun, but find somewhere shady and sheltered.

A lettuce glut is inevitable. The obvious solution is to try your hand at some cooked lettuce dishes. Soups, of which there are endless permutations, are especially good – potatoes, fresh herbs, peas, courgettes and crab make the best. Braised lettuce has its enthusiasts, though I am not fond of it myself, finding its inherent wateriness and stringiness comes too much to the fore. Lettuce shredded and used in a stir-fry has more possibilities. In all cooked dishes, remember to use only the best leaves and tender hearts – gardeners can afford to be discriminating. Second-rate leaves are better relegated to the compost heap, or fed to the rabbit.

For notes on lettuce salads see p. 61.

Lettuce and red pepper summer gazpacho

This soup comes from an idea in *The Light Eater's Cookbook*, published by the British Iceberg Growers' Association.

½ *red pepper, deseeded and chopped*	*To serve*
¼ *cucumber, deseeded and diced*	*diced red pepper*
2 *ripe tomatoes, chopped, plus 1 tsp*	*diced cucumber*
tomato purée	*chopped spring onions*
½ *pt (300ml) chicken stock*	*croûtons*
2 *tsp chopped basil*	*iced mineral water*
2oz *(60g) shredded lettuce*	2–3 *tsp basil vinegar*
	ice cubes
	jug of olive oil

Simmer all the ingredients except the lettuce for 5 minutes. Add the lettuce and simmer another 2 minutes. Blend, cool, and chill. To serve, put the vegetables and croûtons into small bowls or arrange separately on a platter so everyone can help themselves for adding to the soup. Dilute the soup with iced mineral water to a thinnish consistency, sharpening with basil vinegar to taste. Serve with an ice cube in each bowl, handing round the olive oil separately.

Summer cannelloni

8 sheets lasagne (preferably
  homemade) or bought cannelloni
  tubes
For the filling
4oz (120g) courgettes, cut into 1in
  (2.5cm) strips
2 tsp olive oil

4oz (120g) finely chopped crisp lettuce
4oz (120g) ricotta cheese
generous grating of nutmeg
To finish
shavings of butter
a few tbsp chicken stock or water
freshly grated parmesan cheese

Cook the lasagne or cannelloni in simmering water until just soft. Drain carefully and lay out on the working surface. Toss the courgettes in the olive oil over a high heat in a nonstick pan for 1–2 minutes until barely soft and just wilted. Mix with the other ingredients to make a stiff paste. Spread over the lasagne sheets and roll up, or stuff into the cannelloni tubes. Arrange in a buttered gratin dish, moisten with broth or water and cook in a hot oven, 200°C/400°F/gas mark 6, for 5–7 minutes; just enough for the lettuce to wilt and everything to heat through. Serve as a first course with parmesan cheese scattered over.

Lettuce cakes

The idea for these crisp, savoury little patties comes from *The Baghdad Kitchen* by Nina Jamil-Garbutt. This quantity makes 8 small cakes.

4oz (120g) crisp lettuce, finely
  chopped
3–4 spring onions, chopped
2 tbsp chopped parsley, or parsley and
  tarragon, dill, oregano or mint
1oz (30g) plain flour

1oz (30g) fine maize meal
½ tsp powdered cumin
pinch of salt
2 eggs, lightly beaten
vegetable oil for frying

Mix all the dry ingredients, then add enough egg to make a thick batter. Heat 2 tbsp oil in a nonstick frying pan and drop spoons of the mixture into the pan, using the back of a spoon to make a flattish round cake. Cook both sides until golden and crisp. Keep warm while you cook the rest, adding extra oil if necessary. Serve as a first course with bread, pickles or a sweetish chutney.

Onions

Home-grown onions, of whatever size and complexion, are stronger and more flavourful than commercially grown onions. They are a rewarding crop to grow, but take more time and care than is generally supposed. When space is scarce, my advice to the cook would be to persuade the gardener to grow shallots or garlic instead.

The modern way to grow onions is from onion sets, specially raised immature onion bulbs. The soil needs to be fertile and the situation sunny. The first job is to prepare the bed, applying seaweed meal and potash just before planting and raking down the soil to a fine tilth. Plant the sets in spring, 2in (5cm) apart, with 6in (15cm) between the rows; this spacing should give medium sized onions. Check at first – birds have an infuriating habit of tweaking at the tops, pulling the baby onion clean out of its hole. Once the plants are established, about 6in (15cm) tall, dress the bed generously with dried blood, scratching it gently into the surface of the soil using a small fork. This will provide a gentle hoeing. No further hoeing should be undertaken until the plants are mature – the roots lie close to the surface and may get damaged. Mulch at this stage with a thick layer of compost. When the tops start to die back, bend them over gently to the ground to assist ripening. Harvest around the end of August.

Choose a dry sunny day, laying them out on the garden path or somewhere where the soil can dry off easily. Successful storing depends on drying the bulbs thoroughly. This is best achieved in the open air, preferably, we find, hanging the onions upside down, but if the weather is wet, you will need to dry them inside. A greenhouse is ideal. Our own method is to hang the onions from an improvised frame (a slatted picnic table) but they can equally be laid out on a dry floor in a well ventilated covered place on sheets of newspaper. Spread them out so they do not crowd each other and leave them for 2–3 weeks. Once thoroughly dried, clean them before hanging up to store. Although not strictly necessary, this improves the appearance considerably: trim the roots, cut off the excess tops, leaving enough to plait or hang the onions from, and take off the outside muddy skins. Sort them out, setting aside the second best for more immediate use. Plait them onto a coil of butchers' string or hang in bunches. Store in a cold, dark, airy place, not the kitchen.

Properly stored, a well cured onion should last six months or more. Check regularly for signs of rotting. Green sprouting shoots can be used as onion greens, and the papery skins, added to stock, give it an amber colour.

Few vegetables have assumed so much importance as onions. They have been cultivated since prehistoric times, and were revered by the Egyptians, Greeks and Romans. A mummy has even been found holding one in its hand. Apart from a brief lull in Europe in the Middle Ages, in one form or another, they have consistently been popular with just about every cuisine you can think of.

As a vegetable, they are best either stuffed and braised or, when they are small – pickling onions especially – blanched and stewed slowly in butter and a sprinkling of sugar until brown and caramelised. In both cases, slow cooking has a mellowing and sweetening effect on onions, rendering them especially delicious. During cooking some of the compounds present become many times as sweet as sugar. Stewing sliced onions very gently until they melt into a purée.

Onions are also very tasty on the barbecue. Cut them into wedges, divide into layers and thread with other vegetables (or lamb) to make kebabs, brushing with oil and flavourings in the usual way.

If only onions did not make you weep. Home-grown onions are worse. Remedies include peeling and slicing them under water or chilling them in the refrigerator. The first washes away the substance which irritates the eyes; the second reduces its volatility. Letting onion atoms lurk within the salad bowl, animating the whole, as Sydney Smith recommended in his famous poem, is not my style. Apparently their pungency can be reduced by tossing the onion bits in vinegar and salt as soon as they are cut, before adding the oil or other dressing ingredients, or by sprinkling the onion with the Middle Eastern spice, sumac. Tell me if it works.

Except where the recipe specifies, a finely sliced onion produces a more pleasing dish than one which has been coarsely chopped.

Shallots

Shallots are grown in the same way as onions from sets, except they may be planted and harvested earlier, around July, each bulb producing a clump of shallots. Major seed companies now stock them. They are invaluable for the cook, being a mild onion which softens readily on cooking (though home-grown shallots tend to be more pungent). I like them because they are small, which makes them ideal when only a small amount of onion is required. Roast shallots have become popular of late and make an excellent accompaniment to meat dishes.

Peas

The garden pea we enjoy today was developed by Italian gardeners in the 16th century. Before then there had been field peas, eaten not green but dried, and for sustenance rather than pleasure. At first, fresh peas were a curiosity, 'a fit daintie for ladies'. As is well known, meteoric rise to fame came at the end of the 17th century at Louis XIV's court at Versailles, when the ladies gorged themselves on fresh peas. A hundred and thirty years later thay had descended to the masses and William Cobbett could confidently write: 'This is one of those vegetables which all people like. From the greatest to the smallest of gardens we always find peas.'

By the early 19th century, the English pea was well ahead of anyone else's. Thomas Andrew Knight, the eminent Victorian horticulturist, bred an even

sweeter and more tender pea, the marrow pea, forerunner of modern marrowfats. Many new tall, dwarf, early and late varieties were also introduced, so that by the end of the century 173 different varieties of peas had been recorded. Few survive today. To grow a pea with pedigree, or a tall pea like Admiral Beatty or Champion with enormous fat pods and large plump peas, you will need to seek out a specialist supplier like HDRA who maintain a gene bank of old varieties.

The passion for peas quickly extended to earliness. 'Ever since I became a man' – Cobbett again – 'I can recollect that it was always deemed rather a sign of bad gardening if there were not green peas in the garden on the 4th of June.' This was the King's birthday. George III reigned so long that his birthday formed a sort of season with gardeners.

Few modern gardeners would go to the lengths required, or have the time, labour or hot beds at hand to produce peas in early June. For a modern garden with limited space, second earlies or an early maincrop make better sense. These mature approximately ten days later than the early varieties, have longer pods, and thus a higher yield. A new variety, Hurst Greenshaft, is to be recommended.

To produce a crop of early peas, sowings should be made in March in the greenhouse, using guttering pipe, cut into appropriate lengths: fill the pipe three-quarters full with seed compost, sow the seeds thickly, water well, and then cover over with a good depth of damp peat. Soon you will have a thicket of sturdy young pea plants. Plant out when they reach 3–4in (7.5–10cm) high – do not break them up but simply slide the trough out whole into a prepared trench. To do this, hold a small fork against the peas and pull the piping steadily away from them. Keep the peas under cloches or Agryl P17 (see p. 18) until the weather warms up and all danger of late frosts is over. This way, you avoid problems with mice and unpredictable spring weather. Later sowings, from May, should be made direct. Soak the peas in paraffin in advance to deter mice. The plants take approximately 12–14 weeks to mature, giving peas from early July onwards.

Garden peas are a luxury crop even for gardeners. The plants need to be staked, well watered in dry weather, and netted from birds, which peck off the growing tips and damage the pods. In comparison to other vegetables, the yield is small – and then there's all the picking and podding to be done. But think of the reward! And do not deceive yourself for a minute that frozen peas are anything but a poor second best.

Any fresh garden pea makes good eating. However, it is very difficult to tell exactly the moment a pod should be picked, for the pod plumps out before the peas have reached their optimum size. This necessitates much gentle squeezing up and down the row and many an agonising decision. As a general guide, wait until you can feel the firmness of the pea pressing against the sides of the pod: it should be firm but not bullet hard – a sure sign you have missed its moment of glory.

You need to go over the pods regularly; the ripening period staggers over a week or so. As the peas mature further, pods and peas become harder and more floury as sugar is converted into starch. Even perfect peas can lose up to 40 per cent of their sugar within a few hours of picking – one of the reasons I suspect that bought garden peas rarely live up to their promise, forcing people back to the freezer. If you need to keep them, keep them in the fridge, which slows the process of conversion.

The only problem with peas is that there will never be enough of them. On average, 1lb (450g) pods will yield around 6oz (180g) peas, sufficient for two small servings. Tiny immature peas, the sweetest of them all, are an indulgence for private pleasure; eat them secretly and do not tell the gardener.

Peas should be cooked soon after they have been picked – 'alive' as one writer put it, and need the briefest of cooking, 1–3 minutes at the most. A sprig of mint is customary, though I must confess I can never see the point for garden peas in their prime. A perfect pea has the perfect taste.

In small gardens, where room can only be found for a few rows of peas, it is often difficult to gather enough for a respectable serving. The best way to make a virtue out of their scarcity is to cook them in the French style, with a few shredded lettuce leaves, and some finely chopped spring onion and carrot, finishing with a little cream, serving them in small bowls as a first course.

Small quantities can also be eked out in salads and make felicitous additions to soups and risottos. Old floury peas can be turned into purées, or used in braised dishes or casseroles. Pods, too, if you can be bothered, make excellent soups and purées – see p. 126 for the general idea. Their taste can be strong on its own, so tame them with cream or fromage blanc and herbs, or spice them with coriander and ginger.

Frozen garden peas are extraordinarily good, almost as much a luxury as when they are fresh. Follow the method given on p. 124, and blanch for 1 minute. As a stop-gap, peas can also be frozen unblanched.

Summer pea and purslane soup

This recipe is loosely based on one given by Jane Grigson in her *Vegetable Book*. If you do not have summer purslane, substitute claytonia instead.

1oz (30g) purslane
1¼oz (40g) sorrel, midribs removed
4 small sprigs chervil, stalks removed
3 spring onions, white and green,
* finely chopped*

½oz (15g) butter
scant 1pt (600ml) hot light chicken or
* vegetable stock*
4oz (120g) fresh peas

Finely chop the herbs. Melt the butter in a pan, add the herbs and spring onion, cover, and sweat gently for 15 minutes until the mixture melts into a purée. Pour on the hot stock and simmer for 15 minutes, keeping the lid slightly ajar. Add the peas. Cook, uncovered, until just done – they should still retain their bright colour, about 2–5 minutes depending on your peas. Serve immediately.

Pea pod purée

This is a way of making fresh peas stretch further. Cut off the stalks, rinse, and put the pods in a pan with a little chopped onion. For every 1lb (450g) pods, allow about ½ pt (300ml) water, and 1 small onion. Cover and simmer until soft, 15–20 minutes. Blend in batches in a food processor to a rough purée with some of the cooking liquid. Sieve, taking care not to push any of the stringy bits through. Dry out if it is still too liquid.

To serve, enrich the basic purée with a lump of butter or a little thick cream. Aromatics – chopped green peppercorns, chopped mint, a little finely chopped fresh chilli or spring onion, are also good. Serve in small quantities, or use to fill croustades or pastries.

Pea pod purée with ginger and mint

Fry a generous teaspoon of finely grated fresh ginger in a little butter very briefly, 30–45 seconds. Add the pea pod purée, and stir until hot. Finish with finely chopped mint to taste. Excellent with summer duck.

Pea pod soups

Pea pod purée can also be turned into soups. Tip the cooked pods and onion into the food processor with all the cooking liquid and blend and sieve as before. 1lb (450g) pods will provide enough for four servings. Now, proceed as follows:

1 Dilute with light chicken broth/milk/milk and water/cream and water to give the right consistency, add a little chopped mint and serve. If you like, add a sprig of mint when you cook the pods (remove before blending)

2 Cook 1–1½oz (30–45g) sorrel in a knob of butter until wilted to a purée. Add the pea pod purée. Dilute with water or light vegetable stock and finish with milk or a little cream to soften.

3 Stir in plain yoghurt and mineral water to taste. Chill. Add a little finely chopped mint before serving. A beautiful summer soup.

Pasta with fresh peas

Pasta and peas make a perfect combination, either on their own or with other vegetables such as leeks and mushrooms. Serve as a first course. Fresh or homemade pasta is better by far, though undeniably packet shells cup the peas and hold the sauce more successfully.

1 large clove garlic, crushed
5 fl oz (150ml) single cream
8oz (225g) pasta shells or fresh
*   tagliatelle*

8oz (225g) fresh peas
6 basil leaves, shredded into strands

Simmer the garlic in the cream in a small pan for a few minutes and then remove. Cook the pasta and the peas (the peas can go into the pasta water when the pasta is nearly done). Drain and toss in the sauce. Divide between four hot plates, scatter over the basil and serve immediately.

Beef braised with new peas

In the 1930s, the government introduced a scheme to encourage British housewives to buy more home-grown produce. The National Mark Movement was born and meant the sign of quality. National Mark eggs, flour, fruit, vegetables, meat and poultry became a feature of British life for a time. With the campaign came the *National Mark Cookbook*, written by Ambrose Heath and D. Cottington Taylor, director of the Good Housekeeping Institute. This is one of their recipes, the kind you can make anywhere given a pot and access to fresh peas. I have a feeling it was used often – it cropped up again in a newspaper a couple of years ago. Any piece of beef is suitable. The original recipe recommended fillet but added – wisely – a cheaper cut could be used. The instructions could not be pithier.

Choose a pot, preferably a heavy earthenware casserole, which takes whatever sized piece of beef you have. I generally use silverside or topside; a 2½–3lb (1.25–

1.5kg) joint should be ample for 4. Seal the beef all over in butter. Fill all the space around with fresh peas – allow 1½–2 lb (675–900g) shelled weight for 4. Put extra dabs of butter on top. Season if you want, though this is not necessary. Cover tightly and pot-roast very gently for 2½–3½ hours, depending on the size and quality of meat. I cook the dish at 140–150°C/275–300°F/gas mark 1–2, testing the meat after the first 2 hours. Do not add any liquid: the beef and the peas will make their own delicious gravy. Accompany with freshly made horseradish sauce.

Fresh pea and coriander tabbouleh

Cracked wheat or bulgur is of one of the most useful grains to have in the store cupboard, ideal for summer salads and quick pilafs. The grains are partially cooked and need only to be soaked before using. This is a variation of the classic lemon juice and parsley tabouleh.

4oz (120g) cracked wheat
2oz (60g) cooked tender peas
2–3 spring onions, chopped
1 ripe tomato, chopped
4 tbsp chopped coriander

1–2 tsp mint
2–3 tbsp olive oil
lemon juice
salt

Soak the cracked wheat with water to cover by 1in (2.5cm) for about half an hour (if you are short of time, use hot water and leave for 5–10 minutes). Rinse, and squeeze dry in your hands. Mix all the ingredients together lightly, adding lemon juice and salt to taste. Leave for 30 minutes to let the flavours marry and arrange on a platter set in a fringe of lettuce leaves. Serves 3–4.

Sugar snap peas

These are a favourite pea in our household, the ones we have grown until recently in preference to mangetout. With both, you eat the entire pod, but there the similarity ends. The sugar snap pea pod is sweet, fleshy and succulent; it snaps as it breaks – hence the common name, revealing fully formed peas inside. It is not as attractive as the mangetout, a mannequin among peas, but is especially delicious raw.

You could be forgiven for thinking that the sugar snap pea is a new kind of pea, for certainly it is being hailed as such. Not so. Gardeners have appreciated this pea for over 250 years. This is what a lady correspondent from Suffolk has to say in the early 18th century, published in Part II of *The Country Housewife and Lady's Director*, by Richard Bradley in 1736:

'You have mention'd in one of your books a sort of pea, which is called the Gourmandine, or Gourmand; which I suppose one may call, in English, the Glutton's Pea, because we eat all of it. For the pods of it are very sweet and have no film, or skin in them, so that the cods may be as well eaten as the peas themselves; . . . the best way, is to cut them cross, as you do French beans, and stew them in gravy with a little pepper and salt, there is not anything in my opinion can eat better. . . .'

Glutton's pea is a good name. The peas are sweeter than ordinary peas and have the added attraction of being enclosed in a juicy coat. Cooks will like them for they need only to remove the stringy bit down the side, and gardeners love them for the yield is twice as high and they last twice as long as ordinary peas. Unlike the latter, they need to be picked when they are mature and the pods full. Before this the sweetness has not developed properly. Test a few as they progress. Once ready, they last about a week on the plant – do not leave them to get old. Pick them regularly and new pods will keep forming.

Sugar snap peas are best raw served in a bowl as crudités. They can also be used chopped in salads or soups. Personally speaking, I find their sweetness overpoweringly cloying once cooked, but you may not agree.

Potatoes

More than any other vegetable save tomatoes, potatoes have suffered most from modern horticultural and commercial practices and preferences. Almost invariably, the kind you buy are a mockery of the real thing. Though a rearguard consumer backlash may save us yet, if you want a potato with depth and character, with nuances of flavour, texture and cooking appeal, you must grow your own. Nor does the matter end there. For if you are a cook, there are still very many varieties to choose from, though the less common ones need searching out. Until his death in 1988, the keeper of all our potatoes was D. Maclean of Dornock Farm, Crieff, Perthshire. It was he who supplied potato enthusiasts with the Shetland Black, or Kipplestone Kidney, Jersey Royals, May Queen and the extraordinarily meaty Golden Wonder, in addition to well established and promising new varieties. Efforts are being made to save his collection. Meanwhile, HORA have published a booklet, *The Potato Finder*, listing all the varieties currently available in the UK and their stockists; support them, or many more varieties will be lost.

New gardeners could be forgiven for thinking there is nothing to growing potatoes. You will always get some potatoes, no matter how poor your soil or what kind you grow. But potatoes vary wildly, and a variety which does well in one soil may be a waste of effort in another. This is the reason old gardeners saved their seed and why so many different varieties of potatoes emerged in the past. The season and general fertility of the soil affects yields, and all three affect eventual flavour.

Many gardeners don't have room to grow all the potatoes they would want. For small gardens the best solution is to grow a few rows of earlies to enjoy through the summer, supplemented by second earlies, which should store until Christmas. Both will be ready in time to leave the ground free for a second crop of winter brassicas or oriental vegetables. Few crops give as much satisfaction or are as interesting as potatoes. No matter how few you have room for, always try two or three different varieties, balancing a dependable all-rounder like Wilja with more unusual varieties, or a salad potato like Pink Fir Apple. Seek advice from your supplier, taking into account your soil and general situation.

Early potatoes are easy to grow compared to maincrop, which are plagued with many ills. Sow the tubers in early April, as soon as the land is suitable, taking out a hole for each tuber and mixing in well rotted compost or peat. This helps to reduce the number of blemishes. Rub out the smaller eyes to leave 3–4 well developed ones and plant a trowel's depth, 4–6in (10–15cm), allowing 15in (38cm) between the plants. You need to protect against any late frosts. This can either be with cloches or sheets of polythene, but the new material Agryl P17 (see p. 18), used by Jersey potato growers, is far the best, giving you potatoes two weeks earlier. On deep beds there is no need to ridge potatoes, though check and cover any growing tubers peeping through the surface with extra soil. This will help prevent greening caused by exposure to light. New potatoes should be ready around the end of June. Dig up a root to try. Second earlies will be ready up to four weeks later. For an extra early crop, sow a few spare tubers in large pots in good compost in the greenhouse in late February.

Digging potatoes is utterly pleasurable, reminiscent of childhood games of seek and find. Prise the fork – never use a spade – into the ground gently, and well away from the centre of the plant, and ease out a good ball of soil, grasping the haulm with your other hand. Two people are better than one. Most of the potatoes are to be found around the centre, clinging by their stems to the parent plant, but appreciable numbers will be found in the surrounding soil. Fish around diligently, turning the soil over gently, a forkful at a time. On deep beds, if just a few potatoes are wanted, a lazy method when time is pressing is to scratch away the soil and pick out those closest to the surface, leaving the plant intact. Ideally, and especially with new potatoes, you should dig and eat your potatoes without delay, with the smell of earth still clinging. Truly, there is no finer dish in the world.

One never knows how many potatoes a plant will yield; some as little as ½lb (225g), others 2lb (1kg) or more. Similarly, tuber size will vary. Sort them out, arranging them by size and using any damaged ones first. When it comes to harvesting second early or main crop potatoes, choose a dry day, laying the potatoes out for a few hours to dry the skins. Then clean them, brushing off the surplus dirt with a soft kitchen brush or kitchen paper. This takes time, but is satisfying work. Pick and sort, and store somewhere cool and dark in strong brown paper sacks. These allow potatoes to breathe and excess moisture to escape. Do not attempt to store potatoes in plastic bags for any length of time. Check stored potatoes regularly, removing any that show signs of mould, and remember to close the bag each time you open it.

Maincrop potatoes are generally left in the ground for as long as possible until the haulm has withered, allowing the potatoes time to grow larger and the skins to toughen. In practice, much depends on your soil and prevailing weather conditions. In wet seasons or on heavy soils, it is better to harvest early than risk damage and rotting.

New potatoes straight from the garden have paper-thin skins which rub off easily. Cook them simply, either in sufficient water to cover by 1in (2.5cm) or so, or by stoving them in butter or olive oil with no water and a tight lid over a gentle heat, shaking the pan often. Undercooked potatoes do not make pleasant eating any more than potatoes boiled to a mush. If you prefer to boil them in a minimum amount of water, you must watch them like a hawk – potatoes take longer than you think, and easily burn. Another way of cooking tiny new potatoes is to pop them in the oven wrapped loosely in foil with dabs of butter and sprigs of mint, allowing 35–40 minutes cooking.

The obvious superior flavour of homegrown potatoes is evident however you cook them. Mashed potatoes, blended with only their own cooking liquor and perhaps the top of the milk, can be superb. With roast potatoes, the inside is not merely soft but has real flavour. In casseroled dishes a well flavoured garden potato adds genuine character. It is the same with potato soups, which are generally not sufficiently appreciated. Make the tomato and potato soup on p. 132 with stale potatoes and watery tomatoes and it will be indifferent; make it with tomatoes and potatoes from the garden and it comes alive.

The skins of potatoes are the other thing which has engaged attention in recent years. It has now become accepted cooking practice to leave the skins on, and to encourage your family to eat them. Nothing is more pleasurable than the crusty skin of a well baked jacket potato. Skins from home-grown potatoes can be enjoyed with relish but commercial potatoes are sprayed during storage to prevent them from sprouting, and residues remain on the skin. My advice when using ordinary bought potatoes is either to peel them first, or to remove the skins before eating.

Potatoes cooked in a devil

The potato devil, or *diable*, is an attractive double-ended pot-bellied unglazed pot from southwest France used to cook potatoes and chestnuts without any liquid or fat. Elizabeth David wrote about them in *French Provincial Cooking* almost 30 years ago, and they have recently become generally available here (Habitat stores and good quality kitchen shops stock them). After an initial rinsing, the pot is never washed, and over time becomes charred on the inside from the cooked potatoes. It is a lovely homely pot to use. The cleaned and scrubbed potatoes are put into the bottom half, the other half of the pot put on top and the *diable* is put in the oven. Halfway through, you turn the pot upside down. In a moderate oven, medium sized potatoes take 1¼–1½ hours. It may also be used on top of the stove, where it serves as a tiny clay oven. Keep the heat low, using a diffuser mat (if the heat is too strong, the potatoes will burn) and turn the *diable* frequently. The method is far slower than boiling and the potatoes acquire a very different flavour. You will find them slow to cook at first, but they cook more quickly as the *diable* heats up; check them regularly towards the end. Once cooked, the potatoes will keep warm for up to half an hour.

The point of the potato devil is simple. The clay absorbs some of the moisture content of the potatoes, and they emerge crisp, flecked with brown and with a good earthy, fireplace flavour, as one writer put it. Being enclosed, it also affords the possibility of adding aromatics – thyme, whole cloves of garlic, caraway seeds – which impregnate the potatoes with their fragrance. For shop-bought potatoes, the potato *diable* can be a great improver of flavour, which is why I include it here. For homegrown potatoes, the *diable* is not so successful. The earthiness of the *diable* tends to mask the natural flavour of the potato and all but ruins the delicacy of a new potato.

Fast-boiled potatoes

Discussing ways of cooking potatoes one day, a colleague reminded me of this: cut your cleaned, scrubbed potatoes, peeled or not as you want, into thickish slices. Put in a pan with enough water to come halfway up. Add a lump of butter or 1–2 tbsp olive oil, jam the lid on tight and boil briskly over a high heat until done, about 10–15 minutes. Check the water level towards the end, adding extra if the potatoes look like drying out too soon. As the potatoes cook, they imbibe the flavour from the fat and form their own sauce. Transfer to a serving dish, not forgetting to pour over all the juices.

Note If too much liquid remains, transfer the potatoes to the dish and boil down to form a thick sauce. Pour over the potatoes as before.

Tomato, leek and potato soup

I believe it must have been M. Boulestin in his book *Simple French Cooking for English Homes*, published in 1923, who first introduced this soup here. Why it is not found more often is surprising, for few soups are better when made with good ingredients. As far as I am aware, only Elizabeth David has given it, in her *French Provincial Cooking*, from which my own version has evolved.

8oz (225g) leeks, white part only, sliced
½oz (15g) butter
8oz (225g) ripe red tomatoes, coarsely chopped
8oz (225g) potatoes, peeled and diced into small cubes

1 tsp sugar
To finish
a little creamy milk or single cream
finely chopped parsley or chervil

Begin by softening the leeks in a heavy covered pan in a little butter: 'Half the success of the soup depends upon this first operation,' writes Mrs David. 'If the butter burns instead of just melting or the leeks brown the flavour will be spoilt.' Add the tomatoes, cook a little longer until their juices run. Add potatoes, water and sugar, bring to the boil, cover, and simmer until the potatoes are soft but not overcooked, about 20–25 minutes. Now, push the soup through a mouli – a blender is wrong for this soup – and return to the pan, making sure you have scraped up all the vegetable mass which tends to stick to the underside of the blade.

Finish with a little creamy milk or single cream, enough to soften the acidity of the tomatoes but without making it too bland. For me, the beauty of this soup is its everyday simplicity and fine harmony of flavours; too much cream and the effect becomes too muted. The finished consistency should be that of thin cream. Add a spot of extra water if necessary. Stir in a *very* little finely chopped parsley or chervil and serve.

Potato, tomato and mint gratin

Gratins make the very best savoury vegetable dishes. Judge the quantities by appetite – people's capacity for potato dishes vary, my own being considerably larger than most.

1½–2lb (675–900g) waxy potatoes, washed but not peeled
1¼–1½lb (570–675g) ripe tomatoes, coarsely chopped
smallish handful of mint and parsley

2 cloves of garlic, chopped
2 tbsp pine kernels
soft brown breadcrumbs
olive oil or mixture of olive oil and butter

Boil the potatoes in their skins until almost done. Peel and slice thinly. Grease a suitably large shallow ovenproof dish, and arrange the potatoes, overlapping them slightly so they fit into a single layer.

While the potatoes are cooking, prepare the tomato topping. Chop herbs, garlic and nuts to a fine paste. Mix with the tomatoes and spread over the potatoes. Cover with a layer of breadcrumbs, dribble with oil or dot with butter. Bake in a moderate oven, 180°C/350°F/gas mark 4 for 45 minutes or until the potatoes are soft. The topping should be pleasantly charred here and there – if necessary, crisp the surface under the grill for a couple of minutes. A lovely dish in summer to serve with lamb.

Spiced and savoury potato cakes

Potato cakes exist in various forms. These are the simplest you can make, a plain potato base to which you add any savoury or spiced mixture you have to hand and which is appropriate for the rest of the meal. You need very little flavourings – a couple of spoonfuls of cooked mushrooms or ham, a handful of chopped herbs, and only a couple of teaspoons of spice mixtures. Add these as you go along, tasting until the balance of flavours seems right. The final cooking is merely to brown the outside and heat the cakes through – remember this when devising fillings. Different coatings can be used to alter flavour and crispness.

1½lb (675g) floury potatoes, washed but not peeled
For the flavouring
finely diced ham/cooked mushrooms/ spring onion mixed with tomato purée/grated cheese/grated horseradish/chopped herbs/ground

cumin mixed with a little chopped garlic or chilli/fried onion/caraway seeds/poppy seeds, etc.
beaten egg
wholewheat or plain semolina/ cornmeal/dried breadcrumbs

Cook the potatoes in their skins until very soft. Peel when cool enough to handle and mash with a potato masher or fork. Blend in the chosen flavouring, mixing well. Form into patties about 2in (5cm) across and ½in (1.25cm) deep. Have the coating mixture ready on a plate. Dip the patties first into beaten egg and then the topping mixture, using a palette knife to press the topping lightly but firmly into place. Leave to firm up in a cool place for 30–60 minutes, then fry in a non-stick pan with a little butter, olive oil or bacon fat, giving them 5 minutes either side, enough to brown and crisp the outside and heat the potato cakes through. Good with any grilled meat or fish.

Potato bread

No one did more to encourage the acceptance of potatoes as a staple food in France than Antoine Augustin Parmentier (1737–1813), the French philanthropist, economist and agronomist. Today, we acknowledge the debt in the names of potato dishes bearing the title 'parmentier'. During the Seven Years' War (1756–63), he was taken prisoner by the Prussians and survived by living on potatoes. Realising their potential, he worked tirelessly to popularise their cultivation and use, on one occasion offering a bouquet of potato blooms to Louis XVI and Marie Antoinette, who wore one in her hair. He wrote extensively on the subject, expounding on the virtues of potato bread, in his book *Le Parfait Boulanger*, published in 1778. Though it was seen as a substitute for wheat bread in times of shortage or economy, potato bread was highly thought of, especially toasted, by some 19th-century writers. Parmentier recommended substituting half the flour with cooked potato, a proportion which does not produce the kind of bread we are accustomed to or would necessarily enjoy today. A lesser proportion, say a quarter to a third potato, however, produces a good loaf of moister texture than ordinary bread and which does not noticeably taste of potatoes. This recipe is for a brown loaf, but you can use all white flour, or any proportion of either you prefer. The potato should be free of lumps and mixed thoroughly with the flours. Otherwise, the bread is straightforward and is made in the usual way.

6–8oz (180–225g) *potatoes, scrubbed*
5 fl oz (150ml) *warm milk*
¼–½oz (7.5–15g) *fresh yeast*
6oz (180g) *wholewheat bread flour*

6oz (180g) *white unbleached bread flour*
extra flour as necessary
1 tsp *salt*

Begin by cooking the potatoes until very soft. Skin, mash and combine to a purée with the warm milk. Cream the yeast with a little extra milk and few grains of sugar. Mix the flours and salt in a warm roomy bowl. Mix the potato purée, flour and yeast and knead to a softish dough, adding extra flour as needed until the dough is no longer sticky. Cover with a plate or wrap in a plastic bag and leave until doubled in bulk. If it suits, knock back and give the dough another rise. Knock back gently and put into a large warmed loaf tin. Prove in a warm place until well risen. Bake in a hot oven, 220°C/450°F/gas mark 7 for 15 minutes, turning down to 190°C/375°F/gas mark 5 to complete the cooking, another 15–20 minutes. Cool on a rack.
Note The steamy warm atmosphere ideal for proving is often difficult to achieve at home. The best solution I have found is to set the tin on a thick wooden board (I use the breadboard) over a pan of gently simmering water, arranging a plastic bag loosely on top. A wooden board is necessary because it is a poor conductor of heat and stops the bottom of the bread tin from becoming too hot. To allow the steam to rise and envelop the tin, the board should not cover the pan completely. The method works well for sluggish doughs or when the kitchen is cold.

Spinach

Spinach is a relatively late arrival to kitchen gardens. The Persians grew it first in the 6th century, then the Arabs, who called it the prince of vegetables and took it with them when they conquered Spain. It was probably from Spain that spinach first arrived in England. The herbalist Turner mentions it in 1538 as well known in England, and an early recipe for 'spynoches fryed' appears in the *Forme of Cury*, written by Richard II's cooks in the late 1390s. It would not be out of place today: boiled, drained and chopped spinach, fried in oil and sprinkled with 'powdour douce', mild sweet spices such as cinnamon and nutmeg. The Elizabethans were fond of it as a boiled salad, in sauces and in sweet tarts; later generations favoured eggs and fried sippets of bread.

It is easy to see why spinach caught on with cooks and gardeners alike. Few vegetables offer so much reward for so little effort. Spinach is one of the easiest plants to cultivate. It is one of the best catch crops to plant between anything which does not mature until later in summer, such as brassicas, broad beans, or even peas. The best is grown in spring, while the days are cool and moist. Sow as early as you can in April, thinning the plants to 6in (15cm) apart (these can be added to early summer salads). Protect with cloches or, better, Agryl P17 (p. 18), and the crop will grow much faster, resulting in even finer spinach. It matures in approximately 8–10 weeks. Depending on the weather, expect two or three decent pickings before it runs to seed.

Home-grown spinach has a natural buttery taste and a beautifully creamy texture. Much work has been done in recent years by plant breeders to produce varieties with less oxalic acid, such as Dominant, a truly excellent spinach. These are the ones to grow. Spinach is not a good high summer crop. It is a plant of temperate regions and bolts readily in hot dry weather. Over the centuries, gardeners have struggled with this problem, without avail. For later summer use, spinach chard is a much better plant for the kitchen.

Winter spinach is actually a misnomer. It refers to varieties which are sown in autumn and then overwintered as immature plants. These start into growth early in spring and give a crop 2–3 weeks earlier than spring sown varieties, but the quality is not as fine. For spinach-type leaves to pick during the winter, leaf beet spinach is the answer. This also gives a flush of new leaves in early spring.

Spinach should be picked regularly. Go over the plants, each in turn, plucking the leaves gently, stacking them neatly in the picking basket. Though it leaves the plant looking odd, it is less work in the kitchen if you sever the leaf where it joins the stalk.

Once picked, spinach quickly becomes limp. In Chinese markets, fresh leafy greens are constantly sprinkled with water to keep them bright and turgid. This is a useful tip if you need to keep the picked leaves waiting for a little while. Pick over, and remove any damaged leaves. If you are not going to use them straight away, do not wash, but stuff them immediately into a plastic bag. Loosely tie the top and keep in the salad drawer of the refrigerator. Like this, the leaves will remain reasonably turgid and succulent for 3–4 days, and can sometimes keep in good condition for up to a week with hardly any loss of flavour when cooked.

In dry weather, often the leaves require no more than a quick wash under running water, and sometimes not that. Only if it is muddy will they need the thorough washing so often necessary with bought spinach. Trim off the stalks if they remain. If you can be bothered, remove the midribs from the larger leaves.

Freshly picked spinach is one of the most delicious vegetables. Your own should be enjoyed for the luxury it is, cooked simply and plainly, for as little time as possible. It needs neither butter, cream, nor seasonings of any kind. Served with sweet quartered oranges arranged around the dish, nothing is finer.

The English way to cook spinach is with no other moisture than that adhering to its leaves after washing. The French method is to blanch it in a quantity of boiling water. The natural reaction, I suppose, is to think that our way must be best. This is not necessarily so. When properly carried out, there is little between the two. Blanching spinach takes a fraction of the time – a minute at most – compared to 5–7 minutes gentle cooking in its own moisture (add a spot of water to the pan to allay fears of any sticking or burning). Nutritionally, the balance tips in favour of the shorter method, despite the quantity of water used. Whichever you adopt, far better results will be obtained by cooking only small quantities of spinach at a time, in two or three batches if necessary.

Too much handling when expelling the excess moisture destroys its natural creaminess. Drain it very well, and squeeze thoroughly but gently, not so much to leave the spinach dry and unappetising.

This is how to treat prime spinach. Later, when the plants have started to bolt, the leaves become smaller and more angular. These are better suited to soups, stuffings and long-cooked spinach dishes.

Quantities for spinach are difficult to give. For home-grown spinach, 12oz (340g) is not too little for two people to enjoy as a vegetable course. For salads, 12–16oz (340–450g) is about right for four.

Freezing spinach

Spinach is an excellent vegetable to freeze, one of the very few which seems to suffer minimally in the process. For this reason alone, it is worth growing as much as you can. Freezing also fits in well with the general growing pattern as spinach tends to come in short but prolific flushes. Ideally, pick and freeze without delay. As long as you have everything organised beforehand, a good picking – about 9lb (4kg) or so – can be frozen in little over half an hour. The procedure I adopt, and which has served me well for a number of years, is as follows:

1 Wash the spinach quickly in a large washing-up bowl and leave to drain on the draining board. Open the windows.
2 Have two of your largest pans full of boiling water, ready to go on top of the stove. You also need a colander with a soup plate underneath to catch the drips positioned at the side of the stove, a large perforated skimmer to scoop out the spinach, a roomy plastic bowl to put the cleaned spinach in, and the sink full of clean cold water (if you have two sinks, so much the better – fill them both with cold water).
3 Turn the heat on full under the pans of water, and collect a bowl of spinach. When the water has reached a rolling boil, throw 2 small handfuls of spinach into the first pan. Wait until the water comes back to the boil – this should be almost immediately. Give it 15–30 seconds, then scoop out the spinach with the skimmer into the waiting colander. Throw in a second batch of spinach into the second pan. Without delay, tip the blanched spinach into the sink of waiting cold water. By the time you are at the stove, the second batch will be about ready to be scooped out into the colander and the next batch put into the first pan. (Or you can use both pans at once, which makes the business slightly more hectic, or a single pan, which takes slightly longer overall.) Repeat the process two or three times, then turn off the heat.
4 Next, deal with the spinach in the sink. Using your hands, scoop up the spinach, a handful at a time. It should now be quite cold. If not, run it under more cold water. Squeeze gently, removing all the excess moisture. Leave to drain on the draining board. Fill the sink with fresh cold water in preparation for the next batch.
5 Repeat the blanching and cooling process in this way until all the spinach is used up.
6 Bag the spinach, either chopped first, or left as whole leaves, label, and freeze.

Once you have tried this, you will find the method both quick and easy. The important thing to remember is *only blanch small quantities at a time*. Blanching is then completed in the quickest time possible, conserving the maximum amount of nutrients, and the vegetables are frozen in peak condition.

Spinach that has been frozen needs no further cooking, though it will need drying out. Reheat gently either defrosted or from frozen, or cook as the recipe indicates. Defrosted spinach is excellent in cooked spinach salads or any recipe which calls for blanched or cooked spinach.

Raw spinach salads

Until you have grown spinach yourself, it is impossible to know how good raw spinach is. Maybe this is why we do not find raw spinach much in salads. Limp spinach never has the same appeal – nor does it taste so appetising. Spanking fresh from the garden, it is one of the best vegetables for early summer salads, either on its own or mixed with other salad greens. Choose perfect leaves, wash, dry, and lay out on a plate. Team them with complementary ingredients and flavourings – lightly cooked chicken livers, frizzled bacon, oranges, capers, anchovies, olives, walnuts, diced tomatoes – add a dressing, and serve as a first course. Or try the Spinach and strawberry salad, and Spinach parcels below.

Spinach and strawberry salad

Strawberries and spinach mature at the same time and combine well; so well, it is odd that they are not found together more often. Lay some fine spinach leaves on individual plates and dot liberally with sliced ripe strawberries. If you like, add some finely sliced button mushrooms as well. Moisten with freshly squeezed orange juice or a mixture of yoghurt and strawberries puréed together, sharpened with a flavoured vinegar and spooned over the salad in pretty pink blobs. Serve immediately, and encourage everyone to eat with their fingers, wrapping the spinach around the strawberries.

Spinach parcels

This is no more than an extension of the wrap-around policy, but here the leaves are raw rather than cooked, providing a crisp crunch as you bite into them.

Fillings

shavings of mild cheese plus diced tomato

cooked rice or bulgur wheat mixed with pine kernels/diced tomato/ herbs/chopped olives/raisins/dates/ chopped hard-boiled egg/strips of ham or chicken

chopped banana and frizzled bacon

chopped avocado pear and cooked rice

cooked buckwheat/spring onions/ beetroot/sour cream

cooked lentils

cottage cheese/fresh pineapple

herbs/soft cheeses

Choose medium to large freshly picked leaves. Wash and dry if necessary, or wipe them over with a cloth and lay them smooth side down. Nip out the stalk with a knife making a small V in each leaf. This makes them easier to roll. Put a small amount of filling in the centre, roll up tucking the ends underneath. Stack them tightly together on a serving dish (the rolls have a habit of unwinding) and serve. Alternatively, provide two or three fillings, pile the prepared leaves on a plate and let everyone make their own parcels.

Cooked spinach salads

Cooked spinach salads are easy. Avoid leftover dull green leaves. The spinach should be freshly cooked, bright and lively. Blanch briefly – 30 seconds or so – and drain thoroughly, gently squeezing out the moisture. Slice into thick neat wedges. Alternatively use your own defrosted frozen spinach. Dress with one of the following:

Lemon and garlic dressing

Infuse a crushed clove of garlic in the juice of half a lemon sweetened with 1 tsp honey. Leave for 1–2 hours. Remove the garlic, spoon over the spinach and serve well chilled.

Mustard dressing and radishes

Mix 1 generous tsp mild mustard with a good pinch of sugar, 1 tbsp olive or nut oil, and 1 tbsp lemon or lime juice. Toss the spinach and chill. To serve, mound the spinach in little heaps on plates. Decorate with slivers of stoned black olives, tuck in thinly sliced radishes. Eat with rye bread or hot dry toast. For a more substantial salad, arrange lettuce leaves on a plate and heap the mounds of spinach around. Briefly cook thin strips of lamb's kidney with chopped spring onion in oil and butter for a minute or so. Deglaze with marsala and spoon over the centre of the salad. Decorate with thin slices of radish and olives as before.

Hard-boiled egg

Dress the spinach with a simple olive oil vinaigrette and chill. Arrange finely chopped hard-boiled egg over the top, with slices of egg around the sides. Serve.

Spiced sesame seed dressing

Dry-roast 1 tbsp sesame seeds and ½ tsp cumin seeds over moderate heat for a minute or two, covering them with a lid when they start to pop. Do not let them burn – the idea is to release their aroma. Crush lightly with a good pinch of salt in a pestle and mortar. Sprinkle over well chilled spinach and serve. Or mix into thick sheep's milk yoghurt, or half yoghurt, half cream, and spoon over the spinach as usual.

Yoghurt dressing

A Middle Eastern salad, best made with homemade yoghurt. Mix the spinach with a few raisins plumped either by steeping them in hot water or by frying them in a spot of oil or butter for a minute or two. Softly fried onion and garlic is another possibility. Beat the yoghurt with a pinch of salt and spoon over the spinach. Serve plain, well chilled, sprinkled with cinnamon. Another variation I like is to flavour the yoghurt slightly with saffron. Either toast 2–3 strands until dry, and crumble to a powder, or use a pinch of powdered saffron. Mix into the yoghurt and spoon over the salad as before.

Lemon cream dressing

Flavour a little thick cream with lemon juice, sugar, and a scrap of finely grated lemon peel. Spoon over chilled spinach and serve.

Spinach au jus

Spinach mixed with the juices from a roast joint of beef, veal or lamb is delicious. Blanch and drain your spinach in the usual way. Mix 1 tsp potato flour with some of the meat juices. Put the spinach in a pan with the juice and flour mixture, or use the roasting pan, mopping up the fat first. Reheat to boiling, gently turning the spinach over in the juices. The potato flour will bind the two and soak up any extra moisture from the spinach, which should not be wet or bathed in a sauce but glisten nicely.

Spinach purées

Leanline purées have become very much a part of modern cooking. Their attraction is simplicity of execution matched with clear flavours which allow ingredients to speak for themselves. They can be used as a sauce or to accompany simple grills and roasts and steamed or poached fish, also very much part of today's cooking. For busy cooks, they can be prepared in advance and reheated gently, or kept warm in a bain-marie.

You need not confine yourself to one vegetable for these purées. Try a mixture of spinach and leek; spinach, garlic and mushroom; or spinach and fresh pear. The procedure is simple. Cook each vegetable separately (but use the pear raw), purée, and then blend together to achieve the right balance of texture and flavour, enriching with a little butter or cream if appropriate.

Spinach, chickpeas and pasta

A favourite pasta meal at home; Swiss chard makes a similarly excellent dish.

1 clove of garlic, chopped
olive oil
4oz (120g) cooked chickpeas
4oz (120g) cooked or frozen spinach,
  drained and chopped

salt
8oz (225g) wholewheat pasta shapes,
  or homemade pasta
parmesan or pecorino cheese

Fry the garlic in 1 tbsp olive oil for 2–3 minutes. Do not let it burn. Add the chickpeas, turning them over in the garlic, followed by the spinach. Cook a couple of minutes longer to heat through and amalgamate the flavours. Season lightly with salt.

Meanwhile, cook the pasta and have hot soup or pasta dishes at the ready. Toss everything together and serve, passing round a jug of olive oil separately; forget the rules, and hand round cheese also. Serves 2.

This glorious mixture can also be used as a salad. Serve at room temperature dressed with olive oil and a squeeze of lemon juice, seasoning with salt to taste. A liberal scattering of parsley can also be added.

Tomatoes

The arrival of the first ripe tomatoes is always a high point in the gardening calendar. We are too far north to grow outside tomatoes, but accommodate as many as we can in the greenhouse, three or four different varieties occupying the whole of one side, with basil planted in front and marigolds in between. They usually start to ripen around early August, lasting well into October. The plants are then pulled up, and the remaining trusses laid out in boxes in the spare room, continuing to ripen sometimes until Christmas.

Our tomatoes, you will have noted, are late. Though heat is applied in the early stages to get the plants established, thereafter they mature and ripen naturally, as the season dictates. It is this gradual unhurried ripening which helps to produce tomatoes of real quality and flavour denied to so many consumers today. Before the advent of commercial horticulture, and the development of year-round tomatoes, this was the way the best tomatoes were always grown; forced tomatoes, even a gardener's, will never achieve the same depth of flavour nor fully attain the necessary balance between acidity and sweetness.

Tomatoes vary enormously in flavour, texture and crop yield. For this reason alone, it makes sense to grow a range of varieties and to try at least one new variety every year. Harbinger, a thin-skinned old gardening favourite, is a reliable cropper and amongst the earliest to ripen. It has become our standard tomato. Shirley and Gardener's Delight are also excellent. The yellow fleshed varieties, which were popular during the 19th century, are sharp and refreshing, and look most attractive mixed with red tomatoes in salads.

It was, in fact, the yellow varieties which were first introduced from the New World into Europe in the early 16th century, a decade before the red varieties became known. The new vegetable was christened *pomo d'oro*, golden apple, the name Italians use today (our name comes from *tomatl*, the Nahuatl name used in Mexico). Their disadvantage is their poor yield, hence they have never found commercial favour. Another of the original tomatoes brought from Mexico is the cherry tomato. These are not to be judged by commercially grown cherry tomatoes, which have no taste at all and are tomato-like in colour only. Even tiny home-grown ones are supremely sweet. Nothing looks more attractive in the salad bowl except perhaps the pea-sized redcurrant tomatoes, another 19th-century favourite. We grow Sweet 100. This is a popular American-bred variety, with the bonus of twice as much vitamin C as other tomatoes.

For every tomato that pleases, however, there will be more that do not. Here, commercial interests are largely to blame. Shape, yield, and disease resistance are the parameters modern growers know and seek. One of the most depressing things I read in the course of writing this book was a bulletin from the MAFF on tomato production. Flavour is not recorded in the list of desirable characteristics. It talked of flavour only once, in connection with the variety Gardener's Delight. 'There is a demand,' it said, 'for small highly flavoured fruit. This is mainly from multiple stores rather than through wholesale markets. Outlets should therefore be determined before embarking on production.' A dismal prospect for consumers and gardeners alike.

To grow decent, well flavoured tomatoes needs care. Even if the right varieties can be found, plants bought from garden centres are rarely satisfactory. It is much better to raise your own from seed. Sow three seeds to a pot under heat, around mid-March, thinning to the strongest seedling. When the roots start to stick out of the base of the pot, plant out with as little disturbance as possible in the greenhouse in good soil 18in (45cm) apart. An alternative method which we employ is to plant the tomatoes out in growbags, three plants in each, with the bases slit. This provides necessary drainage and allows the mature plants to grow into the soil, giving the roots a free run. Thereafter they need under rather than over-watering and a well ventilated atmosphere.

Tomatoes need dry, airy conditions if they are to do well and not fall prone to disease. Once the plants have reached 2 ft (60cm) in height they should be fed regularly every ten days. Avoid too much nitrogen, which results in excess leaf growth at the expense of fruit. As the season progresses, pick off any leaves showing botrytis, which can be a major enemy. And don't forget the marigolds, the organic remedy for keeping away whitefly, which works remarkably well.

Never judge tomatoes by bought specimens. These go flabby and squashy and become less and less interesting. As a home-grown tomato ripens, it develops a rich full flavour, keeps better, and retains its eating quality far longer.

Garden tomatoes can be picked as required, so storage is rarely a problem. For salads, pick them warm and red, ripe but still firm. For sauces and soups, you can leave them longer; unless the weather is against you, and the fruit splits or develops moulds, a tomato will happily stay on the plant for two weeks. They also continue to ripen and stay in good condition off the plant. Pick them either singly with their stalk intact or by the truss and keep them in the larder or somewhere cool, ideally at about 50°F (10°C). Never store tomatoes in the fridge. They are sub-tropical plants and suffer physical deterioration in cold conditions, eventually leading to loss of texture and flavour.

You will never have your fill of garden tomatoes. At the end of the season, pull up the plants and remove the leaves. Either lay the stalks with their trusses of unripe fruit in a box, or hang them from a hook in the ceiling in a dry warmish back room (it is warmth not sunshine which ripens tomatoes). There is no need to wrap them in paper or do anything except to inspect them now and then and remove any which become damaged or bad. The last few will be wizened, but are richly flavoured and fine for cooking in soups and sauces.

Surplus tomatoes should be frozen, whole or cut in half, or as a cooked or raw tomato sauce. The texture of frozen tomatoes is ruined but the flavour is reasonable. One more useful point. Try not to waste tomato pips: the highest concentration of vitamin C is to be found in the surrounding jelly-like material.

Skinning tomatoes

A very ripe tomato, especially a thin-skinned variety, will peel easily; if the skin does not give immediately, try gently rubbing the tomato with the back of the knife first to loosen the skin. For salads, peel them thinly with a serrated knife or potato peeler. The other method is to pour boiling water over the tomatoes. The tomatoes are apt to become mushy, so you need to work quickly if they are to be used uncooked and still retain their texture. Count to ten and no more. Rinse under the cold tap and the skins should slip off easily.

For much of the time skinning tomatoes is an unnecessary refinement. There are occasions, in a barely cooked fresh tomato sauce, for example, when the skin gets in the way of a dish, but mainly it is a matter of personal preference. I rather like mine on; for most soup and sauces, they can be sieved out at the end if needed.

Much is made of the flavour of the skins. In my experience, it is the tomatoes and not the skins which count.

Tomato salads

It seems impossible to tire of tomato salads from the garden. Sliced or cut into rough chunks, still warm, with olive oil, basil, olives and bread, they make the perfect summer meal. A simple sliced tomato and hard-boiled egg salad, and the wonderful Greek salad of tomatoes, cucumbers, and feta cheese (see p. 102) is so familiar in my household as to be part of our daily existence.

Such salads rely purely on the quality of the tomatoes, which should be at the peak of ripeness. Judging that moment comes with experience, a combination of smell, feel – firm but gently yielding – and colour. For raw tomato sauces or tomato vinaigrette, slightly over-ripe tomatoes are best. These are also excellent chopped up in any form of mixed salad.

Until recently, I was not aware how good unripe garden tomatoes can be in salads. The surprise is that they are not sour, but have a sharp, clean taste, as thirst-quenching on a hot summer's day as homemade lemonade.

Green tomato salad

This is the salad that Susan Jones makes at the Ryd-Gard-Wen Hotel in Dyfed. She serves it on a large glass Victorian platter, which enhances the cool quality of the salad and makes it especially attractive.

Choose tomatoes which are on the turn, showing their first blush of pink. Slice and arrange on a bed of pale green lettuce leaves with a few thinly sliced rounds of orange, pith, peel and pips carefully removed. Dress with vinaigrette. Strew with a liberal quantity of fresh dill and serve.

Tomato juice: drinks and cocktails

Another pleasure of having your own tomatoes is fresh tomato juice for summer drinks and healthy pick-me-ups. It's an ideal way of using very ripe tomatoes, and with a blender or food processor drinks can be made in a matter of minutes. Always serve them well chilled and stir just before serving.

These recipes are based on two in Rosemary Hume's *Party Food and Drink*, published in 1950. Do not be alarmed at the colour – more rosy pink than processed red.

To make the base, blend 1¼lb (570g) very ripe tomatoes to a slushy liquid. Sieve. Depending on the juiciness of the tomatoes, you should get around 1 pt (600ml) of juice, sufficient for 4–6 servings. Now add one of the following:

1 The scrubbed rind and juice of half a lemon, plus a seasoning of good vinegar, Worcestershire sauce, sugar, salt and pepper – enough to give piquancy. Chill thoroughly for 1–2 hours. Remove the lemon rind and stir before serving. If the purée is very thick, dilute with a little chilled still mineral water.

2 The juice of two freshly squeezed oranges, plus 3–4 sprigs of lightly bruised basil. Chill thoroughly for 1–2 hours. Remove the basil before serving. Stir, and taste – a pinch of sugar can often bring out the flavour. Pour into glasses, decorate with a slice of orange and a tiny leaf of basil, and serve.

Note This can easily be turned into an iced sorbet to serve as a first course. Chop the basil finely and season with salt and a healthy dash of wine or basil vinegar. Freeze until set, and then blend in a processor until smooth. Scoop out rounded spoonfuls and serve immediately with thin slices of avocado, or refreeze until required, allowing it to soften slightly first.

Tomato and yoghurt drink

Combine equal quantities of tomato juice and still mineral water. Stir in yoghurt to taste. Add a large sprig of mint, crushing it with the back of a spoon to release its flavour. Season with salt and chill. Remove the mint before serving, or before if the flavour seems right.

Tomato and almond sauce

A Sicilian sauce for pasta, taken from the *Guardian* a couple of years ago, and much used since. The riper the tomatoes the better.

1lb (450g) ripe tomatoes	*2 tbsp olive oil*
3½oz (100g) ground almonds	*3 basil leaves, chopped*
1 large clove of garlic, preferably fresh,	
finely chopped	

Dip the tomatoes briefly in boiling water, then remove the skins. Chop to a sauce-like consistency. Mix in the other ingredients to a pinkish paste. I sometimes add a splash of marsala. Either toss in the hot pasta, or serve separately in a bowl at the table. Serves 4–6.

It's not obligatory, but the flavour of the sauce is improved with freshly ground almonds: skin the almonds by scalding them in boiling water, taking them out one at a time to peel off the skins. Grind in a coffee grinder and proceed as before.

Tomato and frizzled parsley sauce

A quick savoury sauce to make in autumn. Chop a clove of garlic with a large handful of parsley until reduced to green speckles. For each person, take one sun-dried tomato, the kind preserved in salt, and cut into little strips, and 1 large ripe, coarsely chopped fresh tomato. Fry garlic, parsley and sun-dried tomatoes in a little olive oil over a brisk heat for 1–2 minutes. Do not let the garlic burn. Add the fresh tomato, cook for 2–3 minutes longer, until the tomatoes begin to wilt and give up their juice. Have your pasta waiting in a hot dish. Top with the sauce and serve immediately, handing round extra olive oil.

Tomato, *chilli and mint sauce*

A high summer sauce. Serve with fresh sardines or mullet grilled on the barbecue.
  Sweat a small chopped onion in olive oil together with a chopped green chilli. Add 1lb (450g) chopped tomatoes, 1 tbsp tomato purée and a big sprig of mint and cook steadily for 20 minutes until you're left with a rough chunky sauce. Remove the mint, add some more, freshly chopped, and serve.

Spiced tomato sauce

An aromatic sauce, taken with minor adaptions from Julie Sahni's *Classic Indian Vegetarian Cooking*. It can be used for all kinds of vegetables, fish, and pancake dishes, or as the base for an easily made meat stew.

1lb (450g) fresh ripe tomatoes, puréed with skin on	*2 tsp ground cumin*
	¼ pt (150ml) water
3oz (90g) onions, chopped	*1–2 tbsp coriander, finely chopped*
1 tbsp vegetable oil	

Soften the onion in the oil in a small pan and cook until light brown. Add the cumin, stir for a few seconds, then add the tomatoes and water. Cook over a steady heat, uncovered, for 15–20 minutes or until the sauce becomes agreeably chunky. Turn off the heat and stir in the coriander. For a smoother sauce, blend before adding the coriander.
  The sauce can be made without the fresh coriander. In this case, leave to mellow for 24 hours before using.

Lamb, chickpeas, spinach beet, and tomato stew

1–1¼lb (450–570g) lean lamb, taken from the shoulder or leg	*4–6oz (120–180g) cooked chickpeas*
	spiced tomato sauce made with 1lb (450g) tomatoes (see above)
4–6oz (120–180g) spinach beet, blanched for 3–4 minutes	

Cut the lamb into neat steaks, about ½in (1.25cm) thick. Wipe a piece of trimmed fat around a heated nonstick frying pan and brown the pieces of meat on both sides. Add all the other ingredients. Bring to the boil, transfer to an ovenproof casserole, cover, and slip into a low oven, 130°C/275°F/gas mark 1. Cook for 1–1½ hours until the meat is very tender. Turn off the oven and leave the stew to mellow for a few hours, until the next day if possible, before serving. Serve from the casserole with rice and a small dish of finely chopped fresh coriander passed round separately. Spinach or Swiss chard leaves can be used if no spinach beet is available.

Tomato and mussel chowder

One of the easiest and best fish soups I know.

1½lb (675g) mussels
1½lb (675g) very ripe tomatoes,
   coarsely chopped
1 small onion/2 shallots/white part of
   1 leek, finely chopped
1 tbsp chopped parsley
about 5fl oz (150ml) wine or water

To finish
1 packet powdered saffron
up to 5fl oz (150ml) single cream
1–2 tsp potato flour
a little extra finely chopped parsley

Have your mussels scrubbed and prepared in the usual way, discarding any which do not close when tapped sharply with a knife. Put into a large pan with the tomatoes, onion and parsley and enough wine or water to moisten the bottom. Cover with a tightly fitting lid and cook steadily for 5 minutes. Poke about and discard any mussels that haven't opened.

Meanwhile dissolve the saffron in some of the cream. Stir in 1 tsp potato flour. Stir the mixture into the chowder, adding extra cream to taste. Finish with a little extra finely chopped parsley. Pour into a tureen or soup plates and serve immediately, with good bread to mop up the delicious sauce.
Note The potato flour serves to bind the sauce, which should be only slightly thickened. If the sauce is still runny, add a further 1 tsp, slaked in cream as before.

Bruschetta

Bread doused in olive oil takes on many forms. In Italy, when the laborious work of harvesting and pressing the olives is over, and the clear, fragrant, dense green oil begins to trickle out of the rush mats stacked in the presses, thick slices of bread are toasted over the open fire, rubbed liberally with fresh juicy garlic, and drenched in the virgin oil, rich reward and celebration of the new harvest. This is bruschetta, (also known as *fetta unta* or *fettunta*). It is said to be one of the most popular appetisers in Tuscany. Often it is topped with slightly crushed ripe tomatoes, which turns it into more of a meal. If you find yourself near the Coltibuono Estate, which is set in massive chestnut woods not too far from Radda, the heart of Chianti district, order one from their restaurant. The open fire has been replaced by an oven, but the bruschetta – served in a limpid green pool of their own oil – is quite delicious.

With the necessary requirements – good homemade bread, ripe tomatoes, sweet garlic and decent, fruity olive oil – a memorable bruschetta can be made on the barbecue. After much trial and error, this is the method we follow: make sure the fire is properly prepared, the coals gently glowing and showing white ash on the surface before you begin to cook.

Slice the tomatoes in half and set on the grill to heat through and soften somewhat. Cut the bread thickly and toast on one side only. This will take only a few moments, and you must watch it does not burn. Hand round the bread toasted side up, let each person rub in the required amount of garlic and moisten his or her slice with olive oil. Remove the skin from the tomatoes and squash each into the prepared bruschetta. Using a fish slice, carefully return the bruschetta to the grill and toast the other side. Again, be careful not to burn the slices. They taste best eaten off wooden boards, as does all barbecued food. Transfer each to a waiting plate (or board), dribble extra olive oil over the top; eat immediately.

Summer turnips

White summer turnips bought from shops can be a disappointment, but picked from the garden when about the size of a golfball, live up to expectations well. Ours come at the end of June or early July from a sowing in mid-April. Their papery thin skins do not need peeling. Wash them gently and trim off the tops.

Young turnips need gentle cooking, about five minutes, if they are sliced, and not more than 10 if left whole. The best way is to stew them gently in a covered pan with a little butter and a sprinkling of sugar. Add a spot of water if you are nervous of them burning, and watch them towards the end, for they collapse quickly once cooked. Serve them with their caramelly juices on their own or to accompany lamb. Another way is to squeeze the juice of one or two fresh oranges over them in the pan, and cook them as before, or to bake them in the oven with dabs of butter, covering them with foil.

Never let summer turnips get too big. Their attraction is their mildness, only a hint of pepperiness showing through. As they get older, or if the weather gets hot, their flavour becomes more pronounced and more like winter turnips. Should this happen, blanch them first for 3–4 minutes. Peel away the skins if they are tough and proceed as before.

Braised young turnips with spinach

Baby turnips and spinach are a happy pairing. Serve either hot as a separate vegetable course or at room temperature as a starter.

8 baby turnips, trimmed and scrubbed
1 tbsp light soy sauce
1 tbsp honey
1 tbsp mirin (rice wine)

1lb (450g) spinach, washed and stems removed
4 tsp lightly toasted sesame seeds

Begin with the turnips, which are cooked in the Japanese fashion. Slice each into thin segments, cutting vertically from top to bottom. Put into a pan with the soy sauce, honey and mirin. Add enough water to cover and simmer until just cooked. This should take 4–5 minutes – watch them at the end and do not let them collapse. Cool in the liquid.

Blanch the spinach for 30 seconds in a large pan of boiling water. Do this in batches. Drain, press out the excess moisture and spread out neatly on to 4 plates. Meanwhile, reheat the turnips. Arrange on top of the spinach, fanning them out prettily. Boil down the liquid to a thin syrupy glaze, and dribble over the turnips, dividing the glaze equally between the plates. Scatter with sesame seeds and serve.

Turnip and dill salad

This is a pretty salad to serve as a garnish with cold fish dishes or cold roast beef. Shred young turnips (taste first to see they are not too strong) on the julienne shredder of a food processor, mix with chopped dill, and moisten with sweetened lemon juice, approximately 2 parts lemon juice to 1 part sugar. Arrange in small mounds to the side of the plate and serve. For 4, allow 4oz (120g) turnip, mixed with 1 tbsp dill, 1 tbsp lemon juice, and 2 tsp sugar.

Roast summer turnips

Blanch and peel off the skins as above. Cut into wedges and surround the joint, turning them over in the fat. Cook until well browned, 30–45 minutes.

Vine leaves

A vine brings the Mediterranean into your garden. Trained over an arbour on the patio or outside the garden door with clematis or roses, nothing surpasses its dappled shade in summer. For table grapes to ripen successfully here, vines need to be grown in a greenhouse, but the vine itself is a hardy, vigorous scrambling plant, withstanding temperatures well below zero. For the cook, there is the bonus of a ready supply of fresh vine leaves. These can be used for summer dishes of dolmades, to wrap around barbecued or braised fish (or mushrooms), or to provide a chewy lemony casing for small birds such as quail, roasted in the oven.

Fresh vine leaves can be picked throughout the summer, though they toughen considerably as they get older. Old leaves are fine to line the pot or to use as a casing which you then remove, but for dishes where the vine leaf is intended to be eaten, choose tender blemish-free leaves. June and early July are the best time to pick them, when they have reached a respectable size but are still young and supple.

Vine leaves will keep for a week or so wrapped in a plastic bag in the refrigerator. To use, blanch them first for 2–5 minutes in a large pot of water.

Blanched vine leaves freeze well. Pack them in plastic bags in convenient numbers and freeze in the usual way.

Stuffed vine leaves

Go for medium sized, good looking leaves. Pick a handful of large ones to line the pot. Taking care not to tear the leaf, make an inverted V shape nick at the base, where the stalk and other veins meet up. Next, blanch the leaves, in batches if necessary, in a large pot of boiling water for at least 2 minutes. Drain in a colander and leave to cool. Unfold the leaves, spreading them out flat on the work surface, dull side uppermost with the base of the leaf towards you.

Heap a teaspoon of prepared stuffing in the centre of each leaf, making a little ridge. Fold the bottom of the leaf over the filling. Bring the sides over the middle and roll up gently like a cigar, tucking in the edges to give a neat finish.

Line a spacious pot with the large leaves – this is a traditional precaution to help prevent the stuffed leaves from burning. Pack the stuffed leaves, joins underneath, closely together, wedging them in neatly in layers. Cover completely with water, adding a little olive oil and some lemon juice. Tomato purée or other aromatics such as garlic, chilli or bay leaves can be added too. Put a saucer or small plate on top to prevent the parcels from moving around while cooking. Bring to the boil, cover, and cook gently for 30–60 minutes, depending on the filling. Halfway through cooking time, check the water – if it looks like drying up add more. Cool in the pan, and serve at room temperature with some of the cooking juice and a little extra olive oil, or a bowl of plain yoghurt and sprinkling of fresh herbs. Meat fillings are generally served hot.

Stuffed vine leaves may also be cooked in a low oven. They keep well for a few days in the refrigerator and will freeze successfully.

Fillings

These mixtures will fill 25–30 leaves.

1   Dried apricot, rice and fresh coriander

3oz (90g) dried hunza apricots
3oz (90g) uncooked long-grain rice, preferably Basmati
6 spring onions or Welsh onions, finely chopped

1½–2 tbsp finely chopped coriander
½ tsp ground cinnamon (optional)
2–3 tbsp olive oil
juice of half a large lemon

Pour boiling water over the apricots and leave to cool. Remove the flesh, chopping or tearing it into small pieces, and add to the rice and other stuffing ingredients. Mix well. Blanch and stuff the leaves as described above. Arrange in a pan, pour over the soaking liquor, top up with enough water to cover, and add the olive oil and lemon juice. Tuck in any coriander stalks down the sides, weight with a plate and cook until tender.

2 Lamb, bulgur and cumin

6 spring onions or Welsh onions, finely
   chopped
1 tbsp olive oil
1 tsp cumin seeds
3oz (90g) lean cooked lamb,
   preferably underdone
1oz (30g) bulgur
1 tbsp chopped parsley, mint or dill

For the sauce
2 fat cloves of garlic, sliced
2 tbsp tomato purée
2 tbsp olive oil
juice of half a lemon
1 bay leaf

Soften the onion in the oil. Stir in the cumin, cook for a minute, then add lamb, bulgur and herbs. Mix thoroughly and take off the heat. Prepare and stuff the leaves as before, adding all the sauce ingredients to the pot with water to cover. Cook until the leaves are tender. Transfer to a serving dish, boil down the sauce until thick and pour over the stuffed vine leaves.
Note The leaves can be left to cool in the liquid and reheated later.

3 Courgette, feta cheese and mint

A slightly different treatment for young, very tender leaves that require no further cooking. The stuffing keeps its freshness in a way I find most attractive. Blanch the leaves for a few minutes, drain and spread out as before. Prepare the stuffing as follows.

6oz (180g) courgettes, wiped and
   grated
1 tbsp olive oil
3oz (90g) feta cheese

2 tbsp cooked but firm white rice
1 tbsp finely chopped mint
lemon juice

Cook the courgettes over a high heat in the olive oil, stirring constantly for 1 minute until they begin to wilt. Transfer to a bowl. Add the other ingredients, crumbling the feta cheese finely. Mix well. Stuff the vine leaves, roll up and lay on a serving dish. Moisten with olive oil and a squeeze of lemon juice and serve at room temperature. Eat Fresh.

Hannah Glasse's vine leaf fritters

Vines were first cultivated seriously in England in monasteries during the 7th and 8th centuries. By the 11th century, 38 vineyards were recorded. This proliferation continued throughout the Middle Ages. All the royal households and nobility had their vineyards, as well as the great abbeys and cathedrals. It was always an unpredictable business (the Romans thought the climate too unsuitable; an edict allowing vines to be raised in England was only granted in AD 280). In the 14th and 15th centuries, the weather worsened, and this together with changes in farming and the devastation of the Black Death, contributed to the decline of commercial vineyards. From then onwards vineyards became domestic affairs, planted by enthusiasts, and attention turned towards the growing of grapes for the table.

But what of the vine leaves? I have come across a 17th-century recipe for 'Delma' or dolmades, which must have been brought from abroad, and there are various mentions of vine leaves in recipes for preserves, where they were wrapped around walnuts or boiled with apples in the belief it kept them green. Gervase Markham, in *The English Housewife* (1653), used them as a stuffing for roast pigeon, but the only other English recipe I have come across is this, from Hannah Glasse's *Art of Cookery made Plain and Easy* published in 1741 when fritters of all kinds were popular. Try them for the fun of it.

baby vine leaves	*For the batter*
a little brandy	*1oz (30g) plain flour*
finely grated lemon peel	*3 fl oz (90ml) medium sweet sherry or*
caster sugar and cinnamon for	*sweet wine*
strewing	*1 egg white, stiffly beaten*

'Take some of the smallest vine-leaves you can get, and having cut off the great stalks, put them in a dish with some French Brandy, green lemon rasped, and some sugar; take a good handful of fine flour, mixed with white wine or ale, let your butter be hot, and with a spoon drop in your batter; take great care they don't stick one to the other; on each fritter lay a leaf; fry them quick, and strew sugar over them, and glaze them with a red-hot shovel.'

Use baby leaves, 1–2in (2.5–5cm), which are still soft and pliable. Moisten with brandy and mix with lemon peel – leave the sugar till later. Make a thick batter with the flour and sherry, then fold in the egg white. The batter should be very thick, almost the consistency of a mousse. Dip the leaves, making sure each side is well coated. Deep fry in batches, taking care not to crowd the pan. They need only 45–60 seconds. Drain on kitchen paper, sprinkle with plain or flavoured caster sugar and eat immediately.

Grilled goat's cheese in vine leaves

Choose soft or semi-soft goat's cheese, allowing 1–1½oz (30–45g) and one blanched vine leaf per portion. Paint both sides of the leaf with olive oil. Form the cheese into a round and wrap in the vine leaf. Grill under a hot grill, keeping the parcels 3–4in (7.5–10cm) away from the heat source, until the surface of the leaf begins to brown. Serve immediately, either as a first course with salad, olives and chopped fresh tomato moistened with an olive oil vinaigrette; or for dessert with a fresh apricot sauce, made by stewing peeled chopped ripe apricots with a few tablespoons of water and vanilla sugar to taste. Accompany with a glass of chilled dessert wine.

AUTUMN

September, October, November

The variety of crops that can be grown through autumn and into winter is prodigious. Indeed, there is no reason why any kitchen garden cannot be almost as productive during these months as it has been over summer. In our own garden, only two of the eight beds become empty. Brassicas, leeks and root crops fill half the available space, the rest is given to winter salad stuff, spinach beet, Swiss chard, and a selection of oriental vegetables. Many of these crops need protection, some will not survive, or perhaps will not perform well because of the weather, but even allowing for this, the range and choice at my disposal is far greater than my local greengrocer could provide.

The most important job in autumn is harvesting. This involves anything from hanging up the final batch of tomatoes or peppers or marrows in the garden shed, to major harvesting of bulky root crops. Until fairly recently, in rural communities and on the large country estates, ensuring crops were safely stored for winter was laborious, painstaking work. In *Cottesbrooke, an English Kitchen Garden*, Susan Campbell describes potato and carrot clamps being made for 8 hundredweight of carrots and over 50 hundredweight of potatoes – this gives some idea of the immense scale involved. For today's kitchen gardener, the motivation lies not in necessity but in the satisfaction of having home-grown vegetables for the family to eat. For this reason harvesting and storing is worth doing well and taking time over.

For practical purposes, root vegetables fall into two groups, those which can be left in the ground and those which are not frost-hardy and must be lifted. Storing crops in situ is a mixed blessing. Provided that they are adequately covered (a severe frost will damage most root vegetables), and your soil does not suffer from slugs, they will remain fresh, nature providing its own refrigeration. They should be checked periodically and lifted if they begin to deteriorate badly. Bringing them into the kitchen straight out of the earth presents problems once the bad weather arrives. It is then that time spent in autumn cleaning and storing the crops repays the effort.

Drying out is the main form of deterioration in storage, but otherwise root crops remain in good condition. Save for parsnips, which improve considerably once frosted, we store all surplus root crops in strong paper sacks. Despite your best intentions, the first hard frosts will inevitably catch you unprepared. Most autumn crops will stand a slight frost but no more. Be warned, and do at least make sure that crops needing protection have their cloches over them in good time, and that those which are especially vulnerable are safely gathered in. For advice about storage, see individual vegetables.

I find it odd that cooking in autumn and winter generates so little enthusiasm. Maybe this is one reason why the shelves are filled with unseasonal courgettes. Cooking autumn and winter vegetables is every bit as pleasurable as preparing summer ones. With summer produce, simplicity and freshness is the thing, and cooking is often reduced to a minimum. In autumn and winter the urge is for robust flavours, warming spicy food, comforting stews and positive combinations. With salads, the emphasis changes to sharper, slightly bitter tastes. This mirrors exactly what you will find in the garden. Who needs courgettes?

SALADS

For the last three hundred years, autumn and winter salads have taken a back seat in British cookery. It is time this view was changed. Given pride of place, they become as important to the enjoyment of food during the cold season as warming stews and thick hearty country soups.

Early autumn salads are a coninuation of summer salads, small salad plants – rocket, claytonia, land cress, and herbs such as buckler leafed sorrel, parsley and the last of the tarragon, chervil and mint, signalling the first change to sharper, more robust flavours. As autumn progresses, the shift continues with endives, chicories, and tender young leaves of Japanese mizuna and Chinese cabbage. Salads for autumn and winter can draw also on the autumn harvest in other ways. From mid autumn, root and cabbage salads begin to appear. These are not generally appreciated enough as salad material, yet I value them as much as green salads. One of the best ways to use them is in winter hors d'oeuvres as described on p. 227. Such salads are quite my favourite food of autumn.

Autumn salad with confit of duck

Making confit has become part of autumn kitchen work. The way I enjoy it best – and which stretches it furthest – is as a first course with salad leaves. Arrange your salad leaves on large plates. Some bitter leaves – chicory, endive or sorrel – should be included. Leave plain or dress with a little walnut or olive oil. Take some confit, cut into strips, put in a dish and grill until crisp and brown. Scatter over the salad, not forgetting to share out the delicious fat also. If you have them, scatter over grattons of crisp duck skin, also heated through. Serve immediately.

If no confit is available, the salad can be made with left over roast duck or game. Grill the pieces as before. If you do not have duck grattons, use frizzled bacon cut into tiny dice, or croûtons. Chopped ripe tomato, dressed as above, and arranged around the outside adds a sweet element which complements the slightly salty taste of the meat.

FRESH HERBS FOR AUTUMN AND WINTER

For the kitchen gardener, the supply of fresh herbs through the colder months is limited mainly to the perennials – rosemary, sage, thyme, pot marjoram. Their qualities are warmth, and a sharply aromatic pungency. All are appetite stimulants and have digestive properties. Whereas summer herbs are used freely and liberally, these are to be approached more like spices, with deliberate thoughtfulness. Because of their perennial nature, their use is not restricted to one particular season – rosemary twigs can be thrown on the summer barbecue, for example – but their strong flavours and forceful character render them particularly suited, I find, to the braises and solid hearty fare of autumn and winter.

Parsley, chervil and mint (see spring herbs, p. 26) are other herbs which are to be had easily. Mint and parsley can be dug up and replanted in the greenhouse, or potted up and brought inside. Chervil is sturdier than its delicate appearance indicates and is generally hardy.

Parsley

Parsley is a hardy biennial and comes into its prime in September. With protection, it survives most winters. The simplest method is to dig up one or two plants (the root balls are large) and transplant them under cover or repot them and bring them inside. Both flat and curly leaved varieties can be treated in this way. Come spring, they will grow with renewed vigour, providing enough parsley until the new season's crop is ready.

The English have always had a great affection for curled parsley, an affection I share. Ann Scott James in *The Cottage Garden* writes of the efforts that amateur gardeners made at the turn of the century to improve strains by repeated diligent selection of the best plants to produce crisper, curlier and greener varieties (earlier efforts were not so scientific, and included rolling the plants with a roller, or treading them down with heavy boots). More recently, varieties of continental flat leaved parsley have made a comeback. From a gardener's point of view, flat leaved parsley is larger and hardier, and better for standing as it does not collect the snow and rain like curled parsley does. There is little between them in flavour; certainly nothing like the difference sometimes credited. The leaves of flat leaved parsley are apt to be tougher; being flatter they are slightly easier to chop. Try them both, sowing in March, under gentle heat in small pots. Thin the seedlings progressively until three are left in each pot. Transplant in June after all danger of frost, in the same clumps of three into open ground, 9in (23cm) apart. This saves any disquiet about the slow, notoriously erratic germination of parsley seeds when sowed direct. Once established, parsley is a sizeable and prolific plant. Three clumps will provide ample for everybody.

Parsley soup

Parsley was one of the best loved of medieval flavourings. *The Feate of Gardeninge*, written in the mid-15th century, devotes a whole section to it, indicating its importance at this time. It was used lavishly, especially to flavour green porrays, simple broths made with boiled leaves and herbs. Parsley soup has a delicate taste and is a useful standby.

2 shallots or 1 small onion, chopped
½oz (15g) butter for frying
1 large bunch of parsley, including
*   stalks, washed and roughly chopped*

2 pt (1.2l) milk
a little beurre manié or 1 scant tsp
*   potato flour slaked in 2 tbsp water*
additional finely chopped parsley

Soften the shallot or onion in the melted butter until transparent. Add the parsley and milk and simmer very gently for just 5 minutes. Liquidise and then sieve, pressing hard against the sieve and scraping all the bright green specks on the underside of the sieve back into the pan. Reheat, thicken slightly with a few flakes of beurre manié or potato flour, check the seasoning and serve immediately, garnished with a very little finely chopped parsley.

For a richer embellishment, briefly liquidise a small amount of double cream with some chopped parsley leaves until it solidifies. Just before serving, place a small blob in each bowl. Serves 4–6.

Chicken breasts en persillade

An unapologetically garlicky dish, easy to prepare, suitable for both summer and winter eating. Be careful over your choice of mustard and go for the sweeter milder kind, either French Dijon or German.

4 chicken breasts, skinned and boned
5–6 large sprigs parsley
4 cloves of garlic
2–3 tbsp mild mustard
5 fl oz (150ml) well flavoured chicken
*   stock*

2 tbsp tarragon vinegar
To finish
2–4 fl oz (60–120ml) single cream
½–1 tsp potato flour slaked in little
*   water*

Begin by making the persillade. Remove the tufts of parsley from the stems and chop the garlic and parsley into a mass of green and white speckles. If you have one, a mezzaluna makes light work of this kind of chopping. Coat both sides of the chicken with mustard. Take a shallow oval ovenware dish and sprinkle the base with half the persillade mixture. Lay the chicken breasts on top and sprinkle over the rest of the mixture. If more convenient, the dish can now be left in a cool place for a couple of hours.

To cook, pour the stock and vinegar around the chicken pieces and bring to the boil on top of the stove. Cover loosely with buttered paper. Cook in a moderate oven, 180°C/350°F/gas mark 4, for about 30 minutes. The meat should remain moist, so do not overcook.

Carefully transfer the breasts to a serving dish, being careful not to dislodge their bright green topping, and keep warm in the turned-off oven while you complete the sauce. Set the cooking juices over a high heat and reduce by at least half, or until the flavour seems right. Finish with cream to taste, and a last-minute binding of potato flour, sufficient to thicken slightly. Pour the sauce around the chicken and serve with plain rice, keeping any vegetables or salad as a separate course.

Fried parsley

Deep-fried parsley is delicious. It frizzles down to nothing, a good thing when parsley is abundant. Have the oil hot, and the tufts of parsley washed and well dried. Do not overcrowd the pan – it sizzles violently – and cook for a few seconds only. If it starts to burn around the edges, the oil is too hot. Lift out with a skimmer and drain very well on kitchen paper. Use with fish, or to scatter over green salads.

Risotto verde

This idea comes from *Grain Gastronomy*, by American writer Janet Fletcher, published in 1988. Make a paste by combining parsley, basil and spinach leaves in the proportion 1:1:3 with 1–2 large cloves of peeled garlic in a food processor, removing the stems and midribs first. Add softened butter, (I allow 1oz (30g) per ½oz (15g) of herbs and 1½oz (45g) spinach), blend well and set aside. Make a plain risotto in the usual way. Stir in the herb paste at the end, together with parmesan if using. This turns out to be a fragrant and most useful paste, excellent stirred into plain rice and grain dishes of all kinds and vegetables such as courgettes, broad beans or fennel. The garlic can be omitted if preferred.

Rosemary

Rosemary is one of the most handsome plants in the herb garden. It grows into a very large bush, so should be positioned accordingly. Its name means 'dew-of-the-sea', and its native home is along the coasts of the Mediterranean. Like many of our herbs, it was introduced here by the Romans and was a favourite with the Elizabethans, who used it profusely as a strewing herb, in juleps and meads, with meat and pottages and comfits. 'I lette it runne all over my garden walls,' wrote Sir Thomas Moore, 'not only because my bees love it, but because it is the herb sacred to rememberance, and, therefore, to friendship.'

Rosemary is not fully hardy, especially in colder parts of the country. It needs a sunny position and a limey, well drained soil to show its best. To be sure of not losing it, strike a few cuttings each summer.

Few people would claim rosemary their favourite kitchen herb. The spikiness of the leaves can be irritating, though I must say I'm becoming partial to them when they are crisped and slightly charred on the barbecue. The Italians are probably fondest of rosemary, and make a virtue of its pungency by partnering it with garlic, anchovies and other robust flavourings. Lamb or pork are obvious partners and the best potato cakes I have ever eaten were flavoured with chopped rosemary. Branches of rosemary have long been used for basting meat grilled over the fire, and I have become fond of chicken with rosemary. It is also pleasant, occasionally, in breads, in sweet and savoury biscuits, to flavour syrups, or made into a fruit jelly to serve with meat. In summer, the flowers can be used to add to salads.

Chicken in vinegar with rosemary and anchovies

This recipe is adapted from Marcella Hazan's book, *Marcella's Italian Kitchen*, published in 1986. It is a good example of how to use rosemary to its full aromatic advantage. The vinegar mellows to produce a deliciously piquant sauce.

4 *chicken breasts or legs, with skin*	1 *tsp fresh, chopped rosemary*
2 *tbsp olive oil*	3 *fl oz wine vinegar*
2–3 *large anchovies*	

If you are using legs, divide each into two pieces, cutting them through at the knee joint.

Begin by browning the chicken, very slowly, in nonstick pan turning often. The chicken legs provide their own fat. Allow a good 20–25 minutes for breasts, and 30–35 minutes for legs, until the skin is well browned and is appetisingly crisp. The success of the dish depends on this operation, so be assiduous in letting the meat brown evenly and gently.

Remove from the pan and wipe out the fat. Add the olive oil, anchovies and rosemary, cook for 1 minute and then replace the chicken pieces, coating them with the anchovy and herb mixture. Pour in the vinegar and let it boil for 1 minute. Turn down the heat to a bare simmer, cover, and continue cooking very gently for another 15–20 minutes until the chicken is cooked and the sauce mellows and matures. Check the liquid from time to time, adding a little water if necessary. There should just be a small amount of sauce at the finish. Sautéed potatoes and spinach make a good accompaniment.

Roast chicken with lemon and rosemary

Rub your chicken with the cut half of a scrubbed lemon, olive oil and rosemary. Stuff the cavity with two or three good sized rosemary sprigs, plus the lemon. Lay a couple more sprigs on top and leave for a couple of hours for the flavours to infuse. Roast in the normal way, approximately 20 minutes on either side, with buttered paper covering the breast, in a moderately hot oven, 190°C/375°F/gas mark 5. Remove the paper, turn upright, and cook for a further 20 minutes or until cooked through and nicely browned. Baste frequently. Leave in the turned off oven for 10 minutes before serving. If you want, make a sauce with the juices, tipping them out of the cavity or serve plain with a creamy garlic purée.

Rosemary and honey oranges

In 1981 The Herb Society, founded by Mrs C. F. Leyel, (who also founded the Culpepper herb shops), published a quartet of small booklets on chives, parsley, rosemary and mint. Snap them up if you come across them in secondhand book shops, for they are charming. This idea is adapted from the rosemary booklet.

4 *large oranges*	1–2*oz (30–60g) honey*
2 *x 6in (15cm) sprigs of rosemary*	5 *fl oz water*

Bring the rosemary, honey and water slowly to the boil and simmer gently for 5–10 minutes until the syrup thickens slightly. Cool. Meanwhile, peel away the skin and pith from the oranges, remove any pips and slice thinly. Remove the rosemary, pour the syrup over the slices and serve well chilled with a few fresh rosemary leaves as decoration.

Sage

The name sage is derived from the Latin *salvere*, to save, and is an indication of the esteem it was once accorded as the herbalists' cure-all. The flowers are especially appreciated by bees. Sage belongs to the same family, the labiates, as mint, rosemary and marjoram. Like them, its native home is the Mediterranean. The plants quickly grow to large shrubby bushes with a tendency to become woody, and should be renewed by taking heel cuttings every three or four years. In the kitchen, it is most commonly associated with fatty foods, where it is an aid to digestion. Use the tender leaves, which are softer and downy to the touch. Though there is some die-back, leaves remain on the plant all winter and can be picked as required.

Although one of our commonest herbs, sage is not used much in British kitchens apart from in sage and onion stuffing. Its brutish assertiveness needs to be approached cautiously, a very little chopped sage being sufficient in most cases. An exception to this are some Italian dishes; *saltimbocca*, for example, where pieces of tender veal are wrapped around sage leaves and cooked gently in butter and wine. Another Italian idea is to cook the leaves briefly in oil or butter. This releases their aroma – they can either be left for those who like them, or removed at the end of the dish. In addition to fatty meats, sage complements basic foods like beans, pasta, rice and bread. The following recipes all have Italian leanings, Italians, I find, having the best sage recipes.

Rice with butter and sage leaves

Have some plainly cooked rice, the round chewy arborio type for preference, ready in a serving dish. Sprinkle generously with freshly grated parmesan cheese. Fry a generous quantity of sage leaves – more than you think you'll need – in butter over a briskish heat for a couple of minutes: magic. The leaves crisp and lose their pungency. Watch they do not burn. Pour over the rice and serve. This can also be used for pasta (with olive oil instead of butter), or ravioli stuffed with ricotta.

Fagioli all' uccelletto

This bean dish is the speciality of Tuscany. It is served tepid and Tuscans seem to eat it with everything. It is the name which is the puzzle – *uccelletto* means a small bird, such as quail, and it is difficult to see any obvious association. My best guess is the one offered to me by a Tuscan cook who explained that the beans should be served surrounding a dish of small game birds which are stuffed with sage and garlic and cooked in a little white wine. My cook's version, and the one I enjoy, includes tomato purée. If this is omitted it becomes *fagioli all' uccelletto in bianco*. Other versions include a chopped onion fried in olive oil before the beans are added, which I do not care for.

1lb (450g) cooked cannelli beans
3–4 sage leaves
1–2 cloves of garlic, crushed

olive oil
2–3 tbsp tomato purée diluted with
water

Fry the sage and garlic in 2–3 tbsp fruity oil for a minute or so over a low heat – the leaves should remain soft. Tip in the beans, give everything a good stir, then add the tomato purée and enough water to make a sauce. Simmer for 5–10 minutes and serve, dribbling a little extra olive oil on top.

Quail with sage

Allow 2 large sprigs of sage and 2 quail per person as a main dish. Wipe the quail, rub with sage and put 2–3 sage leaves in each cavity. Truss up the legs (a rubber band wound around them is satisfactory). Brown evenly in 1–2 tbsp olive oil over a highish heat in a nonstick frying pan. Add the rest of the sage, turn down the heat, cover and cook gently for 15–20 minutes, turning the quail often. They should end up well browned and crisp. Remove the cover, and turn up the heat to finish crisping the quail. Splash with white wine. Cook for a minute or so to let the flavours merge and the alcohol evaporate. Serve with the fried sage.

This dish makes an excellent partner to risotto, or to cooked white beans in the Tuscan fasion. Serve the risotto or beans around the quail, decorating with fresh sage.

Stuff peeled fresh garlic cloves into the cavities with the sage if you like.

Sage and olive bread

Take a piece of dough from your main baking, white or brown, and knead into it a mixture of finely chopped sage leaves and stoned black olives, using approximately half sage to olives. Roll into a long stick 1in (2.5cm) thick. Brush with olive oil, leave to prove on a baking sheet dusted with flour or coarse semolina for 15 minutes and bake in a hot oven for another 15 minutes, or until well risen and cooked through. Serve, sliced into rounds, to accompany autumn and winter hors d'oeuvres.

Thyme

Thyme is one of the great European herbs, a much cherished Mediterranean plant. Together with parsley, it is the herb I use most in winter. There are many varieties, both upright and creeping. Common thyme is the best for general kitchen purposes, but it is worth growing a few different kinds. Two I would single out are lemon thyme, a variegated herb with a sharp lemon scent ideal for chicken, veal, or pork; and caraway thyme, a charming diminutive creeping herb.

All the thymes are very pretty in flower and highly attractive to bees. Thyme dislikes a cold wet soil and needs full sun and a light, well drained, stony or sandy soil to do well. It has a tendency to go woody and the plants will need replenishing. In gardens where it grows well, it self-seeds readily, providing a constant supply of new plants.

Thyme is indispensable for long, slow-cooked dishes, for soups and stuffings. I am particularly fond of it with onions and garlic, with lamb and certain vegetables such as potatoes or sweet peppers, and to add to olives or cheese stored under olive oil. Modern cooks make infusions of thyme over which they steam meat or fish.

Laban with thyme

Laban, labna or lebneh as they are variously known, are little balls of soft cheese made from yoghurt. They are common all over the Middle East, eaten for breakfast and at other meals throughout the day. They are easy to make and can be kept under olive oil with a sprig of aromatic herb (thyme being my favourite) in the same way that French soft cheeses sometimes are. They taste delicious summer or winter spread on some good thick bread or pitta, with some of their oil dribbled over and eaten with olives and salad as a lunchtime snack or part of a mezze.

Laban are made from cow's or goat's milk yoghurt. The latter are the more distinctive and the kind I like best. If possible, start with homemade yoghurt. Bought goat's milk yoghurt is very satisfactory but commercial cow's milk yoghurt, especially if made from skimmed milk, is too synthetic for these delicate cheeses. The procedure is simple, though you may need one or two trials to judge when the curd is sufficiently drained.

Spread a square of double thickness muslin over a sieve and tip in a quantity of homemade yoghurt. Salt very lightly, draw up the corners of the muslin and suspend the bag from a hook overnight, or for several hours, with a bowl underneath to catch the whey. A thick rubber band wrapped first around the muslin and then over the hook is usually sufficient. Next day unwrap the curd, mould it into shape and wrap in kitchen paper for a couple of hours to absorb any remaining moisture.

Roll the curd into little balls about the size of quail's eggs. They can be eaten immediately, sprinkled with olive oil and a little crushed dried mint or chopped thyme, or stored under olive oil with a sprig of thyme and kept in the refrigerator.

As with all homemade cheeses, the yield is small. Expect somewhere between a quarter and a third of the original amount of yoghurt.

Braised shin of beef with wine and brandy

Slow, patient, aromatic braised meat dishes are without peer in winter. Shin of beef, a much underestimated cut, is the perfect choice for such a dish, yielding a rich, savoury sauce. As with all cuts of meat that need long cooking to become tender, timings are difficult. The best plan is to prepare the dish in advance, re-heating later. The flavour mellows during the wait.

Flavourings of garlic, bay leaf, chopped tomato, carrot, celery and onion, diced bacon, and orange peel are common, but as the years go by I have come to prefer the less fussy versions, relying on thyme as the aromatic and the long slow cooking to achieve the desired end.

4 large thick slices shin of beef
1 tbsp beef fat or olive oil for frying
2 fl oz (60ml) armagnac or brandy
8 fl oz (240ml) reasonable red wine
large sprig of thyme

strip of pork rind (optional, but
 include if possible)

To finish
1 tsp potato flour slaked in a little
 water

Melt the fat or oil in a nonstick frying pan and seal the meat on both sides over a high heat. Lower the heat, pour in the brandy and ignite – stand well back – shaking the pan to ensure that the alcohol is burnt off, leaving only the aromatic essences behind. Pour in the wine, bubble up, and cook for a minute or two. Transfer the contents to a heavy ovenproof casserole, tucking the thyme well down into the liquid. Add the pork rind if using. Seal well, inserting a sheet of greaseproof paper between pan and lid. Cook in the lowest possible oven, 130–140°C/250–275°F/gas mark ½–1, for 3–4 hours; the meat should be tender but not cooked to rags. Leave the meat in the turned-off oven until the time comes to finish and serve.

Discard the thyme and arrange the meat in a serving dish. Bind the sauce, which by now will be dark and rich, with a little potato flour slaked in water, adding it gradually to give the desired thickness, and pour over the meat.

Serve with pasta and a garnish of either thin batons of carrots fried in a little butter and olive oil until nicely browned at the edges, or mushrooms stewed gently with some finely chopped garlic and parsley for about 10 minutes, finishing with 1 tbsp brandy swilled around the pan.

VEGETABLES

Beetroot

I am fond of beetroot. It may not be a vegetable one wants everyday, nor in appreciable quantities, but it's no bother to grow and like carrots fits neatly into summer and winter eating.

Seed catalogues now offer four types. The round beetroot we are all familiar with. Long cylindrical varieties such as Forono are less well known but becoming increasingly popular. These look rather like purple coloured Mooli. They stand proud of the soil and give good value where space is limited. Recently, an Italian variety, Barbabietola di Chioggia, has been introduced. This is grown primarily for its attractive striped pattern when sliced crosswise raw. Alas, the effect is transitory, for the colour fades to all over pinkness when cooked. Finally, there are golden yellow beetroot. These were a popular Victorian beetroot, renowned for their sweetness. One of their attractions is that the colour does not bleed – an obvious advantage in salads. The tops of the yellow varieties are also fleshier and more succulent, approaching spinach beet in quality, and the best kind to add to soups or stuffings. The variety available here is Burpee's Golden, named after a famous 19th-century American seedsman. All four seem to have much the same flavour, though today I find it is the red rather than the yellow which have the edge on sweetness.

Beetroot belongs to the goosefoot family, which includes the chards, mangolds, good King Henry and seakale, and is of North African origin. The wild form is the sea beet, *Beta maritima*, a seashore plant found around the Mediterranean and Atlantic coasts of Europe and North Africa. Until I looked into the matter I had assumed – no particular reason why – that the leaf varieties had developed from the garden beetroot but this is not the case. It is the garden beetroot which is the newcomer, arriving sometime in the 14th or 15th century. The best guess is that it was developed by German gardeners, gradually spreading across Europe. It reached Italy and Britain in the 16th century, one herbalist, with machiavellian flourish, describing the root 'within and without wholly red, suffused with bloody gore, sweeter to the taste'. It went by the name Roman beet and its arrival signalled in part the demise of the leaf forms. Gerard was convinced that this red and beautiful root, as he called it, would be a boon to the curious and cunning cook. He was right. A hundred and fifty years later beetroot had become firmly established in kitchen gardens everywhere.

Nothing could be simpler to grow than beetroot, but do not rush to sow them too early. For the cook's purposes, medium sized beetroot are far preferable to those which grow woody and large. Sow clusters of seeds 1in (2.5cm) apart in early June, thinning to 3in (7.5cm) apart to give you decent sized beetroot by mid–late October.

Beetroot do not stand frosts well and are better lifted as soon as they have matured to a respectable size. Harvest as for carrots (p. 92), and store in peat or sand. If you have only a smallish amount, they can be stored in brown paper bags. The optimum temperature for storing beetroot is 4°C/39°F, the temperature of a domestic fridge. They tend to dry out and should be checked regularly for mould which can appear on the whiskery root tail. Take care also to cut the tops off as close to the root as you can. These quickly rot and become an unpleasant slimy mess, and should be removed before they cause further rotting.

The main question the beetroot presents in the kitchen is whether it should be boiled or baked. Considered opinion favours baked beetroot, though I do not entirely agree. Baking beetroot is a slow process, up to 3–4 hours in a lowish oven. It produces a more concentrated flavour, darker colour, and denser, though not necessarily better, texture. Boiled beetroot is ready much sooner. Baby beetroot may take as little as 15 minutes; small beetroot 25–30 minutes; medium beetroot 45–55 minutes, and so on. They need to be soft –

their sweetness comes through better – but should not be overdone. Try one towards the end of the cooking time, by inserting a skewer, and gauge the others accordingly. If they are almost done, they can be left to cool in the liquid. By the time they have cooled they will be ready. Cooking in their liquid also produces a deeper coloured beetroot. If cooked properly, they will not be watery. Once cooked, the skins slip off easily. Beetroot does not soak up fat, which serves instead to add additional flavour and give a gloss to the surface of the beetroot.

There are other ways of preparing beetroot: peel, grate, and toss in a frying pan with a little butter or flavoured oil for a few minutes, adding, if you like, a little finely grated lemon or orange rind. A few tablespoons of marsala or port can be poured on at the end. Messy but quick and flavourful.

The custom of using beetroot tops, strange to us now, has not entirely disappeared outside Britain. I remember on holiday in Tuscany seeing neat bundles of young beetroot leaves tied in raffia on sale in the markets. They are a common ingredient for pasta stuffings. The yellow varieties are especially suitable, either fresh or blanched and frozen for later use. Choose only the best of the leaves. Their taste is that of coarse spinach – I often use them in green frittatas or in minestras. If you use the ordinary kind, do not be surprised if your soup turns faintly purple – beetroot vermilion is something we all have to live with.

Traditional British cookery has not served beetroot well. In fact, it has not served it at all. Boiled beetroot dressed in vinegar may have been a grateful winter salad in the 17th century, but one would have hoped for more 300 years later. To find interesting and enjoyable ideas for what can be a fine vegetable, you will need either to look further afield to Northern Europe or the Baltic countries, or at ideas from the new vegetarian cookery writers who turn beetroot's forthrightness to good advantage.

Beetroot is a valuable vegetable prized in raw juice therapy for its powers in promoting health and combating cancer. The problem is that for general use its aggressive nature when raw renders it unpalatable except in very small quantities. It is best grated very finely or put through the julienne shredder of the food processor, combined with a softening element such as cream or a sweetener such as honey to temper its earthiness. The striped varieties are especially attractive, turning a pretty shade of violet when finely grated. Grating beetroot is a messy business. Make sure you don't cover everything else with specks of purple juice.

Raw beetroot salad with honey and garlic dressing

Marinate a crushed clove of garlic for a couple of hours in lemon juice sweetened with honey to taste. Remove the garlic. Toss finely shredded beetroot in the dressing and leave for a little while for the flavours to mingle. Serve piled into small mounds as part of an autumn or winter hors d'oeuvre.

Raw beetroot, potato and horseradish salad

Prepare equal quantities of grated beetroot and peeled, diced warm potato. Moisten with thick creamy yoghurt/yoghurt and sour cream/mayonnaise to which a little freshly grated horseradish has been added. Mix everything together lightly, adding a few drops of vinegar to sharpen slightly. Strew finely chopped hard-boiled egg over the top. Serve on its own with chicory and endive leaves, or as a side salad to accompany soused herrings. A lovely salad.

Raw beetroot with orange juice and caraway seeds

Moisten finely grated beetroot with fresh orange juice. Add a little sugar if necessary. In a dry pan, toss a generous sprinkling of caraway seeds for 2–3 minutes until crisp. Scatter over the beetroot. Serve in small mounds as part of an autumn or winter hors d'oeuvre.

Beetroot and banana salad with allspice dressing

Dress neat fingers of cooked beetroot and banana with a lemon juice and olive oil vinaigrette to which a hefty pinch of freshly ground allspice has been added. Set in a frill of lamb's lettuce, or small salad leaves.

Tomato, beetroot and tarragon salad

Mix diced cooked beetroot and chopped tomato with chopped tarragon and bind with a little thick mayonnaise – the juice from the tomatoes will dilute the dressing. Serve set in salad leaves, corn salad or slightly bitter leaves for preference, or as part of a mixed autumn hors d'oeuvre.

Butter bean and beetroot salad

Butter beans and beetroot are a good combination. Allow equal quantities – something like 8oz (225g) cooked beans and 2 medium or 1 large beetroot cut into small neat fingers should be sufficient for four. Arrange in a shallow dish with, optionally, a little chopped spring onion. Pour over a vinaigrette made with 2 tsp lemon juice, 1 tsp honey, salt, and 2 tbsp olive oil. Mix very lightly – not enough to blur the colours – and serve at room temperature.

Simple ways with hot beetroot

I can never understand why beetroot is served so unenthusiastically in restaurants, when all it takes is a little effort and imagination. Peel and slice – or better, I think, dice – and then toss with a little finely chopped onion or garlic softened first in a knob of butter, finishing with a dusting of parsley or mint, as described by Elizabeth David in *French Provincial Cooking*. Or try a squeeze of orange juice, a few drops of tarragon vinegar, or a little chopped and seeded tomato. With only slightly more effort, you can produce the other dishes below.

Beetroot with lemon juice and capers

An idea from Constance Spry. Toss cooked beetroot in a little butter, finely shredded lemon rind and 1 scant tsp sugar. Add the juice of half a lemon, some finely chopped parsley and 1 heaped tbsp drained capers per beetroot. Allow all to heat through and serve immediately.

Beetroot in cream

Toss cooked beetroot in a little butter in a small pan. Depending on the quantity of beetroot, pour over 2–4 tsp cider or wine vinegar, raspberry or tarragon flavoured if possible, followed by enough cream to moisten well. Don't worry if the cream curdles, it will right itself as it boils. Boil up and serve.

Sugared beetroot

An odd combination but one that works. For 8oz (225g) beetroot, melt ½oz (15g) butter and stir the beetroot around until hot and coated. Sprinkle over 2 tsp soft brown sugar. Shake for 30 seconds before the sugar has time to melt; it should form a slightly grainy coating. Good with strong flavoured game.

Beetroot with ginger, cumin or caraway

From *Food of Love* by Guislane Morland. Cook your beetroot, keeping them slightly underdone. Peel and slice or cut into thin chips. Toss gently in a covered pan with a little butter and some julienne shreds of ginger, or a generous pinch of either cumin or caraway seeds. Cook for a few minutes only. Serve like this, or with a little thick yoghurt or sour cream stirred around just sufficiently to give a pretty marbled effect.

Red and yellow spiced rice

A winter warmer, based on an idea from Richard Cawley's *New English Cooking*.

12oz (340g) brown rice	pinch of salt
1 small onion	4oz (120g) each of cooked beetroot,
1–2 tbsp vegetable oil for frying	red pepper, skinned tomato,
1 scant tsp cumin seeds	chopped into small even dice
1 tsp turmeric	

Cook the rice for 5 minutes in water to cover by a depth of 1in (2.5cm). Drain. Soften the onion in a little vegetable oil, add the spices and cook for 30 seconds. Add the rice, turning it over to collect the spices. Add enough water just to cover, season lightly with salt, and simmer for 10–15 minutes – the water should be nearly but not quite absorbed. Turn off the heat and leave for 10 minutes for the rice to finish cooking in its own steam.

Mix in the vegetables and leave on a hot plate or in a warm oven to heat through for another 5 minutes. The finished dish will be quite moist but not soggy and the rice nicely cooked.

Cod steaks with beetroot and apple

Fish and beetroot is another combination not sufficiently taken advantage of in British cookery. Try it with white fish and salmon as well as soused herring or mackerel.

4 cod steaks of even thickness
½oz (15g) butter for frying
2 medium crisp eating apples, peeled, cored and diced
1 large cooked beetroot, skinned and diced

pinch of caraway seeds (optional)
3–4 tbsp single cream, yoghurt, or a mixture of the two

Wipe the fish with kitchen paper and cut off any fins. Seal in hot butter on both sides over a brisk heat in a nonstick frying pan. Turn down the heat, cover and cook very gently until just done (look for the white curd), anything from 7–10 minutes, depending on the thickness of your steaks. Let the fish rest briefly and then transfer to heated plates and keep warm.

Quickly deal with the sauce. Boil down the fish juices, add the apple and cook for 2–3 minutes, stirring until the dice soften. Follow with the beetroot and caraway seeds if using, and heat through. Finish with enough cream or yoghurt to bind the mixture and produce a small amount of sauce. Spoon around the fish. Serve immediately with saffron or turmeric tinged rice or plain potatoes dusted with parsley. Either way, the colour is stunning.

Carrots

Carrots belong to the same family as caraway, chervil, coriander, cumin, dill and parsley – an association which will be appreciated immediately by cooks. Their long history is complicated and confusing. Early carrots were not orange, but white, yellow, red, purple, or even blackish, and are believed to have been domesticated originally in Afghanistan, where the greatest diversity has been found. But though eaten since antiquity, primitive carrots would not have made particularly good eating, and must have been little better than the wild forms which are pale and tough with no root at all to speak of.

The early cultivated carrots spread westwards and eastwards: into Asia Minor in the 10th and 11th centuries, Arab-occupied Spain in the 12th century, China and northwestern Europe in the 14th century, reaching England in the 15th century. Great improvements were introduced by Flemish gardeners in the late Middle Ages. At the turn of the 16th century efforts were made to breed an orange coloured carrot from the yellow varieties. By the early 17th century the transition was complete and the long orange carrot had been established. The colour was a winner. From these came the improved Horn varieties, from which all modern western varieties are derived.

Carrots – which from the outset were hailed as sustaining food for peasants instead of bread or meat – have been an important feature of kitchen gardens ever since. Maincrop carrots are richer and fuller flavoured than summer ones. As with early carrots, they come in three lengths: short or stump rooted, said to be best for clay or impenetrable soils; intermediate carrots; and those with long tapering roots. Though not everyone agrees, as far as flavour goes, I am increasingly of the opinion that variety is less important than soil and growing conditions. In America, intensely coloured carrots are now being bred containing three times the amount of carotene, which points the way for the future perhaps. Carrots should never be grown on freshly manured ground. This causes them to fork and split. They succeed best on lighter sandy soils.

Most people sow maincrop carrots too early. This has a tendency to produce woody specimens. Mid-May is soon enough. At first the plants seem impossibly spindly, but as summer progresses they grow fast, reaching a respectable girth by October. Thin them twice, to 1in (2.5cm) and then 2–3in (5–7.5cm) apart, remembering to burn or discard the thinnings well away from the carrot row, as these attract carrot fly (see p. 126).

Maincrop carrots are usually harvested around mid-late October. As with summer carrots, the important thing is to watch how the flavour develops. A week or two can make a perceptible difference. Pick a cool, dry day. Lay them out on a garden path or somewhere where they can dry off for a few hours, after which they should be gently but thoroughly cleaned. Twist off the tops and lay neatly in cardboard boxes sandwiched in layers of peat, taking care not to let them touch each other if you can help it. Close the box and store somewhere cool and dark.

Stored this way, carrots will last 2–3 months. Towards the end, the tops will start to sprout and the carrots dry out, taking on a wizened appearance, but the flavour will be fine, (unlike sweetcorn or peas, the sugars do not turn to starch in storage) and the carrots perfectly usable for soups and the stock pot. Take them out as you need, shaking off the peat and washing and scrubbing in the usual way using a stiff brush.

Cooking without carrots is unthinkable. They are an essential ingredient for soups, stockpots and braises, a natural partner with beef, and an outstanding vegetable in their own right. Few root vegetables are as versatile when it comes to marrying spices and seasonings, and their natural sweetness makes them especially invaluable in salads. They harmonise particularly well with other root vegetables and with Chinese leaf vegetables for stir-fried dishes.

Carrots are wasted by boiling. Cook them in their own juices with a knob of butter in a tightly fitting pan over a gentle heat until the centres are just soft, either whole or cut into thin or thick triangular wedges. Depending on their size, they should take around 5–10 minutes. Despite their sweetness, a pinch of sugar sprinkled over towards the end brings out the flavour remarkably. Or you can cook them in stock in the oven or wrap them in foil with butter, a few tablespoons of water and herbs. When you are short of time, grated carrot tossed over heat for a couple of minutes in butter or one of the nut oils just until the bulk begins to soften makes an excellent dish. It is one of my favourite vegetable dishes, especially to accompany bulgur or rice pilafs.

Carrots are a highly nutritious vegetable, rich in carotene (which becomes vitamin A), and contain other important vitamins and minerals. They are just as delicious raw as cooked. Take advantage of this as often as you can.

Gujerati carrot salad

One of the best carrot salads, from Madhur Jaffrey. This is the version I use.

12oz (340g) grated carrot   1–2 tbsp vegetable oil
good squeeze of lemon juice   1 tbsp black mustard seeds

Mound the carrot onto a serving dish and squeeze over lemon juice to taste. Heat the oil in a small frying pan. Add the mustard seeds, cover, and cook briefly for a few seconds until they pop. Pour the lot in a swirl over the carrot and serve.

Carrots with crushed coriander

Scrub and scrape or peel your carrots and cut into even sized wedges. Put in a pan with a knob of butter and a spot of oil, plus 1 tsp lightly crushed coriander seeds per person. Cover and cook very gently, shaking the pan frequently, until almost done. Depending on the quantity, sprinkle over 1–2 tsp soft brown sugar, replace the lid and continue to cook until done and the carrots and juices nicely caramelised. Watch they do not burn. If they start to catch, turn off the heat for a little while to let the pan cool somewhat. Then put back over a gentle heat and continue cooking. This tip works for all root vegetables cooked in this style.

Carrot and hazelnut roulade with cream and sage filling

12oz (340g) prepared carrots, chopped
5 fl oz (150ml) chicken stock
1oz (30g) hazelnuts
2 egg yolks
4 egg whites

For the filling
about 5oz (150g) sour cream/thick
    drained yoghurt/curd cheese or
    cream cheese and thick yoghurt
    mixed/ricotta cheese plus a little
    cream
1–2 tsp finely chopped fresh sage

Cook the carrots in the chicken stock in a covered pan until very soft. Purée in a blender and then return to the pan to dry off if necessary. Cool slightly and set aside. Meanwhile, lightly toast the hazelnuts, crush and then chop finely – or, for a less gritty texture, grind in a food processor or coffee grinder.

Have a Swiss roll tin ready lined with clingfilm. Mix the carrot purée and hazelnuts and beat in the egg yolks. Whisk the egg whites until stiff, and fold into the mixture. It should not be too thick. Spread the mixture evenly on to the prepared tin. Bake at 220°C/425°F/gas mark 7 for about 10 minutes until *just* firm; the inside should still feel slightly creamy to the touch.

Mix the chosen filling, which should be of a thick spreading consistency, with the sage, and spread over the roulade, keeping it well away from the edge. Keeping it flat, transfer to a hot serving plate. Now roll up carefully – it is more fragile than most roulades – easing it away from the lining as you go. Serve immediately, either as a first course, or as part of a vegetable meal. No sauce is really necessary, but if you have some, a little fresh tomato coulis or tomato vinaigrette made with olive oil is a pleasant accompaniment. Serves 3–4.

Lemon and sherry carrots

1lb (450g) carrots, peeled
½oz (15g) butter
2 tsp soft brown sugar

3–4 fl oz (90–120ml) medium sherry
juice of 1 lemon

Cut the carrots into thickish strips or else thin wedges fashioned into miniature carrots by rounding off the edges with a potato peeler – the first is quicker, the second more appealing. Melt the butter in a heavy pan, add the carrots, cover, and cook gently for 5 minutes, stirring them round now and then. Sprinkle over the sugar, then pour in the sherry. Bubble up and reduce a little. Add the lemon juice, cover and simmer for 15–20 minutes. There should be just a small amount of sticky glaze at the finish – check towards the end that the liquid does not dry up, adding extra sherry or water as necessary. Alternatively, if too much liquid remains, boil down. The taste should be refreshingly tangy. Good with roast pork or veal, or as part of a vegetable meal surrounded by a bed of Swiss chard or spinach beet.

Oxtail braised in Guinness with orange and carrots

Oxtail is a much maligned and under-used cut in British cookery. If it were more expensive, no doubt we would see it differently. Nothing produces more heartwarming succulent winter fare, or is better tempered.

8 good pieces of oxtail (buy 2 tails, saving the end bits for soup)
1 large onion, sliced
1 small bottle (270ml) Guinness
2 tsp tomato purée
sugar

1 medium orange
8oz (225g) carrots, cut into small wedges
a little butter
1–2 tsp potato flour, slaked in a little water

Trim the oxtail of excess fat and seal in a dry pan, an ovenproof casserole if possible. Remove the oxtail and brown the onions, adding a little rendered down fat from the oxtail if needed. Replace the oxtail and pour in the Guinness. Add water to cover, the tomato purée and 2 tsp sugar. Bring to the boil, cover tightly and transfer to a very low oven, 120°C/225°F/gas mark ½. Cook until the meat parts from the bones, which may take 3 hours or so. Turn off the oven and allow to cool, overnight if it suits. Remove the fat.

Meanwhile, make the orange garnish. Using a zester, pare the zest into spillikins, blanch for 5 minutes, drain and reserve. In a small pan, heat 2 tsp sugar with 1 tbsp water. Cook until the mixture caramelises – watch it when it turns. Off the heat, add the orange spillikins. They will sizzle furiously, but there is no need to be alarmed. Stir and leave to cool (it will harden), then add a little extra water to dissolve the caramel and soften the spillikins.

To finish the dish, reheat the oxtail in the sauce, this time uncovered, in a moderate oven, 160–180°C/325–350°F/gas mark 3–4, for about 45 minutes. If the sauce looks like drying up too much, add extra water as necessary. Cook the carrots in a little butter, mix with the orange spillikins and reserve.

Transfer the oxtail to a serving dish. Thicken the sauce with potato flour, adding it cautiously, a little at a time. Add orange juice to taste. It should be dark, rich and reasonably fruity. Pour the sauce round the oxtail and scatter the carrots on top of the sauce. Serve with pasta or polenta.

Cauliflower

Cauliflowers are something the English have always excelled at. They arrived here, via Cyprus, sometime in the 16th century. A little over 100 years later, there was already a vigorous export trade to the continent with early 'colly-flowers' grown by London market gardeners fetching 2–3 shillings apiece. Even then, cauliflower could be had for six months of the year. By the 19th century, expertise had reached fever pitch. Cauliflower was an all-year-round vegetable, one it seemed we never tired of. 'In London,' wrote Vilmorin-Andrieux in *The Vegetable Garden*, 'it is hardly possible to overstock the market with this vegetable.' The same might be said of Leicester markets today.

Cauliflower began life as an early mutant of the cabbage. A drawing in the *Herbal* of Rembertus Dodonaeus, written in 1554, shows the Cyprus cabbage as it was then called, recognisably a cauliflower but with a mean and wizened head enveloped in a mass of kale-like leaves. Selective breeding over the centuries has produced desirable fat creamy curds, but at a price. The cauliflower is a well-bred freak, its curds a mass of tiny sterile delicate florets which need cajoling and persuasion to bloat themselves into large heads. It is easily the most difficult of the brassica family, precocious by nature, demanding exactly the right conditions and intolerant of any kind of check. A rich fertile soil with a high potash content is essential.

For the kitchen gardener, success is more likely with summer and autumn cauliflowers. Summer cauliflowers mature July/early August. Recommended varieties are the long established All The Year Round and a new variety, Snowball. Autumn cauliflowers mature September/October. Here, the Australian varieties are very reliable. Half a dozen or so well grown cauliflowers are rich reward. To ensure a succession you will have to choose different varieties with different maturing times. Cultivation is as for other brassicas. Sow the seeds in seedtrays, February/March for summer cauliflowers, and during May for autumn maturing cauliflowers, experimenting to see how late you can sow them to suit your conditions. Transplant in about 4–5 weeks to 15in (38cm) apart, before the young plants become too large. They can be spaced closer, resulting in smaller heads. They grow faster than other brassicas, maturing at about four months. Keep well watered in dry weather.

Bending the leaves to form a protective shield over the developing curds is a long established practice, mentioned in all the early gardening books. The curd is extremely delicate. Heavy rains will ruin it and even touching the curd may cause damage, releasing a sap on which micro-organisms thrive, quickening discolouration and deterioration, and spoiling your hard work.

Harvesting cauliflower requires judgment and precise timing. 'As soon as you observe the outside of the flower beginning to part from the rest, 'tis high time to cut it,' wrote the author of *Adam's Luxury and Eve's Cookery* in 1744. Once the curd has begun to form, it increases in size and matures very quickly over the space of a few days and needs to be watched constantly. Colour is an important indicator. A young cauliflower is milky white and virgin bright, becoming more creamy, then finally yellowing and dulling with age. Once ready, cauliflowers do not stand more than two or three days and should be picked immediately while the curds are perfect and blemish-free. After this time, the curds begin to break up and become looser. Deterioration rapidly follows. If you cannot eat them, pick them, trim the leaves and store somewhere cold. Wrapped in a plastic bag they keep in respectable condition for up to a week in the refrigerator, though the flavour will dull slightly and lack the true creamy finesse of one which has been freshly picked.

A perfect cauliflower will need only a brief rinse just before cooking. Soaking spoils it. Check that no insects have become embedded within the curds. Surface blemishes can often be removed by scrubbing with a stiff brush. Otherwise cut away any damaged parts and cut into florets.

Cauliflower suffers more than most from overcooking. Other vegetables may get better treatment nowadays, but we still cling to our soggy cauliflower and cheese sauce. Properly cooked it should be just the soft side of firm and have no trace of wateriness.

A whole cauliflower looks impressive, but you are likely to achieve better results by breaking it into individual florets. Do this carefully, following the natural breaks and shapes, cutting the larger curds to make sure all cook evenly. Set a frying pan with ½–1in (1.25–2.5cm) boiling water over a brisk heat. Add the florets and cover. Give them 3–4 minutes. At the end of this time, remove the cover and test with the point of a knife: the curd should be firm, just on the point of yielding. If not, cook a little longer with the lid off, testing every 30 seconds or so where the stem meets the curd.

Ideally, the water should dry up at the same time the curds are done, but have a little extra hot water on hand to top up if needed. Arrange neatly – if you like, reform it into its natural shape – and serve immediately. If you have some, a fringe of freshly cooked calabrese set around the edge sets off the creamy curds well.

The cauliflower is a regal vegetable, best enjoyed on its own. Less perfect cauliflowers make good soups, passable salads, and can be enlivened with spices and flavourings. On the whole, though there are exceptions – broad beans, red peppers, potatoes – cauliflower does not easily mix with other vegetables, or with meat or fish. The only classic dishes we have are with cheese. Mashed hard-boiled eggs, and a scattering of fried crumbs, in the polonaise style, is another worthy standby.

Cauliflower salads

I cannot say I care for raw cauliflower in salads. A few sprigs as crudités with dips are pleasant and crunchy enough but lack the succulence and sweetness needed to sustain interest past the nibbling stage. In mixed salads, to be successful, raw cauliflower should be cut very small and used in small amounts, with grains or rice and other vegetables. Cooked cauliflower salads are a much better proposition and a useful way of using up any leftovers. Mix with rice, tomatoes, olives, capers, anchovies, oil and lemon in the Italian way; mayonnaise or mustardy dressings; or spicy mixtures with chilli, ginger, turmeric, coriander and cumin. Chilled cauliflower is no good at all. Serve cauliflower salads at room temperature.

Cauliflower and broad bean salad

Mix dainty, lightly cooked florets and cooked tender broad beans and (optionally) a little finely chopped red pepper. Bind lightly with a garlicky mayonnaise while the vegetables are still hot. The moisture from the vegetables will dilute the dressing slightly. Sprinkle with a little chopped oregano if you have some and serve as a first course while the vegetables are still warm.

Cauliflower and green pepper salad with spicy coconut dressing

8oz (225g) cauliflower florets
1 green pepper, deseeded and diced
   fairly small
1 fresh green chilli, deseeded and finely
   chopped
1 tsp finely grated fresh ginger

2–3 tbsp raisins
2–4 tsp vegetable oil
For the dressing
1 tbsp coconut cream
2 tbsp water
2–3 tbsp thick yoghurt

Make the dressing first. Melt the coconut cream and water in a small pan. Cool, then beat in the yoghurt and set aside.

Cook the cauliflower florets al dente. Chop into small bite-sized pieces and put into a bowl. Stir-fry the rest of the ingredients in a little vegetable oil over a brisk heat for 1 minute. Add to the cauliflower, together with the dressing and mix well. Serves 2–4.

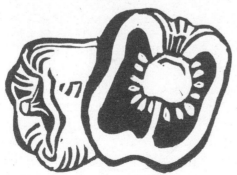

Cauliflower florets with roasted peanuts

A way of finishing cauliflower in the Chinese style: toast some peanuts lightly under the grill or roast for a few minutes in the oven, then rub off their skins. Toss cooked florets (divide them so they are small) in a little sesame seed oil in a frying pan so that they crisp. Serve the cauliflower florets topped with the peanuts, and seasoned with a sprinkling of salt.

Fragrant cauliflower purée

As with many vegetable purées, the addition of a little cooked potato is a good idea, giving cohesion and body without altering the flavour noticeably.

1 large cauliflower, divided into sprigs
1 small – medium hot potato diced,

1 tsp ground coriander, or more to taste
1 tbsp fresh chopped coriander

Reserve a few of the best sprigs of cauliflower. Cook the rest until just soft – about 5 minutes. Blend with the cooked potato, adding a little of the cooking water or milk if necessary to obtain a smooth purée. Add the spices to taste and check the seasoning, adding a little salt if required. Meanwhile cook the remaining sprigs. Arrange the purée on a serving dish, tuck in the florets around the edge, sprinkle over a little extra fresh coriander and serve immediately.

Cauliflower and almond soup

A light delicate soup.

8–10oz (225–285g) cauliflower,
  broken into small florets
1oz (30g) ground almonds
½ pt (300ml) each of chicken stock
  and water

1 large bay leaf, fresh if possible
To finish
a little cream or creamy milk
2 tsp lightly toasted almonds
  (optional)

Simmer the first four ingredients for 15 minutes, or until the cauliflower is soft. Remove the bay leaf, and blend in two batches until the soup is smooth and creamy. Return to the pan, finish with cream or creamy milk. Serve either plain, or with a few toasted almond flakes scattered on top.

Cauliflower with peaches or apricots and tarragon

Take a fine cauliflower and divide into florets. Cook briskly in a little water, keeping it on the crisp side. Melt a knob of butter in a smallish pan and soften 2 tbsp chopped spring onion. Add 1 ripe peach or 2 ripe apricots, diced small. Cook for a couple of minutes, stirring the pieces around. Add the cooked florets and 1 tbsp chopped tarragon. Toss everything together until hot. Turn out onto a serving dish, arranging the fruit mixture on top, and serve immediately.

Cauliflower is spicy tomato sauce

Turn to p. 146 and the recipe for spicy tomato sauce. Don't add the fresh coriander when it says, but divide the florets and cook the cauliflower in the sauce until soft. Sprinkle with fresh coriander and serve.

Cauliflower and potato pie

This excellent vegetable dish – more of a flat cake than a pie – is adapted from *Italian Vegetarian Cookery*, by Paola Gavin, published in 1986.

1lb (450g) floury potatoes, scrubbed
1lb (450g) cauliflower, cut into small
  even florets
2–3 tbsp cream
freshly grated nutmeg

small knob of butter plus 2 tsp olive
  oil
½oz (15g) finely grated parmesan
  cheese (optional)

Boil the potatoes until cooked. Peel when cooled enough to handle and mash with a potato masher. Meanwhile cook the cauliflower al dente. Chop finely by hand or in a food processor. Mix with the potato, adding the cream, and seasoning vigorously with nutmeg. Mix well. Spoon the mixture into a large shallow buttered gratin dish, spreading it evenly to a depth of ½–¾in (1.25–2cm). Melt the butter with oil. Brush the surface, dribbling over the remainder. Sprinkle with parmesan if using and bake at 180°C/375°F/gas mark 4 for 30–35 minutes until the edges are beginning to brown and the top is golden. Serves 4-6.

Celeriac

Celeriac is a specialised form of celery, bred for its bulbous swollen starchy lower stem, hence the description 'turnip-rooted celery'. Both, ultimately, are developed from the wild form, smallage, found growing in the south and east of England, by all accounts a rank smelling, spindly umbelliferous plant.

Credit for the transformation into the cultivated forms belongs to French and Italian horticulturists in the early 17th century, who introduced it to the rest of Europe. There is an account by a Neapolitan, Jo Baptista Porta, said to be the first we have, of celeriac growing in Apulia. He called it capitatum, and described the bulb as nearly the size of a man's head, 'very sweet, odorous and grateful'.

It has always been a novelty vegetable here. The naturalist Gilbert White was one of the few who bothered to try it: 'Bought three plants of curious celeriac from Waltham,' reads his entry in his *Garden Kalendar* for 27

August 1760. 'The leaves are jagged like curled parsley.' He had tried it two years previously, raising the plants from seed. But it was not a stalwart like cabbage or endive or melons or cucumbers, and we hear no more of it after this time.

Nor, apparently, has it struck a chord with many gardeners since. Yet a pleasant surprise awaits anyone who grows their own celeriac. The flavour is sweeter and altogether fresher than that of the bought vegetable, which can seem jaded and coarse by comparison. It is not an easy plant to grow well – think of it as celery rather than a common root. It needs a rich moist soil, full sun and a long growing season. The plants are particularly averse to cold. Success seems to depend on raising strong healthy plants for planting out 9in (23cm) apart under cloches mid-late May.

Sow the seeds under glass, with gentle heat, in late February in a peat-based compost in soil blocks or individual pots. Keep well watered in dry conditions. A liquid feed in summer is beneficial. Later on, the outside leaves start to split at the base and fall away from the plant. Strip them away from the bulb when this happens – it is supposed to encourage the bulb to swell.

If they show brown patches in the centre when cut open, a boron deficiency is probably the answer. Celeriac discolours on cooking depending on the amount of anthocyanin pigment present in the tuber, and this differs according to the variety. Look for varieties such as Iram, where the seed packet specifies tubers which do not discolour on cooking.

A mild frost can improve the flavour of celeriac, but it will not stand hard frosts and should be harvested sometime in late October/early November. Often, the bulbs put on considerable girth towards the end of their growing season; do not to let them get too large, for the centres become woody and the flavour can coarsen somewhat. I am not sure I agree with the general advice to pick them when about the size of a tennis ball. There is a considerable amount of waste on celeriac, which cuts down the usable quantity appreciably, so they should be allowed to grow a little larger.

Celeriac is more difficult to harvest than it appears. The tuber sits on top of the soil, but has a densely matted fibrous root system which spreads extensively around the plant, anchoring it firmly in the ground. You need to dig round it with a fork, and prise it out with some force. Twist off the tops and hack away the worst of the root system before bringing it inside. Store as for other root vegetables in sand or peat, unless you intend to use them fairly quickly, in which case they can be left uncovered in a cool place. Celeriac stores well, and can last up to five months in good conditions.

Garden celeriac is a brute to prepare for cooking. Scrub vigorously under running water with a stiff brush. Leave to drain and pat dry. If necessary, it can now be stored like this in the salad compartment of the refrigerator or the vegetable rack until needed. Wastage can amount to a quarter of the total weight, and it is often better to judge quantities by eye when you are preparing it. As a rough guide, 8oz (225g) prepared weight should be enough for two decent helpings.

Peel, cutting away all the knobbly bits with a knife. Any sound but unusable bits make excellent additions to the stock pot. Slice or dice into even pieces. Unless you are particular about colour, there is no need to drop it into acidulated water. Cook gently with a knob of butter, or braise in stock or wine or orange juice. Either way, allow around 5–10 minutes cooking time. Diced celeriac is also good deep-fried. Blanch it first briefly, drain, pat dry and finish for a couple of minutes in oil to cover, trying to piece to see if the centre is soft. Drain on kitchen paper and serve immediately with a seasoning of salt or celery seeds. Celeriac can be cooked quickly in a frying pan, shredded into julienne strips, or grated and tossed over a high heat in flavoured oils or butter for 1–2 minutes, either on its own or with other complementary vegetables.

Smaller specimens can be cooked whole. The colour goes rather greyish but the flavour is unaffected. Scrub well and cook with water to cover for 30–40 minutes, until a skewer inserts easily. Run under a cold tap, and the skin will peel off easily. The outside layer tends to get mushy, and needs scraping away also. Slice, dress while warm and serve as a salad.

Its colour when cooked, a rather unappetising greyish beige, is the only thing not in its favour. Celeriac is more pleasantly nutty than celery, positive, but mild enough not to be aggressively assertive. It is a far more versatile vegetable than the lack of established recipes would indicate, makes one of the best vegetable purées I know, and is a particularly fine accompaniment to game.

Celeriac tops – which resemble dark green celery stalks, are too strong to put to much use except in stocks; a small piece is plenty.

Celeriac salads

Celeriac is not sufficiently used in salads, which do it great justice. This is probably because raw celeriac discolours quickly, losing its snowy cream appearance. To avoid this, grate it and mix immediately with the dressing. The discolouration is not so bad either if you cut it into strips, and seems less with home-grown celeriac than with the bought kind.

The flavour improves if you blanch it first. Cut the celeriac into strips and blanch very briefly, 30–60 seconds. There is no need to use acidulated water. Drain, toss while warm in the dressing, and it is ready to be used. Alternatively, use a mixture of half raw and half blanched celeriac.

On the whole, creamy dressings suit celeriac better than spicy ones. Nut oils, mustardy vinaigrettes or creamy herb dressings made with thick yoghurt or sour cream are most appropriate. So is a scattering of celery seeds to embellish nut oil or mayonnaise dressings. Its clean nutty flavour teams particularly well with beetroot, carrot, walnut, and chicory, or with sweet vegetables such as peas or red peppers.

Try it also added to coleslaw, tossed in walnut oil and scattered over green salads, or added to ham, egg, smoked fish, or chicken salads.

Celeriac and red pepper salad

Grill a red pepper in the usual way (see p. 206). Mix with an equal quantity – or slightly more – of blanched celeriac cut into the same sized strips, plus a few slivers of garlic. Dribble over olive oil and let the salad marinate for a couple of hours. Scatter over a little finely chopped parsley before serving. Serve at room temperature. Use as part of a mixed hors d'oeuvre.

Celeriac and carrot rémoulade

Rémoulade usually refers to a sauce made with mayonnaise enlivened with chopped capers, gherkins, anchovies and fresh herbs. With celeriac, however, it always refers to a mustardy mayonnaise, and is the best known celeriac salad. This is a variation.

Take equal quantities of very finely grated celeriac and carrot, moistened with mayonnaise, or half plain yoghurt and half mayonnaise, with a generous dollop of Dijon or similar mustard to taste. The salad comes out a pretty pink. If the mixture is too thick, add 1–2 tsp hot water. Serve on a bed of slightly bitter salad leaves, or as part of an autumn or winter hors d'oeuvre.

Celeriac guacamole

Guacamole is the popular Mexican dip, made with mashed avocados and spiced with chillies and garlic. This is a mild version, again to serve as part of an autumn hors d'oeuvre.

Cook your celeriac until very soft. Mash to a purée with a fork with a peeled avocado and a clove of garlic crushed to a pulp with a pinch of salt. Add lemon juice to taste. The mixture should be quite lumpy. Serve at room temperature.

Celeriac polonaise

Toss cooked diced celeriac in mayonnaise diluted with a little hot water. Set in chicory leaves. Top with a very finely chopped hard-boiled egg. Scatter over fried breadcrumbs. One of the best celeriac salads.

Celeriac niçoise

One of the virtues of celeriac is that it has the capacity to imbibe flavours without itself being swamped, as in the following dish.

1 large leek
1 clove garlic, crushed
olive oil
8oz (225g) prepared celeriac, sliced
and cut into chunks
8oz (225g) ripe tomatoes, coarsely
chopped

2 tbsp lemon juice
1 tsp sugar
To finish
olive oil
lemon juice
finely chopped parsley

Soften the leek and garlic in 1 tbsp olive oil for a few minutes over a low heat. Add the rest of the ingredients, stir, cover, and cook steadily until the celeriac is soft, about 15–20 minutes. Remove the lid and cook to reduce the sauce if necessary to a thick coating consistency. Cool. Serve at room temperature, sprinkled with lemon juice, olive oil and parsley. Serves 3–4.

Celeriac and chive soup

Celeriac does not as a rule make the most successful soups. It either needs something to soften the flavour, or to harmonize or compete with it to its advantage. This is one soup I have found to be successful, which I generally make at the end of the winter when the first chives are showing through.

8oz (225g) prepared celeriac, diced
into small cubes
1 clove of garlic

1pt (600ml) milk and water mixed
large handful finely scissored chives

Simmer the first three ingredients in a covered pan until the celeriac is very soft. Blend with half the chives until smooth; the soup will be pale and flecked with green. Reheat, add the rest of the chives, make any adjustments to consistency with a little extra milk or cream if you have it, add the rest of the chives and serve.

Celeriac braised with orange

8oz (225g) prepared celeriac, thinly
sliced and diced
juice of 1 large or 2 small oranges

1 tsp honey
2–3 fl oz (60–90ml) water
chopped chives or chervil (optional)

Put everything in a pan, cover and simmer until the celeriac is tender, stirring from time to time – the sauce reduces and thickens and you should be left with a small amount of glaze at the finish. Scatter with chives or chervil if you have some. An appropriate vegetable dish to serve with game. This quantity serves 2 as a main vegetable or 4 as an accompaniment, and reheats well.

Pork with celeriac and prunes

Once you get away from celeriac as a side vegetable, you need to turn to Europe for dishes which feature celeriac as part of the main course. This dish evolved from an Austrian recipe.

4 lean spare rib (shoulder) pork chops
small sprig of rosemary
12oz (340g) prepared celeriac, peeled
  and sliced into chunks

16 pitted prunes, soaked overnight
  with water to cover
5 fl oz (150ml) white wine

Spike the chops here and there with a few rosemary leaves. Choose a large casserole which will take the chops in a single layer and spread the celeriac over the bottom. Arrange the chops on top. Tuck in the prunes and pour over the wine and water to cover. Bring to the boil, cover, and transfer to a fairly moderate oven, 160–180°C/325–350°F/gas mark 3–4. Cook for about 1¼ hours until the meat is tender.

Remove the meat to a serving dish or separate heated plates, surrounding with the celeriac and prunes. Boil down the juices to concentrate the flavour, spooning off any scum or fat that rises to the surface. Pour over the meat and vegetables. If you prefer, you can thicken the sauce with 1 tsp potato flour slaked in a little water; add it gradually and bring to the boil, stirring constantly until the sauce is lightly thickened.

Endives and chicories

Endives and chicories are autumn and winter salad plants par excellence, and in recent years have enjoyed something of a revival. They are more resistant to pests and diseases than lettuce, largely unfussy in their requirements, and will succeed in a variety of soils and growing conditions, although it is often difficult for the amateur gardener to get as good results as the commercial grower. Problems occur especially with blanching the plants and with getting the ball-headed chicories to form a tight head.

Endives and chicories are closely related, both having a distinctive sharp bitter quality. Many home-grown varieties are likely to be more bitter than their commercial counterparts. They rarely stand up well on their own, but as part of a mixed green salad, their robustness is an advantage. A sweetish dressing is often more appealing to counteract their bitterness. Tear rather than cut the leaves and toss at the last possible moment – minor blemishes overlooked during washing quickly become all too evident once dressed. Once harvested, they keep remarkably well, whole plants lasting up to a month in the refrigerator, and individual leaves for 2 weeks or more. Check them regularly, removing rotting leaves.

If you find the leaves too bitter, cut them coarsely and soak in a large bowl of cold water for an hour or longer. This will alleviate the bitterness. It also happens to be the best way of cleaning all dirty or grimy salad leaves. Other bitter or strong tasting leaves (some of the oriental leafy vegetables, for example) may be treated in the same manner.

Endives and chicories may also be cooked. On the whole, I am not fond of eating them this way – garden endives and chicories are rarely good enough quality, but if should you have a surplus, they can be grilled (which I do like), braised, gratinéed or made into soups.

Endives

Endives are annual or biennial plants and look rather like unruly lettuces. Contrary to popular opinion, they are far less hardy than chicories and will stand only a slight frost. They have evolved from the wild chicory and a related plant, *Chicorium pumilum*. The Greeks and the Romans grew them extensively. Early endives were large, broad, flat leaved types, descendants of modern day Batavian endives, known as *escarole* or *scarole*. They are generally hardier than the second kind, the mop-headed curly leaved frisée type, which are believed to have developed perhaps as late as the 15th or 16th century. Several intermediate types exist also.

For autumn and early winter use, endives should be sown from June to August. They prefer a rich, moisture retentive soil high in organic matter, and like chicories succeed best, we have found, grown in a cold frame, which provides necessary protection later on. Thin the young plants to 6in (15cm), then 12in (30cm) apart, using the thinnings in misticanza salads. A mature endive is a large plant, well grown specimens providing enough leaves for 2–3 weeks. Once mature, protect from rain or frost with cloches. Curly leaved varieties are particularly vulnerable to damage.

Chicories

The chicories are a complex and varied group of extremely hardy and ancient plants. Wild forms are common, picked and eaten in Mediterranean countries as they must have been for thousands of years. The first mention of the cultivated types came in a German herbal of 1616. By the end of the century they were in general cultivation, gardeners progressively selecting less bitter types.

They are almost entirely perennial. For salad purposes they may be divided into two broad types, the fat-rooted witloof chicory grown for winter forcing, and those which are grown for their beautiful green, dark red, pink or variegated leaves.

Witloof is the familiar chicory found nestling in blue tissue paper in supermarkets and all good greengrocers. The name means 'white leaf'. It was discovered accidentally around 1850 by a Belgian farmer who threw some large wild chicory into a warm dark stable, found it produced beautiful blanched heads, and began cultivating it.

Bought forced chicory is generally of good quality, but home-grown is much the better of the two, exhibiting a sweetness and succulence often lacking in commercial chicory. Contrary to popular opinion, witloof chicory is easy to grow, particularly the newer varieties such as Normato which form tight compact heads easily.

Sow outside, as early as you can in April, thinning the young plants to 6–9in (15–23cm) apart. The foliage should be cut off ¼in (6mm) above the crown sometime in November. Dig the crowns when required and bring inside for forcing. In wet weather, the roots tend to rot off, and it is better to dig them up and store them in a cool place or cover with a cloche than leave them in the open ground.

Forcing is straightforward: choose good sized roots and place three in a pot of moist peat or soil, burying up to the crowns. Cover with a second upturned pot, check all light is excluded, and leave for three weeks in a cool room. At the end of this time the chicons should be of good size and ready to eat. Unless you want a whole head, pluck the leaves singly, gently pulling at the base, taking a few from each plant. With the new varieties, there is no need to cover over with a mound of soil or peat to induce tight heads. This is doubly advantageous as the chicons need no cleaning and peat has a horrible way of getting stuck under finger nails.

Forced chicory is a great delicacy. Unless you have more than you know what to do with, it seems a waste to use your own chicory for cooked dishes. One or two heads at least should be reserved for the beautiful polonaise chicory salad with chopped hard-boiled egg, moistened with mayonnaise and finished with fried breadcrumbs. Other classic combinations include fruit, avocado, walnut, beetroot, and celeriac.

The outside leaves can be chopped and used in mixed salads. Otherwise, don't jumble the spears as you would torn or small leaves but display them in a radial pattern to show off their shape or stick them in amongst the salad bowl so that they point upwards like unfurling lilies.

Sugar Loaf chicory belongs to the second group of chicories. It is a splendid hardy self-blanching type, forming large dense heads some as large as Chinese cabbages, with broad crisp midribs and pale inner leaves. It has found favour with gardeners since the 18th century and is the easiest of all the chicories to grow, the one that forms the backbone of many of our autumn and winter salads. If you have never grown chicory before, this is the kind to start with. The seeds should be sown in late June – not before, or they may bolt, and the plants thinned to 9in (23cm) apart. If protected, they will withstand several degrees of frost, but when the weather is bad, it is best to bring them inside. Trim off all the outer light green leaves, and store loosely wrapped in a plastic bag in the refrigerator or a cold larder. Like this, it keeps perfectly for 1–2 months, one large plant providing leaves for salad for a good 3–4 weeks.

Sugar Loaf chicory is less bitter than many of the other chicories. Mix it with other leaves, tearing each large leaf into small pieces, or shred and add to Chinese, white or red cabbage salads. When you get to the middle, keep the choice innermost leaves whole. These are delicious on their own with a walnut oil dressing, or in the polonaise style outlined above. It is best candidate, also, for braised or gratinéed dishes.

Red and green leaved chicories are all very hardy and grown as for endives, except the final spacing can be closer, about 9in (23cm) apart. Take off the largest outside leaves in autumn, leaving the inner leaves to grow on, and picking the leaves from the outside inwards as required. They continue to grow slowly in all but the coldest weather and will last through into the following spring. Keep free of rotting leaves. Once the plant has been cut, the stumps will produce new leaves, with renewed growth during spring. An easy kind is Grumolo Verde, an extremely hardy variety from the Piedmont region of Italy. This forms a rosette of leaves which hugs the ground. The leaves are tough and coarser in flavour, but it is reliable and can be picked continuously throughout the winter. Pick the tenderest leaves gently from the base.

Their bitterness is highly variable. The inner leaves of radicchio, the most popular chicory, are generally mild and should be kept whole. Together with endives, the red forms are the best for grilling. Shredded, and softened in olive oil with onion or other ingredients such as mushrooms, they can be used to make simple pasta dishes.

Blanching endives and chicories

Blanching endives and chicories mollifies the natural bitterness considerably. It is a practice which has engaged the attention of many a noted and respected gardener. The garden calendar which the 18th century naturalist Gilbert White kept for 40 years, shows that he must have spent countless patient hours tying his endives with twine, but I often wonder how successful he was, for it is not an easy thing to achieve under garden conditions.

Whether you blanch under pots or tie with twine it is imperative to keep the plants dry and free of slugs. Pots result in better blanched plants, but the plants are likely to rot more than those tied up to look like a stuffed cabbage. All round, this is simplest: truss them up with good strong twine, a couple of plants at a time, and blanch successionally. They will be ready in 10–14 days. Red chicories can be blanched in situ or forced indoors the same way as Witloof chicory. Neither has proved sufficiently satisfactory for us, and we now find it simpler to enjoy them as they are.

A blanched garden endive is a sorry sight. The wastage is considerable, though the heart will be fine and sweet. Trim the plants ruthlessly and bring inside. If you can, store them without washing and drying them first.

Endive with hot bacon and pumpkin seed dressing

This idea comes from Joy Larkcom. Frizzle small cubes of fatty bacon in their own fat until well browned and nicely crisped. Scatter over endive leaves. Add a little wine vinegar (about 1 tbsp per person), plus 2 tbsp pumpkin seeds to the pan, cook for 2 minutes, pour over the salad and serve immediately. Add a few croûtons for garnish.

Endive with ginger and walnut oil dressing

Cook a generous 1 tsp finely grated ginger in 2 tsp walnut oil for 15 seconds until it frizzles. Cool. Add extra walnut oil, a pinch of salt, stir well and toss the leaves until well coated. My favourite endive dressing.

Pomaine's curled endive and black olive salad

This is a salad of endives, black olives and chapons of dry toast rubbed with garlic, dressed with olive oil sharpened to taste with a few drops of wine vinegar. It comes from *Cooking with Pomaine*, published in 1962. Put the dressing into a roomy bowl, and add the croûtes and olives – I prefer to stone and finely chop them first – with washed, dried and torn endive leaves on top. 'Leave the salad to stand for an hour. The oil becomes fragrant with garlic and the olives attract the oil. Stir the salad only at the last moment, when it is already on the table. The pallor of the leaves is flecked with glistening black olives.'

One of the best endive salads. A few strips of crisp fennel can be arranged on top with the last of the cherry tomatoes.

Pigeon and endive salad

A salad for those who like fruit mixtures with their game, to make when Seville oranges are in season.

Endive leaves, roughly torn, or a
  mixture of endive and chicory leaves
4 skinned pigeon breasts
1 tbsp brandy

juice 1 large or 2 small Seville oranges
2 tbsp Seville marmalade (no peel)
2 tbsp pine kernels, lightly fried in
  butter

Arrange the endive leaves on four plates and set aside. Heat a nonstick frying pan and cook the pigeon breasts over a high heat for 2 minutes each side, pressing down with a spatula to make sure the flesh makes good contact. Cover, turn off the heat and leave for 5–6 minutes. The pigeons continue to cook in the residual heat and should be nicely pink throughout. Slice through each breast 3–4 times, stopping short of the edge and fan the pigeon out on top of the endive leaves. Add the brandy, orange juice and 1 tbsp marmalade to the juices in the pan, and boil for a minute or so to form a thin syrup. Taste, adding extra marmalade if it seems too sharp, and dribble over the meat and salad. Distribute the pine kernels over the breasts and serve immediately.

Forced chicory, apple and fennel salad

chicory spears
½ head of fennel, chopped
2 tbsp walnuts

2 tbsp walnut oil
1 medium-large eating apple, peeled
  and cut into small dice

Arrange the chicory spears on four plates, tops pointing outwards to look like a sunflower. Scatter the chopped fennel over the centre. Chop, then lightly crush the walnuts in a pestle, stir in the walnut oil and then mix in the diced apple. Spoon the apple mixture over the salad and serve, dribbling another 1 tsp oil over the leaves if they seem too dry. A few sprigs of watercress make an attractive addition.

Pyramid salad

A bright crunchy salad.

sugar loaf chicory leaves
2–3oz (60–90g) each raw fennel,
 celeriac, celery, red pepper, mooli
 radish, Chinese cabbage, cooked
 beetroot, all cut into slivers or
 shredded
2 tsp sesame seeds

a few chopped walnuts
4 stoned dates, cut into slivers
For the dressing
4–5 walnuts
1 tbsp each mayonnaise and yoghurt
1 tsp walnut oil

Start with the dressing. Pound the walnuts to a paste in a mortar, adding the rest of the ingredients and enough water to dilute to a pouring consistency.

Tear the chicory leaves coarsely and arrange on four plates. Scatter over the Chinese cabbage, followed by the other vegetables, a layer at a time, mounding them up in the centre to form a pyramid. Sprinkle over the sesame seeds and walnuts and decorate the top with slivers of date. Dribble over the dressing carefully and serve.

Chicory and turkey salad with saffron and vermouth mayonnaise

This is the kind of salad which turns left over Christmas turkey into a modest feast. Use either sugar loaf chicory or forced chicons.

2 large sticks of celery
6–8oz (170–225g) diced turkey meat
1–1½oz (30–45g) chopped walnuts
1 tbsp raisins plumped in hot water
1 diced cooked potato (optional)

For the dressing
2 tbsp mayonnaise
2 tbsp dry vermouth
½ packet of powdered saffron
chicory leaves

Peel away the stringy bits from the celery, slice down the middle and then crosswise into thinnish slices. Mix with the other salad ingredients.

To make the dressing, dissolve the saffron in the vermouth, and stir into the mayonnaise, adding a little hot water or extra vermouth to give a thin pouring consistency. Mix the salad with the dressing and set in a frill of chicory leaves on four plates.

Caribbean salad

Exotic fruits bring sunshine to dismal winters. A way of making them stretch further is to incorporate them into winter salads using the sweetness of one to set off the slight bitterness of the other.

mixed endive and chicory leaves
6–8oz (180–225g) ripe paw-paw,
  skinned and de-seeded
½ small red pepper, cut into thin
  strips
2 tbsp lightly toasted coconut flakes

For the dressing
1 tbsp each mayonnaise, single cream,
  yoghurt and smooth mango chutney
1 tsp curry powder
lemon juice to sharpen

Wash and dry the leaves and arrange on four plates. Using a potato peeler or sharp knife, shave off the furry skin surrounding the central core of the paw-paw and dice the fruit into thinnish, small slices. Divide the paw-paw and red pepper between the plates, arranging them attractively. Mix the dressing ingredients, adding lemon juice to sharpen and thinning if necessary with a few drops of water or milk to give a pouring consistency. Spoon over the salad and finish with a scattering of toasted coconut flakes. If you cannot buy paw-paw, use mango instead.

Grilled chicory or endive salad with toasted nuts

This makes a virtue of damaged specimens needing ruthless trimming. Cut the plants lengthways so that the leaves remain attached to the core, dividing into two or four depending on the size. Lightly coat both sides with either olive, walnut or hazelnut oil. Season sparingly with salt; add a grating of pepper if you like it. Arrange in a dish and grill for a few minutes, turning once or twice. The edges should be appetisingly charred here and there and the centres just soft. Halfway though scatter a few walnut halves, hazelnuts, or pine kernels in the dish. Watch the nuts do not burn, and remove when they are crisp. Serve immediately, with a few of the nuts.

Instead of adding the nuts, cover with flakes of fresh parmesan when the leaves are cooked, dribbling extra oil on top. The cheese should just melt on contact with the hot leaves.

Fennel

Fennel is not a vegetable you expect to find in many English kitchen gardens. It has been tried of course – the Elizabethan diplomat Sir Henry Wotton, who first introduced it, sent seeds and instructions on how to prepare it from Italy to Charles I's gardener John Tradescant the Elder, and Stephen Switzer included it in his pamphlet on foreign vegetables in 1726 – but it remained little more than a curiosity.

It is a native of southern Europe, and is not an easy vegetable to grow here, inclined to bolt, especially in our unpredictable summers, or when subjected to cold or dry spells. For English gardens, new bolt-resistant varieties such as Zefa Fino are more reliable. We have found it succeeds better outside than in a greenhouse. July sowings, harvested in autumn, generally give the best fennel. You can also sow in spring, starting the seeds off under cover in individual pots, though these are more likely to bolt and go to seed prematurely.

The fundamental problem with fennel lies in protecting the developing plants from wind and rain. A tall cloche with the ends removed or a cold frame minus its top glass is desirable, otherwise choose the most sheltered spot you can find. Any check or disturbance may cause bolting. Sow the seeds direct or in small pots, thinning to 4–6in (10–15cm) between each plant. As the bulbs develop, draw a little soil around them to afford a degree of anchorage.

A light, fertile, well drained soil is recommended, though ours succeed in heavier soil. The plants seem frail at first but gain strength quickly. The bulb forms above the ground, sitting square on the soil.

Experience so far has shown that the flavour of the mature crop varies. Some bulbs are very mild, others more pungent with a pronounced aniseed punch. Exactly when they are ready is difficult to determine, but is not critical. They stand well without deterioration and can be picked when required. What you are looking for is a fat, well swollen bulb. If they start to become leggy – a sign of bolting – pull them up and salvage what you can.

Fennel brought in from the garden needs no preparation, save chopping off the feathery fern. This is not so pronounced in flavour as fennel herb, but can be used in the same way. The stalks can be turned into soups, used to flavour fish stocks or dried to aromatise the barbecue. Outside layers of fennel are stringy. Use these for soups and sauces, remembering always to sieve at the end to remove the fibrous debris. Save the crisp tender core for salads or eat as a cooked vegetable. Do not wash, but wrap each trimmed bulb tightly in clingfilm and store somewhere cool, preferably the salad drawer of the refrigerator.

Home-grown fennel is altogether a brighter, crisper and more succulent vegetable than the one you will buy. It is one of the best salad vegetables eaten raw where its astringency comes to the fore. When cooked, it mellows considerably and the difference between bought and home-grown fennel is less noticeable.

The great virtue of fennel is its clean, lively, aromatic flavour. In Italy it is often eaten at the end of the meal to cleanse and refresh the palate. The Earl of Peterborough, one of the few gardeners who grew fennel in the early 18th century, is said to have preferred his with salt only – biting into freshly harvested fennel, one can easily appreciate why. Cut into neat strips, following the natural curve, and serve as part of a dish of crudités with aïoli or the hot garlicky dipping sauce, *bagna cauda*, or as an appetizer on its own to dip into olive oil mixed with a few drops of lemon juice.

Finely chopped fennel can be used in much the same way as celery to add crunchy texture and aromatic flavouring to any number of vegetable salads. This is the way I like fennel best.

Potato and fennel salad

Dice freshly cooked and still warm new potatoes and mix with 2 tbsp finely diced fennel. Season with olive oil, salt and chopped tarragon. An alternative is to omit the tarragon and add a few stoned and chopped black olives.

Fennel, apple and walnut or hazelnut salad

Bind equal quantities of diced fennel and peeled and chopped apple lightly with a mixture of mayonnaise and thick yoghurt, and scatter finely chopped walnuts over the top. A pinch of celery seeds or curry powder can be added to the dressing.

Fennel braised with tomato and mozzarella

A robust dish, which can be eaten hot or cold, worth making in quantity.

12oz (340g) fennel, cut into chunky slices, plus a few feathery fronds, chopped
12oz (340g) ripe tomatoes, peeled and chopped
1 scant tbsp dried tomato paste or 2 dried tomatoes
1 medium onion, sliced
1 clove of garlic, crushed
1 fresh red chilli, deseeded and chopped, or 1–2 dried chillies
olive oil
To finish (per person) (see method)
½oz (15g) each mozzarella and grated parmesan cheese

Put everything except the cheeses in a pan with a little olive oil and cook gently until soft and pulpy. If you're using dried chillies, test halfway through for the hotness, removing them when the strength seems right. If you are going to eat the dish hot, divide between four small gratin dishes, cover with the cheeses and brown under a moderate grill until bubbling. Alternatively, omit the cheeses, cool and serve tepid as a salad with a scattering of fresh chopped fronds or parsley and extra olive oil dribbled over. In either case, remove the dried chillies first.

Fennel and saffron risotto with garden peas, *or home-grown frozen peas*

1 shallot, finely sliced
¼–½oz (7–15g) butter
8oz (225g) fennel, thinly sliced and then chopped
8oz (225g) arborio rice
1 packet powdered saffron
pinch of salt
about 1¼ pt (750ml) well flavoured hot chicken stock
8oz (225g) garden peas

Sweat the shallot in the butter until softened but not coloured. Add the fennel, stir around, then add enough water to cover the bottom of the pan. Simmer for about 25 minutes until the fennel is very soft. Stir in the rice, followed by the saffron and salt. Add the chicken stock gradually in the usual way until you judge the rice to be just cooked and the risotto achieves the right creamy consistency, about 20 minutes. Cook the peas in a separate pan. Stir in some of the peas and serve the rest separately, arranged in a border around the risotto if serving on small plates as a first course. Serves 2–4.

Hake with fennel and apple purée

The combination of fennel and apple is a fine one. The purée may also be used to accompany pork chops, cooking it in the same way.

4 hake steaks (buy the largest you can find)
knob of butter for frying
3–4 tbsp vermouth

For the sauce
12oz (340g) chopped fennel
1 large sweet eating apple, cored and sliced
2–3 strips of scrubbed lemon peel
up to ½oz (15g) butter

Start with the sauce. Simmer the first three ingredients in a little water in a covered pan for 20–25 minutes until soft. Discard the lemon peel and blend to a smooth purée. Sieve back into the pan, pressing hard to extract as much of the purée as you can. Continue to cook down until reduced by about a third; it should be thick with no trace of wateriness. Beat in butter to taste and reserve.

Melt the knob of butter in a heavy or preferably nonstick pan. Seal the fish on both sides over a high heat. Turn down the heat to a whisper, pour over the vermouth, cover and cook gently until the fish is just done, about 5–7 minutes, depending on thickness. Now turn off the heat and let the fish relax for 3–4 minutes.

Transfer the fish to a serving dish or hot plates. Boil down the juices until syrupy, add a splash of vermouth and dribble over the fish. Surround with the hot purée and serve with rice.

Grilled fish with fennel, chilli and garlic

A splendid way of cooking whole fish from Leslie Forbes' *Table in Tuscany*. It was originally intended for fish cooked over an open fire but is very satisfactory cooked under an indoor grill.

4 whole fish such as bream, mullet or
  sardines (allow more if using
  sardines), cleaned, gutted and scaled
For the marinade
4oz (120g) fennel bulb and leaves,
  finely chopped
1 clove garlic, chopped

½ fresh hot chilli pepper
3 tbsp olive oil
1 tbsp white wine vinegar
1 tsp sea salt

Pound the marinade ingredients in a mortar to a roughish paste, adding a little more oil if necessary. Lay the fish in a gratin dish, spoon over the marinade and leave for 30–40 minutes, or longer, turning now and then. Grill in the same dish under a moderate heat until done, basting occasionally with the marinade.

Chicken with fennel, tomatoes and potatoes

Part of our annual holidays are spent self-catering in the Lake District, usually around early September. Half the garden goes too – tomatoes, cucumbers, beans, Swiss chard, onion, garlic, carrots, lettuce, beetroot, potatoes, courgettes, a big bunch of herbs, a basketful of gooseberries, and so on. One-pot dishes are the order of the day. This is one I always enjoy.

4 large chicken legs
1oz (30g) bacon, cut into tiny, neat
  dice
1 large bulb of fennel, sliced vertically
  into moderately thick chunks

1 glass each of white wine and chicken
  stock (or use all chicken stock)
1lb (450g) potatoes, peeled, parboiled
  for 7 minutes, and sliced thinly
8oz (225g) ripe tomatoes

Cut each chicken leg into two, slicing through the knee joint with a heavy knife. Take the largest frying pan you can find and dry fry the legs over a moderate heat until browned all over; let this take a good 15 minutes, turning them over now and then. Remove and pour off the surplus fat. Add the bacon and fennel and fry until beginning to brown. Put back the chicken. Deglaze with the wine, pour in the stock. Tuck the potatoes and tomatoes down the sides and in between, cramming them in where you can. Cover and simmer very gently for about 45 minutes, or until potatoes and chicken are tender. Baste occasionally with the juices. Serve from the same pan with crisp French beans and bread.

Fennel braised with cider

For this you need 1 large fat bulb per 2 servings. Trim the top, slice off the root and cut down the middle. Slice each half into 3 segments. Lay in a pan, making sure the fennel fits in a single layer. Pour over dry cider to come halfway up – about 5 fl oz (150ml) for each bulb. Dab with a little butter, cover and braise gently until the fennel is soft but not mushy. Remove to a gratin dish and boil down the juices to a few tablespoons. Enrich with ¼–½oz (7–15g) butter. Spoon over the fennel and grill until browned. Simple and delicious.

Horseradish

Horseradish is a neglected plant. It will grow almost anywhere, in a rich soil and a sunny position quickly becoming a rampant weed. Every gardener should have a clump, if only to experience how indifferent the bottled variety is.

It is a member of the wallflower family and can be found growing wild on waste ground in most parts of England and Wales, easily recognisable by its thin dock-like leaves and unmistakeable horseradish smell. It is a natural antibiotic, appetite stimulant and digestive – herbalists speak enthusiastically of its favourable influence on the liver; and a good source of vitamin C and minerals.

Horseradish is traditionally harvested in late October/November. This makes sound sense. Before then the flavour has not developed its full strength, and you may be surprised to find how mild it can be even in September. Its strength can also vary from one piece to another and from one season to another. At one time gardeners lavished great care on their horseradish in order to produce long fat straight roots. Nowadays, the usual practice is to plant it and leave it alone. This will do, but once the roots start crowding each other and become very forked, take the trouble to read what Vilmorin-Andrieux have to say on the subject, and replant in a bed of rich soil.

Horseradish should always be peeled and grated fresh. Because of the highly volatile nature of its essential oils, its searing pungency quickly diminishes and is completely lost in cooking. One or two of the very young leaves can be chopped and added to salads.

Horseradish is best when freshly dug, but will keep without drying out too much for 2–3 months. No point in making life difficult: dig deeply, pick out the largest, smoothest roots and discard the rest – horseradish is troublesome enough to clean, full of knobbly bits and protuberances. Either wrap in newspaper and keep somewhere cool, or scrub first, wrap in very slightly dampened kitchen paper, and store in a plastic bag in the salad drawer of the refrigerator.

Freshly made horseradish cream is a revelation. It is excellent with fish, particularly smoked fish, and with root vegetables such as potatoes, celeriac and beetroot. It discolours quickly, so mix with the sauce ingredients directly. If you want to temper its strength, make the sauce an hour or so before you use it; conversely, to appreciate the full sinus effect, grate it immediately prior to serving. Horseradish is rarely used in cooking. With some fish recipes, it is added to the poaching liquor where it will impart its flavour.

Avocado with apple, prawns and horseradish dressing

2 ripe avocados
2oz (60g) best peeled prawns
½ red eating apple, cored and cut into
  tiny neat dice
lemon juice

For the dressing
1 tbsp mayonnaise
2 tsp thick creamy yoghurt
2 tsp freshly grated horseradish
tiny sprigs of watercress or twists of
  lemon for decoration

Cut up the prawns roughly, mix with the apple and toss both in a little lemon juice. Make the dressing by mixing all the ingredients, sharpening with lemon juice to taste. Cut each avocado in half, lightly fill with the prawn and apple, spoon over the dressing, decorate and serve immediately.

Horseradish and apple sauce

Horseradish is indigenous to eastern Europe and has been used extensively there since the Middle Ages. In Russia and the Baltic countries it is used to poach fish, with sometimes a bowl of freshly grated horseradish to accompany, and in Germany and Austria to flavour apple sauce to serve with beef, fish, pork or venison.

195

A simple and excellent sauce is easily made by cooking peeled and chopped apples with a couple of tablespoons of water and a squeeze of lemon juice until soft, adding a little sugar, and 1–2 tbsp freshly grated horseradish. The sauce can be enriched with butter or cream, though I think its clean taste is better without. For choice, and to strike the right sweet-sour note, use half cooking apples and half dessert apples such as Cox's; the former will cook to a pulp while the latter retain some of their texture.

This is a stylish way of presenting the sauce to accompany a roast: for each person bake a small eating apple until soft. Cut in half, scooping out the flesh carefully and discarding the pips and central woody bit. Mash the pulp, add grated horseradish to taste – 2–3 tsp should be about right; squeeze on some lemon juice and pile back into the half skin. Put a tiny blob of redcurrant jelly in the centre, and surround the roast with the stuffed apples.

Mashed potato with horseradish

Horseradish gives oomph to mashed potatoes. Mash them as usual with a little creamy milk. Off the heat, stir in 1 generous tbsp freshly grated horseradish to 1lb (450g) potatoes. The pungency fades but the flavour remains. Serve with salt beef, pork or sausages.

Cheese croûtes with horseradish

This is taken from Mr T. Layton's *Cheese and Cheese Cookery*, published in 1971. Use either bread fried in butter or slices of thin dry brown toast. In either case, remove the crusts first.

Mix together 1oz (30g) each of grated gruyère and parmesan with 1 tbsp cream and 2 tsp finely grated horseradish. Add a few drops of tarragon vinegar and a pinch of paprika. Pile onto fingers of fried bread or toast, put in a hot oven for 5 minutes until the cheese is hot and beginning to melt, and serve. If the oven isn't on, pop them under a grill, keeping them a good distance from the heat.

Horseradish dumplings

These are splendid small dumplings to serve with stews or braised pork chops.

2oz (60g) plain flour	1 heaped tbsp freshly grated
2oz (60g) grated suet or half butter, half suet	horseradish
	pinch of salt
2oz (60g) soft brown or white breadcrumbs	½ tsp baking powder
	beaten egg to bind

Stir all the ingredients together thoroughly, first sifting the baking powder with the flour, and mix with sufficient egg to make a firm dough. Using wetted hands, pinch off the dough into 12 portions and roll each into a ball. Poach in barely simmering salted water for 12–15 minutes; if you are unsure, do a trial run first. They should double in size and be light and cooked through. Drain and serve. If necessary, they will keep in the hot water for a few minutes without coming to any harm.

Oriental vegetables

Oriental vegetables have gained in popularity in recent years. As kitchen garden vegetables, they fit in well, coming mid autumn to early winter, adding variety to the usual run of cabbages and roots. This is the time I find them most useful in our pattern of seasonal eating. I have included those we grow regularly. In *The Salad Garden* Joy Larkcom gives a full account of these diverse and interesting vegetables, which I recommend as the best introduction to oriental vegetables as a whole.

Chinese cabbage

Chinese cabbage is also known as Pe-Tsai or Pekin cabbage. It is a popular vegetable in China and Japan and many kinds exist in both countries. Botanically, it is a relative of the turnip and rape family. There is no evidence that it was cultivated in ancient times and it probably evolved along the same lines as cabbage from varieties of rape seed, with gardeners gradually selecting those plants which led to large leaves and which formed a head. Though we are familiar with the long, loaf shaped, pale self-blanching form of Chinese cabbage, many are loose headed or ball shaped.

We first grew Chinese cabbage when we lived in Cleveland, and were immediately impressed. The early Chinese name, 'ox stomach' is a good one: it grew large and hearty and kept almost indefinitely in the salad drawer. Over the years it has become a regular autumn crop and, given a limited choice, the one I should say to grow in preference to others. It first attracted the attention of English and American gardeners in the 1880s and I have a feeling it is the most versatile of the oriental leafy vegetables, the one most suited to European tastes and meals, its mild flavour and juicy midribs making it excellent for salads as well as stir-fries.

Chinese cabbages are semi-tropical marsh plants and are remarkably fast growing. They mature naturally as the days get shorter, in late summer and autumn. In common with all plants which respond to day length for their development, sowing times are usually critical. If sown too early or checked in their growth, they tend to bolt. You will therefore need to experiment to find the best sowing time for your area. Modern F1 hybrids are recommended. These are less prone to bolting and much better suited to our climate. Compact bulbous conical varieties, such as China Pride, are the most successful. They form tight self-blanched hearts and are fatter, sweeter and crisper than the taller types, which tend to greener leaves, thinner and coarser midribs, and are more suited to being cooked than eaten raw.

Chinese cabbages need a fertile soil and dislike acid conditions. In China they are grown intensively in flooded furrow fields on raised beds, a formidable sight which rather reminds me of our own garden in the height of summer. They must be sown where they are to mature as they will not stand transplanting. Sow after the new potatoes have been lifted in the same bed, around mid-July, thinning the young plants to 12in (30cm) apart. They usually last until Christmas. A severe frost finishes them off, so bring them in in good time.

Garden Chinese cabbages are rarely blemish free. Slugs, in particular, love them. Peel away all damaged leaves, saving any usable fat midribs as a vegetable, and keeping the tender hearts to slice thinly in salads. If you need to, wash under running water, using a soft brush. Drain thoroughly, pat dry with a towel and store in plastic bags in the refrigerator. They keep admirably, lasting two months if necessary.

Though you can cook Chinese cabbage European style, I still find it makes much better eating stir-fried in the traditional way. It may also be braised or poached. In China, because of its ability to absorb flavours, it is often served beneath a highly flavoured meat sauce. In Japan it is popular pickled in salt, rice vinegar or rice bran, producing a kind of oriental sauerkraut, I imagine.

I use Chinese cabbage incessantly from November to January in all kinds of salads. The succulent crisp leaves can be shredded finely and scattered on top of a mixed salad or used more substantially in a variation on coleslaw. As one writer commented, it has a mild, zesty pungency which lettuce lacks.

Chinese leaf salad

This is the kind of salad I make in late autumn to serve mid-week with a leftover roast: shred some inner leaves of Chinese cabbage and mix with whatever lettuce leaves you have, also shredded. Add some diced green pepper, tomato, celery, yellow beetroot and mooli. Toss everything in a little mayonnaise let down with hot water. Set in a fringe of beetroot slices and serve.

Chinese leaf, walnut and Sharon fruit salad

Sharon fruit, a persimmon native to China and Japan, is a beautiful fruit, resembling a plummy, pulpy tomato. It is imported here from Israel, where it was developed in the Sharon valley, and is becoming a common sight in supermarkets especially towards the end of the year. It is a good partner for Chinese cabbage in salads. More often than not you will buy Sharon fruit hard and unripe; let them go as soft as you dare and they make much better eating.

4oz (120g) Chinese leaf
1–2 tbsp chopped walnuts
2 tbsp walnut oil
2 soft, ripe Sharon fruit
2 fresh dates, stoned and quartered

For the garnish
thinly sliced mooli
lettuce, chicory, lamb's lettuce

Unless you are using the small innermost leaves, cut the Chinese leaves down the middle longitudinally and then shred crosswise to give bite-sized pieces. Mix with the walnuts and walnut oil and divide between four plates. Cut each Sharon fruit in half, and slice each half into 4 segments. Arrange prettily in a star shape on top of the salad, with slivers of date in between. Tuck the mooli and the greenery round the edge and serve as a first course.

Chinese leaf, pomegranate and mustard seed salad

A colourful winter salad.

6–8oz (180–225g) Chinese leaf
1 pomegranate
1–2 tbsp mustard seed

2 tbsp grapeseed or vegetable oil
lemon juice (optional)

Shred the Chinese leaf and lightly mix with the pomegranate seeds, being careful to discard the yellow pith. Fry the mustard seeds in the oil until they pop (put on lid to stop the seeds from splattering everywhere). Pour over the salad and gently mix. Taste, adding a squeeze of lemon juice if it seems a good idea, and serve.

Basic stir-fried Chinese vegetables

This forms our regular Monday evening meal through autumn and early winter. It comprises a selection of Chinese leaves with other vegetables to give an appetising mixture of colours, textures and flavours, plus seasonings and aromatics such as ginger and garlic. Served with rice, a shredded omelette flavoured with sherry and spring onion, or chicken wings grilled with soy and sesame seeds, it turns into a Chinese meal of sorts.

This kind of cooking is better judged by eye and feel than precise quantities and instructions. Because of the bulk, a wok is really essential to ensure the vegetables cook quickly and evenly. Have everything prepared, including the sauce, and ready to go. I lay the thinly sliced vegetables and aromatics out in separate bundles on large plates, and the green leaves in a large plastic bowl. The greens will wilt down to about a third of their original bulk – make sure you prepare enough.

For the aromatics
1 tsp chopped ginger
1 small fresh chilli, deseeded and
  chopped
3–4 spring onions
1–2 dried mushrooms (optional)
2 tbsp vegetable oil/light sesame seed
  oil/grapeseed oil
For the vegetables
Prepare a selection from carrot, celery,
  mooli radish, beansprouts, fresh
  mushrooms, frozen peas, shredded
  sprouts, cauliflower florets, leek,
  red/green pepper, plus Chinese
  leaves – Chinese cabbage, mizuna,
  Pak, Choi; green cabbage, Swiss
  chard, all shredded.

Sauce 1
1 tbsp each soy sauce and sherry
1 tsp sugar
1–2 tsp cornflour
3–4 tbsp chicken stock or water
Sauce 2
2 tbsp soy sauce
1 tbsp plum sauce
1–2 tsp cornflour
3–4 tbsp chicken stock or water

First amalgamate the ingredients of the sauce of your choice. Heat the wok, add the oil, swirl it round to coat, and stir-fry the aromatics for 30 seconds. Next add the crunchy vegetables and cook for 1 minute. Follow with the leafy greens, mushrooms and frozen peas. There should be a loud hiss, which the Cantonese call 'wok hay', and the volume of which, they believe, is directly proportional to the quality of the finished dish. Stir-fry vigorously until the vegetables have just wilted, pour in the sauce and continue to stir-fry until the vegetables are well coated. Tip into a serving dish and serve immediately.

For a hotter version, add a few drops of chili sauce; if plum sauce is not available, substitute with hoisin sauce.

Pak Choi

Pak Choi is a member of the turnip family and in China many forms are known. The variety commonly on sale here and the ones found in seed catalogues are those with long white mid-ribs which curve and flatten elegantly at the base like Chinese spoons, and which have broad light or dark green leaves. As a cooked vegetable, it is equally as good, if not preferable to Chinese cabbage. Pak Choi is slightly peppery when raw, but mild and succulent when cooked, keeping its crispness well. It is an easy plant to grow but will not stand hard frosts. Cultivate as for mizuna; harvest and store as for Chinese cabbage – Pak Choi can also be sown and pulled when young throughout the summer. It can be stir-fried or braised and is good either on its own or mixed with other Chinese vegetables.

Pak Choi braised with mushrooms

4 Chinese dried mushrooms
3–4 spring onions/Japanese bunching
  onions, chopped
8–12oz (225–340g) Pak Choi, sliced
4oz (120g) fresh mushrooms
2 tbsps grapeseed or vegetable oil

For the sauce
2 tbs each of soy sauce and sherry
1 tsp sugar
1 tsp cornflour

Cook the dried mushrooms in a little water for a few minutes until soft. Chop and reserve the water. Soften the spring onions in the oil, turn up the heat and stir-fry the Pak Choi for a couple of minutes. Add the dried and fresh mushrooms and continue to cook until the vegetables have wilted.

Meanwhile, mix the sauce ingredients with the reserved mushroom liquor. Tip into the pan, stir, cover and cook for another 3–4 minutes, and serve.

Mizuna

Mizuna is a highly decorative plant, one which would not look out of place in the flower border, with its pencil slim white mid-ribs and dark green jagged leaves cascading out from the centre. It is a valuable cut-and-come plant, peppery when raw, and mild, slightly sharp when cooked. The young leaves, 1–4in (2.5–10cm) tall can be used in winter salads.

One of the many leaf mustards, mizuna is hardier than Chinese cabbage, though will not stand severe frosts and needs protection to survive in reasonable condition through the winter. They are easy plants to grow. Sow the seeds in early August for autumn and winter use, thinning the young plants to 9in (23cm) apart. Spring sown plants for summer use are more delicate but are likely to run to seed and need to be cut regularly.

Mizuna is generally picked when required. Cut from the base with a sharp knife, taking as much as you need, leaving the plant to resprout. Pick over and discard any rotten or damaged leaves, setting aside the smallest leaves for salads. Wrap loosely in plastic bags and store in the refrigerator until needed. To clean, soak it first in a large bowl of cold water, then quickly rinse under the tap. Gather it up in your hands and shake dry.

Save for the tender leaves, Mizuna should be cooked. It can be lightly steamed, though I find stir-frying, for 1–3 minutes, coarsely shredded, in a mixed stir-fry with other Chinese vegetables suits it best.

Spicy fried Mizuna

This recipe is amended slightly from the *Complete Book of Vegetables*, published in 1986. Use either a large frying pan or a wok.

2–4oz (60–120g) lean minced beef or lamb
1 small onion, finely chopped
2 tsp curry powder

2 cloves of garlic, chopped
1lb (450g) mizuna, washed and coarsely chopped.
2 tbs oil

Gently soften the onion in the oil. Add the curry powder, stir around to release the aroma, then add the minced meat and garlic. Fry for another 5 minutes or so, until the meat is cooked. Add the greens and continue to cook, stirring and turning constantly until the greens have wilted but are still crisp.

Check the seasoning – I find a dash of soy sauce helps, and serve immediately. *Variation:* use minced pork with 1 fresh chopped chilli and 1 tsp chilli sauce instead of the curry powder and garlic. Cook as before, adding 1 tsp of sugar with the mizuna. Sprinkle with soy sauce and serve.

Japanese bunching onions

The oriental name for these is Hikari Chang Fa and they have been the main garden onion in China and Japan since prehistoric times. They are similar to spring onions but grow straight like a leek. and are longer lasting. If you value a mild onion flavour, they are excellent.

Japanese bunching onions are, in fact, Japanese varieties of our own Welsh onion, *Allium fistulosum*, (whose name has nothing to do with Wales, but derives from the Anglo-Saxon *welise* and the German *welshe* meaning foreign). They are grown extensively throughout southeast Asia. The whole of the young plant may be used raw or cooked or the tops cut and the clump left to grow more side shoots. In Japan and Hong Kong they are often blanched. The variety most commonly available here is Ishikura. Sow the seed quite thickly early in spring, and leave to grow. Pull as required for summer and autumn use. They are not as hardy as spring or Welsh onions and will not stand severe frosts, rotting from the outside.

Use as you would spring onions. They soften quickly when cooked and are thus particularly useful in stir-fried dishes where an onion flavour is desirable but ordinary onions are both too harsh in texture and flavour.

Fragrant noodles

This recipe comes from *A Guide to Chinese Market Vegetables*, by Martha Dahlen and Karen Phillipps, published in 1980.

'Boil noodles in water with salt and a little oil. In a serving bowl, place finely shredded ginger and chopped spring onions (or Japanese or Welsh onions). Pour a little hot oil over these, and season the mixture with soy sauce. When the noodles are cooked, drain and toss them in the flavoured oil).

Try this. The heat mellows the rawness of the onions and ginger and does indeed produce a fragrant dish. A few cooked peas can be added.

Chinese chives see p. 29.

Chinese and Japanese Winter Radish

Recent years have seen the introduction of Chinese and Japanese winter radishes to seed catalogues, both the more familiar white kind – mooli or daikon – and red and brown skinned varieties. All are much larger than summer radishes and may be round, cylindrical or oblong. Every gardener should try them.

For us the most successful have been the plump alabaster white varieties, such as Mino Early. These are splendid. In contrast to the red and brown skinned types, their flavour is consistently mild and succulent, though they are not as hardy.

All winter radishes are easy to grow. Sow in late July/early August, in soil that has not recently been manured, thinning the plants to 6–8in (15–20cm) apart, for autumn and early winter use. They grow fast, and once the root has begun to swell, fatten quickly. Save for slugs, nothing seems to find them of any interest. They can attain great weights, 3–5lb (1.35–2.25kg) being common, and in Japan some reach 10 times this. In the garden, weights of up to 1lb (450g) are more normal – even so, a dozen will be ample, and provide enough to pass on to curious friends.

Winter radishes can stand in the garden until the severe frosts come. Alternatively, they store extremely well and will last for several weeks without deterioration. Cut off the tops, wash them to remove the earth and store in the usual way either in the refrigerator or in a cold larder.

They make a valuable addition to winter salads, their juicy succulence being especially appreciated. The garden kind need peeling first. Slice, dice, shred, grate or make into paper-thin curls with a potato peeler and use as a garnish, part of an autumn hors d'oeuvre, or to add to mixed salads. They are very good in a vegetable stir-fry. In China they are used in soups and in some meat dishes, and the young seedlings are cooked as greens.

In Japan white winter radishes, daikon, are as common a vegetable as potatoes, and highly regarded as beneficial for the digestion. Grated raw and presented in little piles, they are served as a ubiquitous condiment to counteract the oiliness of deep-fried dishes, to accompany rice dishes, or to add to soups. Daikon pickle is the most common and popular of Japanese pickles.

Daikon, carrot and ginger salad

Mix equal quantities of grated white winter radish and carrot with a little finely grated ginger. Sprinkle with a good pinch of salt and slightly more of caster sugar. Mix well and let stand for 30 minutes or more to let the flavours mellow. Use as a salad or relish, heaped up in small mounds on the plate.

See also autumn and winter salads.

Peppers

Sweet peppers are tropical plants, native to Central and South America and the West Indies. They are one of the new wave vegetables that took root in the 60s and 70s in Britain, though they had long been popular in America and elsewhere — and were grown extensively by London market gardeners 150 years ago. What happened during the intervening years we do not know, for British peppers are a recent commercial venture. Thirty years ago peppers were classed as rare and unusual; today, every garden centre has them.

Peppers belong to the nightshade family, *Solanaceae*, as do their cooking partners aubergines and tomatoes. They were discovered by Columbus, around 1493, along with the other kind of capsicum, the chilli. Like all members of the group, they had been developed from the wild forms which are still collected today in parts of Latin America. Among the ancient Mexican Indian populations they were held in high esteem, second only to maize, and archaeological evidence for their domestication dates back to before 5000BC.

We are most familiar with the red, green and yellow bell peppers, but they also come in white, orange, purple and browny black. As a group they show a remarkable diversity of form and size, and vary in taste from bland to spicy-sweet through to sharp and vigorously hot, depending on their capsicin content. All are an excellent source of vitamin C, which increases as the fruit ripens.

Peppers thrive on warmth. They require a long growing season with no checks. Peppers are grown like tomatoes, though there is a strong case for buying in plants that have been raised in ideal conditions of warmth and light. The drawback is the small selection available. Bell Boy, the most common variety, will produce lots of peppers but their flavour can be disappointing.

Start seeds off in February/March, under heat, in individual pots, planting out in the greenhouse in May. Ours go next to the cucumbers in growbags with the bottoms cut out, three in each bag. Plant marigolds between the plants to deter whitefly, and keep well watered, especially once fruiting has begun. The stems are extremely brittle. Stake the plants to help support the stems as they become heavy with the weight of the fruit. Wind twine around and between the stems, trussing them up as best you can.

In a good year peppers continue to produce and ripen until well into October. How large they grow is difficult to determine but few are likely to compare with those bought from the supermarket. You can start picking the first peppers about the size of a tennis ball to encourage others to set and develop, though the flavour of these early peppers can be sharp and they are better cooked than raw. To pick them, twist the stalk gently or cut with a knife. Irrespective of size, they store extremely well. At the end of the season, pull up the plants, strip off the excess foliage and keep them somewhere cool, where they will stay in good condition, slowly ripening for several weeks to come.

Do not hurry to use your peppers green. Red or yellow peppers are far more interesting. Given time, the majority will ripen, even very small peppers, gradually deepening in colour. Examine the skin to see if there is a small patch showing the barest hint of colour change. If so, put these on one side, using the others first.

Home-grown peppers have a lovely shine to their skins and feel very firm to the touch. The skins are inclined to be slightly tougher and they are rarely as sweet, but they are cleaner in taste and crisper in texture than their commercial counterparts. Left on the plant until their flavour has developed, you will find them more concentrated than commercial peppers, both sharper and stronger and less watery, a desirable quality when it comes to making piperades and stews. Red peppers are more digestible than green, or so I find.

Chopped peppers add bite to late summer and autumn salads. Cooked, they lend a subtle sweetness to soups or vegetable dishes.

Roasting peppers

Roasting peppers in a hot oven or under the grill until the skins are blistered softens and sweetens them. Peppers prepared this way are delicious marinated in olive oil and garlic, and can be kept under olive oil for a couple of weeks in small glass jars. Use them as additions to salads or cooked dishes, or turn into a simple sauce for fish. A bonus is the oil, which becomes flavoured. The charring of the peppers helps to produce the characteristic flavour, but they can also be softened by leaving in a low oven for half an hour or so. To skin, put the peppers into plastic bags, tie the top and leave for a few minutes. The skins will then peel easily.

Prawn, pepper and coconut gazpacho

6oz (180g) finely grated fresh or desiccated coconut (see note below)
¾ pt (450ml) boiling water
4oz (120g) prawns, drained on kitchen paper and coarsely chopped

½ green pepper, de-seeded and finely chopped
1 ripe tomato, peeled, de-seeded and cut into tiny dice
1oz (30g) bulb fennel, finely chopped

Pour the boiling water over coconut and leave to cool. Whizz briefly in a blender and then sieve, pressing hard to extract all moisture from coconut. This is the coconut milk. Stir all the other ingredients into the milk. Serve well chilled in iced bowls. The coconut debris can be used in cakes.

Note: Freshly grated coconut makes far the best coconut milk. It's a fiddly operation but keeps indefinitely in the freezer and can be used from frozen. Drain the liquid from a coconut, then smash into pieces. Prise the white flesh away from outer shell using small very sharp knife – this is easier if you heat outside skin under the grill for a few minutes. Slice off the brown inner skin, rinse, pat dry, and blend the lumps in a food processor until finely chopped.

Piperade

Piperade is the famous dish of tomatoes, peppers and onions, cooked to a creamy mass with eggs. It is the national dish of the Pays Basque, served usually with a generous slice of fried Bayonne ham or long thin spicy loukenkas sausages. For preference the Basques use a long tapering green pepper known as *espellette*, grown around the village of the same name. Locals will tell you these are superior to bell peppers and far less watery. Recipes for piperade vary. Some use red peppers, others a mixture of red and green or green alone. Some include garlic, and some may be spiced with cayenne. The basic mixture, sauce basquaise, can also be incorporated in all kinds of meat dishes and soups, or eaten with grilled fish. It freezes admirably.

This version comes from the Hotel Arce in St Etienne de Baigorry.

For the sauce basquaise
2 large green peppers, de-seeded and coarsely chopped
1 large onion, chopped fairly finely
2 tbsp oil, or duck or goose fat

1–1¼lb (450g-570g) very ripe tomatoes, skinned and coarsely chopped.
For the piperade
6–7 eggs, lightly beaten

Begin by softening the peppers and onions in the oil over a gentle heat for about 15 minutes. Add the tomatoes and cook steadily for another 15–20 minutes. Season if necessary and set aside. This quantity makes about 1 pt (600ml) sauce.

Unless you have a really large frying pan, divide the egg and sauce into halves and make two separate piperades. Reheat the sauce, draining off the excess liquid. (This is important for the omelette to cook properly; the sauce should be chunky and not watery. Save the liquid for soups.) Add the hot sauce to the eggs, mix well and tip into a hot frying pan, preferably nonstick, lubricated with a little oil. Make an omelette in the usual way, keeping it runny in the centre. Fold, divide into two and serve on hot plates with slices of chorizo sausage, fried in their own fat, or bacon. Accompany with salad and bread.

Poulet à la basquaise

Brown jointed chicken pieces evenly in their own fat over a gentle heat until almost cooked through, turning them frequently. Give them a good 20–25 minutes. Drain off the fat. For four people, add about 1pt (600ml) sauce basquaise. Turn the chicken pieces in the sauce, cover, and cook until tender. Serve with rice and salad.

Bean salad à la basquaise

Take some cooked white beans. Season lightly with salt and moisten with sauce basquaise. Dribble over olive oil and finish with chopped parsley. Serve at room temperature.

Ginger, pepper and sweetcorn stir-fry

2 large corn on the cob, cooked
  (approx 8oz/225g stripped weight)
1–2 tbsp vegetable oil
1 fresh green chilli, de-seeded and
  finely chopped
2 tsp finely grated fresh ginger
2 green peppers, de-seeded and cut
  into very thin strips

2 tsp finely chopped preserved ginger
few drops of chilli/tabasco/hot pepper
  or soy sauce
2 spring onions, green and white part,
  finely chopped (optional)

Strip the corn from the cobs and set aside. Heat the oil, add the chilli and ginger and sizzle for 30 seconds. Add the green pepper. Stir-fry for 2 minutes over a high heat. Add the sweetcorn, toss to heat through. Pile onto a serving dish, mix in the spring onions if using, sprinkle lightly with a few drops of chosen sauce (go very easy on the hot variety) and serve immediately.

Note. Cooked prawns can also be added. Add with the sweetcorn and cook until heated through.

Peppers stuffed with hake and saffron rice

This comes from a Spanish tapas idea.

2 large green peppers
6oz (180g) de-skinned fillet of hake,
  cut into small dice
3oz (90g) undercooked long grain rice,
  preferably basmatti

1/8 tsp saffron
2 skinned and chopped ripe tomatoes
a little olive oil

Soften the peppers under a moderate grill or in a low oven. Cut in half, reserving the juice. Take out the pith and seeds, and arrange in a greased ovenproof dish which will just take the peppers comfortably. Gently mix the saffron into the rice until the rice is well coloured. Add the hake and tomato. Pile the filling into the peppers, pour over the reserved juice and finish with a teaspoon of olive oil dribbled over the top of each pepper. Pour a little olive oil into the dish plus a few tablespoons of water. Bake in a moderately hot oven, 190°C/375°F/gas mark 5 for 20–25 minutes, until the fish is cooked. Serve as a first course or with other vegetables.

Note: the moisture from the tomatoes and fish keeps the rice from drying out. If using whole peppers, proceed as above, slicing off the tops and removing the insides, increasing the quantity of stuffing to 8–10oz (225–285g) of hake, and the rest of the ingredients proportionally. Red peppers can also be used.

Preserved green peppers

I do not generally care for preserved vegetables of any kind, but a colleague, Thane

Prince, introduced me to this Italian way of preserving peppers under oil. The preliminary blanching in spiced vinegar and water gives them a slightly pickled quality, appropriate for winter eating.

4–6 *peppers, green or a mixture of*   3–6 *small dried chillies*
    green, red, and yellow, washed, de-   2–3 *cloves of garlic, peeled and sliced*
    seeded and sliced   ½ *tsp salt*
5 *fl oz (150ml) each vinegar and water*   *olive oil*

Put the peppers in a pan with all the ingredients except the oil; there should be sufficient liquid to just cover. Bring to the boil and cook for 2 minutes. Drain, and spread peppers and seasonings on kitchen paper until dry. Pack tightly into small sterilised jars. Add a few strips of sun-dried tomato if you like. Cover with olive oil and seal. Store somewhere cool and dark and keep for a month to mellow nicely before using. Use up within 3 months. The oil will be flavoured, and can be used in soups, salad dressings, and vegetable dishes.

Serve the peppers in a little dish, or use to scatter over mixed green salads, dribbling some of the oil over the leaves. Try them with lightly cooked florets of cauliflower and chopped olives, or with raspings of crisply fried bacon, duck skin, or croûtons. Another good idea is to use them in onion frittatas: gently cook sliced onions for 45 minutes or so in a covered pan with some of the oil and some strips of preserved pepper, adding if you like a little diced fresh red pepper. Cool slightly, beat in the eggs and make the frittata in the usual way. Serve cut into wedges with a few plain boiled potatoes to accompany.

Cauliflower florets can be preserved and used in salads in the same way.

Winter salad with celeriac and preserved green peppers

This is the kind of salad that can be put together for a first course using peppers preserved by the above method. Arrange whatever salad leaves are available in an attractive jumble on separate plates. If possible, include some bitter leaves, tearing them into pieces. Blanch thin strips of celeriac for 30 seconds, toss immediately in a little walnut oil and leave to cool. Prepare thin strips of preserved green pepper, a few thin slices of mushroom, some finely diced celery taken from the heart, and a few stones and chopped olives or segments of fresh orange. Scatter the ingredients over the leaves, dribbling over a little of the green pepper oil. Serve with toasted croûtes of walnut bread.

Swiss chard

Swiss chard is a strikingly handsome plant: magnificent dark green shiny crinkly leaves with thick cream midribs reach 2 ft (60cm) or taller. It has always been an uncommon vegetable in England. Why remains a mystery. 'The plant of this class the most deserving of culture in the cottage garden,' wrote J. C. Loudon, 'is the Swiss chard, which produces abundance of succulent and most nutritious foliage.'

The nomenclature can be confusing. Swiss chard, *beta vulgaris cicla*, is sister to spinach beet and belongs to the same family as spinach, good King Henry (wild spinach), orache (mountain spinach), samphire and fat hen. The ancients referred to it as *beta*, a name which stuck into the 18th century. Both this and spinach beet are early forms of beetroot, but are grown for their leaves, and in the case of Swiss chard, the thick central stems, commonly known as chards. Some authorities think Swiss chard is the oldest form of beet for it was being grown as far back as 700BC in the gardens of King Merodach-Baladan II of Babylonia. You may also come across it as silver or seakale beet, the brilliant red-ribbed variety ruby or rhubarb chard, and an orange one, rainbow chard.

Few plants are more rewarding; but there is a snag. Not all seeds available here produce thick midribs or perform as well as those available in America or France. The leaves can be coarse and the plant variable, sometimes prone to bolting. The American variety, Fordhook Giant, is excellent.

Sow the large round seeds ½in (1.25cm) deep in late April/early May, thinning the plants progressively to 12in (30cm) apart. This will give you Swiss chard from late summer onwards, the time it is generally most useful. If you want a June crop, raise the plants in pots in early March to produce particularly mild, tender tasting leaves. It may also be sown in late July/August in a cold frame to mature late autumn. This has been most successful in our own garden. The plants grow slowly but continuously throughout winter and keep producing new leaves until they run to seed sometime in late spring. A tall cold frame or greenhouse is needed. Remember that a very severe frost will kill the plants.

Half a dozen plants will be ample, and if well grown, three or four may easily suffice. It is a long cropping plant and succeeds best on a fertile soil – an occasional liquid feed over the summer is beneficial.

Young plants, taken as thinnings, about 12in (30cm) high, are a delicacy. Otherwise, do not start picking until the plant is mature (two months). Pick as required, taking the choicest leaves, a few from each plant, breaking or cutting them evenly at the base. This is the best plan for normal domestic use, but you will find Swiss chard a vigorous grower. If you need to contain the plant, or want large quantities of leaves, the plants can be stripped of all but a few inner leaves and will grow again. There is usually no need to store Swiss chard. When the weather turns very cold, protect with cloches. If you want to keep it for a few days, separate ribs and leaf, wrap in a plastic bag, ensuring a tight seal (this helps to prevent wilting) and keep in the refrigerator or somewhere cool.

In Swiss chard you get two vegetables for the price of one. The thick midribs, which many favour, can be steamed or lightly cooked and then finished with creamy embellishments or gratinéed. Remove the papery stringy outer skin with a vegetable knife before you cook them. I find them rather insipid on their own, preferring in general to use them in conjunction with the leaves, or finished with butter or a fruity olive oil.

The leaves are a different matter. Their flavour is that of coarse spinach, less sharp perhaps, and not as delicate (except in early summer). They are invaluable as an addition to soups, pâtés and any number of stuffings or pies where their resilient texture stands up far better than spinach. They are excellent in frittatas, or in stir-fried vegetables, and quite the best green for autumn minestras, bean soups and pasta dishes.

Wash the leaves if necessary, cut away any blemished parts and peel the chards. Unless the dish calls for both chard and leaf, it is usual to separate the two and cook them independently. Slice off the chard, then cut out the white vein running up the centre of the leaf. If you are serving it as a vegetable, allow 4–6oz (120–180g) trimmed weight of chards and the same of leaves per serving. This will seem an enormous bulk of leaves, but it cooks down to a small handful.

Leaves and chards may be blanched or cooked by the conservative method in a little water in a covered pan, allowing 4–5 minutes for the leaves and 5–8 for the chards. For a sizeable quantity, blanching is easier. Shred the leaves and give them 1–2 minutes in a large pan of boiling water until soft, cooking them in batches. The chards can be cut into lengths and will need 3–4 minutes. Swiss chard freezes well – a useful ploy when the supply of leaves outstrips demand. Use the method given on p. 21 following the blanching times above.

Recipes for Swiss chard are interchangeable with those for leef beet.

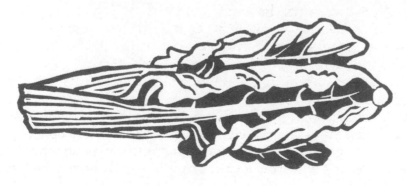

Garden minestra

From mid-August through to October, most days I will make soup for lunch, a thick minestra, using whatever vegetables are to hand, with flavourings such as garlic, sage, thyme, bay leaves, parsley, a little leftover tomato sauce, chopped tomatoes or tomato purée. Shredded Swiss chard or beet leaves and a few peas when available are added at the end. Some days I add pasta. At other times, a few cooked beans or lentils go into the soup. Pesto or fresh parsley is stirred in just before serving. We eat it with bread and a jug of green olive oil, dribbling it over the soup as a final enrichment.

This is a true gardener's soup, the kind you cannot find in cookbooks. It is made instinctively, not to rules or recipes and depends for its success on nothing more than good fresh vegetables. Quantities are not important; aim instead for a variety of vegetables. Follow the general method, and the soup will always turn out well.

Base

*Onion, carrots, celery, plus a selection
from courgette/marrow/pumpkin;
leeks; tomatoes; chard stems; green
pepper; cauliflower; cabbage;
potatoes; green beans; broad beans*
Additional ingredients
*cooked white beans; uncooked lentils;
pasta*

To finish
*a) shredded Swiss chard leaves; fresh
peas; chopped sugar snap peas*
b) pesto/chopped parsely
olive oil

Slice, chop or dice the vegetables as appropriate. Sweat the vegetables and garlic if used in 2–3 tbsp olive oil in a covered pan for 5–10 minutes. Add chosen seasonings, any pulses, and enough water to cover. Simmer with the lid on for 30–35 minutes, adding pasta 3–5 minutes before the end. Add shredded Swiss chard and peas and cook for 2–3 minutes until just done. Stir in pesto if liked and adjust the consistency if necessary with extra water. The soup should be thick with vegetables. Serve in large soup bowls and hand olive oil separately.

Swiss chard and black olive tart

For the pastry
3oz (90g) plain flour
1oz (30g) fine oatmeal
2oz (60g) polyunsaturated margarine,
  or half lard, half margarine
water or beaten egg to bind
For the filling
8oz (225g) Swiss chard, leaves and
  stalks, washed

4 spring onions, chopped
knob of butter for frying
2 large eggs
3–4 tbsp thick creamy yoghurt
1oz (30g) black olives, stoned and
  finely chopped
½–1oz (15g–30g) finely grated
  parmesan

Make the pastry in the usual way. Line a 7in (18cm) flan tin and bake blind in a hot oven, 200°C/400°F/gas mark 6, for 20 minutes. Meanwhile, blanch the leaves and chards separately, for 2 and 4 minutes respectively. Drain and press well. Chop finely, either by hand or in a food processor. Soften the onion in the butter, add the Swiss chard, raise the heat a little and cook for a few minutes, stirring, to dry out any excess moisture. Cool. Beat the eggs and yoghurt and mix with the Swiss chard and the olives. Pour into the flan case, sprinkling parmesan on top. Bake in a moderately hot oven, 190°C/375°F/gas mark 5, for about 25 minutes until firm. Serve immediately with salads and potatoes. Serves 3–4

Swiss chard and parmesan crumble

1–1¼lb (450–570g) tender Swiss
  chard, washed
5fl oz (150ml) single cream
2–3fl oz (60–90ml) water

1 clove of garlic, crushed
1oz (30g) parmesan or pecorino cheese
1oz (30g) fine dry breadcrumbs,
  brown or white

Prepare the Swiss chard in the usual way. Simmer the cream, water and garlic in a small pan until reduced by half. Meanwhile, cook the chard. Shred the leaves and blanch until tender, 1–2 minutes. Drain well, pressing out the excess moisture, and place in the bottom of a shallow gratin dish. Chop the chards into pieces and blanch until tender, 3–4 minutes. Drain, and arrange on top of the leaves. Remove the garlic if you want and pour over the cream – there should be just enough to moisten. Scatter the cheese over the top, followed by the breadcrumbs. Slip under a moderately hot grill until the top is crisp and the chards heated through. Serve immediately.

Midribs persillade

Peel and cut the midribs into 3–4in (7.5–10cm) lengths and blanch in boiling water until just soft, 3–4 minutes. Finely chop a carrot and 1–2 shallots and soften in a little olive oil. Mix with the chards and arrange in a shallow dish. Make a persillade with garlic, a handful of parsley and little finely grated lemon peel. Scatter on top. Add a layer of fine breadcrumbs, dribble over olive oil or dab with butter and bake at 190°C/375°F/gas mark 5 for about 40 minutes, or until the surface is crisp and browned.

Potato soup with Swiss chard

8oz (225g) peeled and diced potato
1 small chopped onion
¾pt (450ml) water

To finish
2–3oz (60–90g) Swiss chard leaves
2oz (60g) bacon or continental
   sausage, cut into neat strips

Simmer the potatoes and onion in the water until soft, about 20 minutes. Purée in a blender or food processor until smooth. Meanwhile, roll up the Swiss chard leaves like cigars and shred as finely as you can, slicing downwards with a serrated knife. In a small pan, frizzle the bacon or sausage in its own fat. Add the Swiss chard to the potato broth and cook for 1–2 minutes. Half the beauty of the soup is its bright green bite, so don't be tempted to cook the Swiss chard longer. Adjust the consistency if necessary with extra water. Ladle into soup bowls. Distribute the bacon and its fat evenly between the bowls and serve immediately with a jug of your best olive oil, to be stirred into the soup at the table.

The potato and onion broth is worth making in quantity and storing in the freezer, to form the basis of many simple garden soups.

Swiss chard and mint filo pastry

4 sheets filo pastry
1lb (450g) Swiss chard (leaves only),
   coarsely chopped
2 large eggs, beaten

4oz (120g) mild crumbly cheese such
   as Wensleydale or Lancashire
1 tbsp finely chopped mint
olive oil for brushing

Oil an 8in (20cm) shallow dish or flan tin and lay the filo pastry over to form a base. Trim away the surplus, leaving a 4in (10cm) rim. Blanch the leaves for 3–4 minutes. Drain, press out the excess moisture and chop finely in a food processor if possible. Mix with the rest of the ingredients and spoon into the pie base, smoothing it out evenly. Cut the edges of the filo pastry at 2in (5cm) intervals back to the rim of the flan case and fold over towards the middle, overlapping the strips neatly to form the top of the pie. Brush with olive oil and bake in a hot oven, 200°C/400°F/gas mark 6, until the top is brown and crisp. Allow to cool a little and serve warm with salads and boiled or jacket potatoes.

Swiss chard and rice torta

Vegetable pies made without pastry are a feature of Italian regional cooking – see also Scarpaccia (p. 99). This recipe is adapted from Marcella Hazan's *Marcell's Italian Kitchen*, published in 1986.

3oz (90g) rice, preferably arborio
12oz (340g) Swiss chard
1 medium onion, finely chopped
olive oil for frying
3 large eggs

1½–2oz (45–60g) finely grated
* parmesan or pecorino*
freshly grated nutmeg
1½–2oz (45–60g) lightly toasted fine
* breadcrumbs*

Cover the rice with water, bring to the boil in a lidded pan, cook 3–4 minutes and turn off the heat. Allow to cool. Prepare the Swiss chard in the usual way and cook in a little water, giving the midribs about 5 minutes and the leaves 2–3 minutes. Drain, squeeze out the excess moisture and chop either by hand or in a food processor. Cool.

Sweat the onion in a little olive oil. Drain the rice. In a bowl, mix the Swiss chard, rice, onion, eggs and half the cheese, seasoning generously with nutmeg. Oil a shallow ovenproof dish and pour in the mixture – it should be about 1in (2.5cm) deep, so do not choose too large a dish. Mix the breadcrumbs with the rest of the cheese and scatter in an even layer over the surface. Dribble olive oil over the top, or dot with butter, and bake in a moderately hot oven, 190°C/375°F/, gas mark 5, for 15–20 minutes until the pie is well puffed and crisp. Cool a little before serving.

Chard, pork and sorrel terrine

The leaves of Swiss chard are admirable in any terrine – use your usual recipe and substitute up to half the meat with blanched chopped leaves. For this recipe, buy decent Cumberland sausages, the kind which are made fresh daily from minced pork and spices.

8oz (225g) Swiss chard leaves, coarsely
* shredded*
2oz (60g) sorrel leaves, midribs
* removed*

8oz (225g) Cumberland sausages,
* removed from their casing*
2 tbsp chopped parsley
1 egg

Blanch the Swiss chard leaves in boiling water for 3–4 minutes. Drain, press well to expel the excess moisture and chop finely by hand. Cook the sorrel briefly in a little water. Squeeze out the excess moisture and chop. Mix everything together in a bowl, beating well. Transfer to an oiled terrine, smooth out the surface. Sit the terrine in another dish containing water to come halfway up the side, and bake in a moderately hot oven, 190°C/375°F/gas mark 5, until the terrine has shrunk away from the sides and the juices run clear, about 45–50 minutes. Serves 4–6.
Note Chopped liver, about 4oz (120g) can be added, with the rest of the ingredients.

Swiss chard, olive oil and sun-dried tomatoes

Buy sun-dried tomatoes preserved in salt rather than under oil. They are sweeter and better flavoured.

Separate the chards from the leaves and blanch separately until just tender. Chop the ribs into lengths. In a separate frying pan, melt a little olive oil and gently fry 1–2 chopped cloves of garlic. Add the chopped chard ribs together with 1–2 chopped fresh tomatoes and 1–2 dried tomatoes cut into little strips. Cook everything together, turning frequently for a few minutes.

Meanwhile, shred the leaves and cook for 4–5 minutes in a covered pan with a little water until wilted. Drain and lay in the bottom of a serving dish. Top with the tomato mixture and serve.

A variation I sometimes make is to omit the garlic and fresh tomato but include a small amount of very finely grated carrot, which gives the dish a pleasant but unobtrusive sweetness.

Swede

The swede was domesticated only a few hundred years ago. It crosses readily with turnips and one guess is that it may have originated in medieval gardens where turnips and kale grew side by side. It was first recorded in Europe in 1620 by the Swiss botanist Casper Bauhin, and introduced here only in the late 1770s. It came to us – of course – from Sweden; hence its name. Its other name, rutabaga, is a corruption of the Swedish dialect term *rota bagge*, red bags, which it could be said to resemble. The scars round its neck, which distinguish it from turnips, are leaf scars, showing that swede is made up partly of the swollen base of the stem.

Do not dismiss swede out of hand – garden swede can be good. Grow a short row and do not let them get too big. A slight frost improves them, but a severe frost damages them irreparably. The trick is in getting them to mature at the right time, in autumn. Avoid sowing them too early; mid-June is soon enough, thinning progressively to 9in (23cm) apart. Pull when required. If they show signs of damage, pull them up in late winter and store somewhere cool – there is no need to be fussy about swedes.

The best swedes, picked during autumn after a slight frost, are sweet. As winter progresses they become ranker in flavour. Their pale yellow orange colour intensifies when cooked. Peel then slice or cube them and cook gently in a covered pan in a little water. Watch they do not cook to a mush – 7–10 minutes should be ample. Leave them plain or mash with a potato masher, incorporating the cooking liquor. They can also be mashed with potato or sometimes carrot. A knob of butter or a little cream improves them. For a change, include a couple of cloves of garlic in the cooking water and mash these with the swede. If you are cooking them with carrot, try tucking a sprig of rosemary in with the vegetables.

Another way: dice and blanch for 2–3 minutes in boiling water. Finish in a pan with butter, until nicely browned, adding, if you like, a few roasted and pounded allspice berries, or some shreds of fresh ginger towards the end.

Swede shoots

'The other day my landlady served me with a delicious vegetable. It looked like very young and tender asparagus in the dish, but peach colour instead of pale green, and it had rather a strong smell. I was quite at a loss to identify it by colour and smell except that it reminded me of walking past a root field. Its taste was not unlike parsnips but not nearly so sweet and it melted in the mouth. It was swede shoots. My shepherd landlord told me he picked them off the sprouting roots when he unearthed the bury. They keep their delicate orange colour till they reach the light. They can only be had just at this time of year (April) and round here the gentry consider them a great delicacy. "Us poor folk don't trouble about 'em," were his words.'

Florence White, *Good Things in England*, 1932

'Some people like the tall soft sprouts of the swede that grow after it has been lifted and stored. These are boiled and served with butter like asparagus'.

Dorothy Hartley, *Food in England*, 1954

I had intended to include these two quotes for their curiosity value, never having stored swede long enough to have large enough shoots to try. Imagine my delight then, when I received the following note from cookery writer Caroline Conran: 'We store our swedes and turnips in peat, and find that they send up pale yellow shoots which are delicate and delicious, if not exactly abundant. They are good mixed with cabbage, chard and/or outside bitter leaves of Sugar loaf chicory, all blanched and fried in oil with garlic.'

Lentil, root vegetable and game broth

Stock made from game can transform ordinary pottage made from a few root vegetables and pulses. The small dark brown lentils or the slate green Puy lentils are best. Sweat a little chopped onion or leek in a little oil, butter or bacon fat with some swede and parsnip cut into very small regular dice. Add lentils, game stock or half stock and half water, a bay leaf, and perhaps a sprig of thyme. Simmer until the lentils are soft. Remove the herbs and adjust the consistency. Check for seasoning and serve.

Swede with sesame seeds and soy

Dice and blanch your swede for 2–3 minutes in boiling water. They should be almost done. Drain, heat a little vegetable oil or light sesame seed oil in a pan, add the swede, sprinkle generously with sesame seeds and toss to coat. Cook for a few munutes over a gentle heat. Serve sprinkled with a few drops of soy.

Swede pot

Root vegetables thinly sliced and baked gently in the oven are a popular side dish in my local restaurant, Weavers at Haworth, and one I am fond of. It's a straightforward homely dish, which doesn't mind keeping if need be and works for any root vegetable (parsnips are especially good). Seasonings can be altered to suit, or meat stock employed instead of cream and water. This is the swede variation.

1lb (450g) prepared swede
1–2 sliced ripe tomatoes

good pinch of chopped thyme
  (optional)
5fl oz (150ml) cream and water mixed

Slice the swede wafer thin using the slicing blade of a food processor or a mandolin. Pile in layers in a deepish dish, slipping in the odd slice of tomato here and there. Stir the thyme into the cream and water mixture and pour over. The liquid should come to the top of the vegetables – add extra if necessary. Cover and bake in a moderate oven, 180°C/350°F/gas mark 4, for 1–1½ hours until the vegetables are meltingly soft and most of the liquid has been absorbed. Serve from the same dish.

WINTER

December, January, February

From our standpoint, winter is the least pleasurable of the seasons. For the most part, our only contact with the garden is to pick and fetch the vegetables, and to clear away the debris of dying foliage – good garden husbandry and a token gesture of respect to a garden temporarily abandoned for the warmth of the fireside.

Seed catalogues are a major preoccupation during January. Their arrival causes a great deal of animated discussion and weighty deliberation. New vegetables seem to appear every year. Different varieties to suit particular soils and conditions hold out promises of improved flavour and quality. The Victorian gardening journalist William Robinson complained bitterly that the mania for size among market gardeners was leading to the rapid deterioration of some of the best varieties. He asserted that flavour was of paramount importance. He also wrote that a common cause of failure in the vegetable garden was too much experimental planting at the expense of things we know and like; his argument rings uncomfortably true today.

While we plan for the year ahead, the garden fends for itself. During the next few months, leeks, brassicas, winter salads and root crops sustain us as they have sustained kitchen gardeners for centuries. The key to a good choice of crops in winter is planning. In small gardens this means hard decisions and some sacrifices, for space which could grow summer crops has to be set aside for winter vegetables. On most deep beds you can get two crops a year, each bed ideally designed to hold crops which mature at approximately the same time. This ensures that the bed can be cleared and more crops follow on. Timing and synchronisation, together with an understanding of the

219

particular requirements of certain groups of vegetables, provide the framework for crop planning. Usually, cropping (cycles) are organised from spring onwards, but if you are concerned to have fresh vegetables throughout the year, a better method we find is to plan what you aim to eat from the garden in November and through the winter, and then work backwards, fitting summer crops into what will be your winter cropping pattern. In practice you will find it almost impossible to achieve technically correct crop rotation in a small garden, but try and organise your cropping to leave at least a year's gap between crops of similar type from the same piece of land or bed.

One of the most difficult aspects of winter gardening is getting crops to mature at the right time. It is always a precarious balance between judgment and luck with the weather. With very few exceptions, crops do not grow over winter, but must either stand or be stored. This means they must reach maturity before the frosts arrive, but not so soon that they are ready too early. Wastage can be a problem particularly once the bad weather sets in. How well crops stand depends on the severity of the season, if they matured at the right time and, in wet weather, how many slugs are lurking in the cabbage patch. In any event, collecting vegetables for the table in winter is rarely a pleasure. As the daily hazards of wind, rain, frost or snow become commonplace, the whole exercise takes on the trappings of a major expedition; sensible cooks get the operation over with as quickly as they can.

WINTER SALADS

A salad made from winter garden stuff is an uplifting experience. In our garden, winter salads centre on endives while they last and chicories, with corn salad, land cress, tiny shoots of Japanese mizuna, chervil, bitter cress, claytonia and perhaps rocket, plus a few small winter lettuces. It is easier, I find, to bring in a batch of each at a time. This then gives me enough material to make three or four little salads over the next few days. Most of the leaves will have some damage and need very careful picking over, before being stored in the salad drawer of the refrigerator. Allow them to thaw first, slowly if necessary. If you can, do not wash until you come to prepare the salad. Where it is necessary, rinse whole plants under the tap, shaking vigorously to expel as much of the water as possible, finally patting dry as best you can. Individual leaves should be washed and dried in a salad spinner.

Meals throughout autumn and winter begin either with soup or a salad hors d'oeuvre. This is always the dish which seems to invite the most comment when people visit, and which they seem to enjoy best. Nothing is simpler or more amply repays the small amount of effort involved.

Aim to provide a selection of 5–6 different vegetables with contrasting textures and colours, some raw, some cooked, padding them out with other savoury ingredients at hand, and to have two or three in a dressing of some kind, though not swamped by it. Make sure the vegetables are cut into thin strips or small dice or grated very finely. To assemble, choose large plates, arranging tiny quantities of each vegetable in an orderly clockwise fashion, with one in the centre. Half the appeal of this dish is not to crowd the plate, or for the hors d'oeuvre to be in any way filling. Think of it more as a colourful and appetising stimulant, paving the way for the main course to follow.

Almost every entry in the book will provide a salad or cooked dish which can be used for autumn and winter hors d'oeuvre. Small amounts of leftover dishes, such as celeriac niçoise, which you might normally throw out, are admirable used in this way.

VEGETABLES

Brussels sprouts

Brussels sprouts are the youngest member of the cabbage tribe. Though there is mention of a 'sproq' in the literature of 13th-century Belgium, the modern form of sprout is believed to have appeared around 1750. By the early 1800s it had reached Britain and France and quickly became popular. English market gardeners in Bedfordshire, where much of the commercial crop is still centred, soon excelled in growing the best brussels sprouts, establishing them conclusively as an English vegetable. There are times when we seem to eat nothing else. A puzzled American, visiting this country for the first time, enquired if we always ate them. He had been in England for a week and had eaten no other greens.

For the gardener, sprouts can be a rewarding vegetable, but they are more difficult than many. Too much nitrogen and they grow too lush, forming leaves at the expense of buttons which then blow apart; too little and the plants make insufficient growth, again resulting in poor buttons. They are said not to succeed on deep beds, though ours succeed magnificently. If you ask my husband the secret of his success he will say he believes it lies in staking each plant firmly with a good strong stake throughout its life.

The seed should be sown in seedtrays in early April. The main problem for small gardens is the space they occupy and the length of their growing season. They need 18–24in (45–60cm) either way, which means only two sprouts per row on a 4ft (1.2m) bed. Variety is particularly important. Modern hybrids form buttons more readily than their traditional counterparts, and are by far the best kind to grow. We grow Fortress and Citadel, both late varieties, aiming for sprouts late November through to the end of February.

Only a gardener appreciates how good a freshly picked sprout is. In recent years, varieties have been bred to mature earlier and earlier so that we now buy sprouts from August onwards. Yet everything about sprouts points to winter enjoyment. As the cold weather sets in, they become sweeter and better flavoured – a simple observation any gardener can make, and due to the natural charges within the tissues: it is nonsense to eat them in August.

Sprouts continue to grow slowly well into winter and are generally harvested when required. It is when the time comes to pick them in bad weather that you value them most. Even from frozen (wear gloves or your fingers will freeze), they can be collected effortlessly. Pick from the bottom upwards, choosing the largest sprouts first.

Towards the end of season, as the weather warms, sprouts deteriorate and their flavour is not appealing. Try to use them before this happens. The sprout tops, when you pick them, can be cooked and served as a green vegetable.

Sprouts do not store well. They keep for a few days somewhere cold, but are better used fresh. Frozen sprouts picked in the morning for the evening's dinner will need to be left in the warmth of the living room to thaw out in time. Well grown sprouts are generally clean. Damaged or blown sprouts can be used for soups, stir-fries or in vegetable stews.

Brussels sprouts are a difficult customer to cook. You have, in effect, a miniature tightly packed cabbage, and the problem is how to ensure that the inside is cooked to a desirable nuttiness without reducing the outside layer to pap. Blanching produces too watery a result. Steaming takes comparatively long (9–10 minutes). Cook them by the conservative method using ½in (1.25cm) boiling water and a large frying pan which will hold the sprouts in a single layer. Choose even sized sprouts. Cover and boil hard, removing the lid after 2–3 minutes, so you can keep an eye on the water level. Test with the point of a knife which should just show a slight resistance as you push it into the centre. 4–5 minutes is generally time enough for small and medium sprouts. Cut larger sprouts in half, or make a deep cut in the base.

Sprouts should be served immediately. Like all brassicas, they are not a vegetable to be kept waiting even if this means leaving the table and attending to their cooking. If you serve them in a covered container, remember they soon lose their bright green colour.

On the whole a decent sprout is best on its own, or with some kind of crisp addition: fried breadcrumbs, frizzled bacon, lightly toasted almond flakes. Try some of the other savoury/spicy mixtures given below. Brussels sprouts can also be shredded and treated as a stir-fry.

Stir-fried brussels sprouts with apple and ginger

This is a useful treatment for large sprouts or the blown kind, which are always difficult to get exactly right. Taking a serrated knife, shred – not grate – the sprouts finely. Heat 1–2 tbsp vegetable oil or light sesame seed oil in a frying pan and stir-fry over a high heat with some finely chopped fresh ginger and a peeled and cored sweet apple cut into small neat dice, for 2–3 minutes. Season with a few drops of soy sauce and serve. Ideally, use equal amounts of apple and sprouts, and don't be overcautious with the ginger – a generous tablespoon should be about right for four people.

Variations Brussels sprouts can be similarly combined with chopped hazelnuts and diced fresh pineapple to accompany duck or pheasant or with shavings of lemon rind, chopped walnuts and walnut oil.

Simple ways with brussels sprouts

Towards the end of the season, when they have lost their new nuttiness and the flavour is beginning to pall, brussels sprouts are better enlivened with a few aromatics. The procedure is simple. Melt 1–2 tbsp oil or fat and briefly fry a few aromatic spices or other tit-bits. Add the freshly cooked sprouts, toss for a couple of minutes to allow them to colour and absorb the flavours and serve. Simple and effective.

Brussels sprouts with cumin and mustard seed

Sizzle 1 tsp lightly toasted and pounded cumin seeds with 1 generous tbsp black mustard seeds in 1–2 tbsp vegetable oil for 30–60 seconds. Add the sprouts and toss for 2–3 minutes. Sprinkle with salt and serve, not forgetting to scrape any remaining spices out of the pan. Try this too with ground coriander and chopped cashew nuts.

Brussels sprouts with bacon and vinegar

Frizzle neat strips of fatty bacon until crisp and well browned in their own fat (add a few bacon rinds if you like). Pour in 2 tbsp good wine vinegar and let it evaporate. Toss in the cooked sprouts and serve.

Brussels sprouts with coconut cream

Shave a small amount of coconut cream into a frying pan and warm through until it has melted. Toss in some freshly cooked sprouts, transfer to a serving dish and finish with a scattering of coconut flakes toasted to a light brown crispness under the grill.

Coconut cream stores indefinitely and is easily shaved with a knife; alternatively it can be melted in a little hot water. It forms a delicious sauce which needs no thickening or exra binding agent.

Brussels sprout and banana omelette

For two people allow approximately 4oz (120g) freshly cooked sprouts and a half a large ripe banana. Dice the sprouts and slice and cut the banana into tiny pieces. Toss both in a little butter until the sprouts have lightly browned and the banana starts to soften. Meanwhile, make two flat omelettes using one egg per person. Spread the filling along the centre, roll up and serve.

Timbale of brussels sprouts

8oz (225g) prepared sprouts	2 tsp finely chopped sage
8oz (225g) ricotta cheese	2 large egg whites

Cook the sprouts briefly until just tender. Blend with the cheese and sage to form a smooth purée and then fold in the stiffly beaten egg whites, incorporating a little at first to loosen the purée and then lightly but thoroughly folding in the remainder. Fill four well buttered crème caramel or other small deep moulds and transfer to a roasting tin half full of water. Bake in a moderate oven, 180°C/350°F/gas mark 4, for approximately 35–40 minutes or until the centre is just firm.

Slip a palette knife around the edge and turn out onto hot plates. Serve either as a vegetable accompaniment or as separate course with a little sauce poured around. The leek and sage sauce on p. 235 is a good one; sauce Bercy another.

Cabbage

Quite when the cabbage emerged as we would recognise it today – the headed rather than the primitive scrawny loose leaf type – is unclear. The wild cabbage is native to the coasts of northwest Europe and the Mediterranean. Early efforts to domesticate it would have concentrated on producing a more palatable and less bitter tasting plant. The wild species are annuals, growing in warm moist winters. As the early cultivars spread northwards, biennials capable of lasting through the winter would also have been selected.

A mid-15th century manuscript gives a vivid illustration of how the cabbage may have been coaxed to form a ball: 'Take young Cabbages and set them in a ground that is greatly dunged, for in manner the ground where they shall be set cannot have too much dung, and let them be set every from other the space of the length of a yard: and always as they grow pluck off the lowest leaves, and so continue to the time that the leaves in the top begin to roll and to fold inwards, and then pluck no more of the leaves but let them grow, and they will grow round.'

The early varieties could not be relied on to form a heart, but by the beginning of the 17th century, this had all changed. As Gerard records in his *Herbal* in 1597, 'There is also found a certaine kinde hereof with the leaves wrapped together into a round head or globe, whose head is white of colour, especially toward winter when it is ripe. This is the great ordinary cabbage known everywhere, and as commonly eaten all over this kingdom.'

During the following centuries, proliferation of varieties gained pace. By the end of the 19th century some 90 varieties were recorded, among them golden savoys, a red-veined marbled Burgundy drumhead, the pointed sugar loaf cabbage, a favourite with many gardeners for 100 years or more, and many others, all of them now lost.

For today's gardener, the headache lies in deciding which type of cabbage to grow and in juggling sowing dates to ensure they mature at the right time. Summer/autumn varieties are sown in spring to mature late summer and autumn. Storable cabbages, again sown in spring and harvested in autumn, are the classic Dutch white cabbages, and can attain great weights. They are most useful, and store up to four months and still make good eating. Winter cabbages are sown in late spring to mature late autumn and stand into the winter. These can be glorious, both the drumheads such as January King, eaten around Christmastime, and the beautiful crinkly savoys for January and February. For both, it is important not to sow too early as success depends on their maturing as late as possible, and this can be achieved only by finding sowing dates to suit your conditions. Spring cabbages are sown late summer to mature the following April/May and can last into June. They are an invaluable spring crop and over the years we have come to prize them highly.

Don't be overzealous with your cabbage patch. Garden cabbages can be weighty things, and a single huge cabbage can last interminably; six plants of each type should be ample. Nor should you buy in cabbage plants and risk clubroot. Sow in seed boxes, or in the seed bed for later varieties, transplanting or thinning the plants to 15in (38cm) apart, and 18in (45cm) for the larger types. The transplanting should be done with care – plant with a trowel not a dibber. Water the hole first. Once the water has soaked away, put in the cabbage plants and firm down gently, scratching the top of the soil lightly so as not to pan the surface.

Cabbages have the ability to sprout again from their base, fine for a cabbage addict or if you have only a couple in the garden, but of doubtful benefit otherwise. The only exception to this is the regrowths which come from spring cabbages. These give quite the best spring greens you are likely to encounter.

Nothing is as good as a cabbage in its prime. However, unless a cabbage has been specifically bred to do so, it does not stand well. It is not a natural storage organ and once past its peak starts to deteriorate slowly. This shows in the leaves, which lose their healthy bloom, becoming increasingly prone to attack from slugs, worms and insects. Not surprisingly the flavour gradually dulls, a fault I have noticed also in oversized cabbages. Like this they are merely boring, as are so many of the shop-bought kind. Further deterioration leads to an incipient rankness. At this stage they become decidedly unpleasant. When a cabbage begins to show signs of wear and tear, it is time to cut it and store it inside. A cold room will do, but if there is space, a refrigerator is better. Wrap it loosely in a plastic bag, and it should keep satisfactorily for a week or two. A cabbage which is picked frozen can be treated slightly differently. In a cold room, large specimens can take up to five days to thaw out, which is sometimes quite useful.

When preparing garden cabbages look out for slugs or brandling worms, which eat their way in from the base upwards. These can usually be flushed out by holding the cabbage under running water. If the cabbage is large, peel away from the outside inwards, saving the heart for another time. Otherwise, cut into wedges, chop or shred as necessary.

Cabbage is a vegetable of extremes. Either you should cook it briefly, as do the Chinese, who understand the quality of crunchiness and simple flavourings, or adopt the French and northern European style of long slow cooking where the cabbage becomes part of the dish, imbibing the surrounding flavours in the process. Both are good. What is not admissible is the British halfway house which reduces cabbage to a watery sulphurous mush. On this point, scientists have confirmed what many of us have suspected. Brassicas are notorious for their volatile sulphurous compounds, many of which increase with cooking, reaching a climax during the 5th-7th minute. This is why cabbages will taste better if cooked briefly, or else cooked sufficiently long for the compounds to break down.

The easiest method of cooking cabbage is as follows: wash, shred or chop coarsely, and cook in a large covered pan containing ½in (1.25cm) boiling water over a brisk heat for 2–3 minutes. Take the lid off, boil away any remaining moisture and serve immediately.

When it comes to adding spices or flavourings, cabbage is remarkably accommodating. Stir-fried, it teams well with flavourings such as cream, fresh herbs, mushrooms and juniper, or with robust spices such as paprika, caraway, chilli, ginger, coriander and cumin.

For long slow cooked dishes, cabbage should be cut into wedges and blanched first in plenty of boiling water for 3–5 minutes. This tempers its natural forthrightness and reduces the volume to a manageable size. Drain, squeeze out the excess moisture, and proceed according to the recipe. Stuffed whole cabbage requires patience, but is worth the effort if you enjoy doing messy jobs occasionally and have time to spare. For this you will need an unblemished cabbage. Otherwise, stuffed leaves make life easier and are just as good to eat.

A good salad in winter

Cabbage salads are rarely the most exciting, but they do have their place and can always be relied on when the salad drawer is empty. Raw cabbage has now been found to be beneficial in protection against stomach cancers. To make any cabbage salad a success, heed the advice of Hannah Woolley, whose recipe is the earliest one I have found (1684). 'Take a good hard Cabbage, and with a sharp knife shave it so thin as you may not discern what it is, then serve it with Oyl and Vinegar.' White cabbages are usually, but not necessarily, the best for salads – much depends on your cabbage.

Cabbage, olive and olive oil salad

My favourite cabbage salad. Quantities are not important, though you should remember that the volume will shrink by half after blanching. Shred some white cabbage as finely as you can and blanch for 1 minute. Drain and refresh, then gently squeeze out the excess moisture. Toss in a little olive oil with some finely chopped black olives, and serve mounded up in little heaps as part of a winter hors d'oeuvre.

Pickled cabbage

Pickled cabbage recipes do not generally excite me but I make an exception for this invigorating spicy recipe from Colin Spencer: 'for lovers of hot dishes which clear the sinuses in one swallow.' Make it in small quantities first, and temper the chilli and ginger accordingly.

half a medium sized white cabbage	1 green chilli, thinly sliced
1 tsp sea salt	½ tbsp sesame seeds
1 tsp caster sugar	1 tbsp rice wine vinegar
1 tbsp sesame oil	
1oz (30g) fresh ginger root, peeled and grated	

'Slice the cabbage thinly, throw into a bowl, sprinkle with sea salt, mix well and leave for a day. Then squeeze out all the moisture with your hands; be vigorous as if wringing clothes. Sprinkle with the sugar. Heat the sesame oil and throw in the ginger root, chilli and sesame seeds. Fry for a moment until the ginger is crisp and the seeds are popping, then pour onto the cabbage. Stir and toss the cabbage thoroughly; finally add the rice wine vinegar. Allow the cabbage to stand for another day. Excellent with smoked fish.'

Crackle cabbage

This is an easy way of preparing cabbage, useful for when the oven is on for another dish. For four servings, allow about 12oz (340g) shredded cabbage – white or green – and 2oz (60g) roughly chopped walnuts. Either use a wok, or cook in two batches if necessary in a nonstick frying pan.

Heat 2 tbsp olive oil and quickly fry the cabbage and the walnuts for a couple of minutes, turning the mixture constantly, until the cabbage just wilts. Transfer to a large shallow gratin dish and pop into a hottish oven until the surface of the cabbage is nicely browned and crackly, 10–15 minutes. Serve from the same dish.

When fresh chestnuts are in season, chop some coarsely and add them to the cabbage and walnuts. Their fulfilling sweetnes contributes to the dish most successfully.

Chicken and cabbage pie

8oz (225g) cabbage, finely shredded (remove the hard central core first)	3–4oz (90–120g) medium fat curd cheese
1 small onion, finely sliced	2 tsp chopped fresh thyme, oregano, tarragon, or basil
butter for frying	
3–4oz (90–120g) mushrooms, washed and sliced	8oz (225g) oatmeal pastry made with 2oz (60g) oatmeal and 6oz (180g) plain flour
8oz (225g) chicken breast meat, or leftover roast chicken meat	

Sweat the cabbage and onion in a knob of butter in a covered pan over a low heat for about 5 minutes until the cabbage has wilted. In another pan, soften the mushrooms in a smidgeon of butter. Set both aside. Cut the meat into bite-sized pieces. If using uncooked meat, seal in a nonstick pan lubricated with a little butter or chicken fat and cook for 5 minutes.

Mix all the pie ingredients and pile into a deep flan dish, making sure there's a good depth of filling. Cover with pastry, make a slit in the top, decorate with trimmings, and brush with egg or milk. Bake in a hot oven, 200°C/400°F/gas mark 6, for 15 minutes, then at 180°C/350°F/gas mark 4 for a further 20–25 minutes. The pastry should be crisp and the filling bubbling. Serve hot with salad and potatoes.

Stuffed cabbage leaves

Stuffed cabbage leaves are very versatile. Almost any kind of stuffing – meat, grain, pulse, cheese, nuts, dried fruit, or vegetable mixtures – is suitable. Herbs and spices add extra flavour and blend well. For meat and vegetable stuffings, raw or undercooked rice, other grains such as bulgur, or bread are usually added to bind the ingredients and act as a stiffener. Follow the procedure for stuffed vine leaves, blanching the leaves for 1–2 minutes first. Shave off the midrib at its thickest part to enable the leaf to roll more easily, put a generous spoonful of stuffing near the base and roll into a neat parcel. Either tie with thread or wedge the parcels tightly together in a casserole dish so they do not fall apart during cooking. A simple tomato sauce or stock flavoured with 2–3 tablespoons of tomato purée is generally used as the braising liquid and reduces down to form a sauce. Add sufficient barely to cover the leaves, tucking in a bay leaf or a sprig of thyme, cover tightly and braise in a moderate oven, 180°C/350°F/gas mark 4 for about an hour.

Recipe books abound with suggestions for suitable stuffings. One I enjoyed particularly in a restaurant once contained a savoury mixture of buckwheat, mushrooms and chopped walnuts, flavoured with miso. Here are two more I find successful.

Stuffed cabbage leaves with pesto

Make some herb pesto in the usual way (see p. 31) but omit the garlic and keep the paste stiffer than normal. Mix with undercooked rice plus a handful of pine kernels, using approximately twice pesto to rice. Stuff the cabbage leaves and braise in a tomato sauce as above for about 45 minutes.

Stuffed cabbage leaves with brown rice, lemon and ginger

The nutty, chewy quality of brown rice comes through well in stuffed dishes of this type. Allow 4–6oz (120-180g) of undercooked rice for 8–10 blanched cabbage leaves. Mix in a generous 1½–2 tablespoons of finely chopped fresh ginger, the rind of 1 well scrubbed lemon and, if liked, a tablespoon of freshly grated coconut .

Moisten with fromage frais, thick drained yoghurt, or sour cream – the mixture should be fairly sloppy. Stuff the cabbage leaves and braise as above for about 45 minutes.

Note: the simplest way to cook brown rice for stuffed dishes is as follows. Add sufficient water to cover by 1in (2.5cm), cover, and cook hard for 4–5 minutes. Turn off the heat and let the rice cool in the liquid, by which time it will be almost cooked.

Hamburg parsley

Hamburg parsley is the variety of common parsley grown for its succulent, delicate tasting root. It looks like a diminutive parsnip and is a relatively new introduction here. Philip Miller, who claimed to be the first to grow it, called it the great-rooted garden parsley in his *Gardener's Dictionary* of 1754 and remarked how common it was in Dutch markets. He imported some seeds from Holland in 1727, though it took some years before he could persuade his customers to try it. Its leaves are flattish rather than curled, and slightly coarser, remaining green and abundant throughout winter. They can be used in exactly the same way as ordinary parsley, though the taste is stronger.

You will sometimes find Hamburg parsley referred to as turnip-rooted parsley, but parsnip-rooted is the better and fairer description, for there is nothing in its shape, taste or texture reminiscent of turnip. It has much more of the textural softness of the parsnip, and something of its sweetness. Its flavour is best described as parsley combined with something like salsify. Large roots are milder. In northern Europe, where it was first developed, it forms an indispensable ingredient of the *Suppengrün*, a little bundle of herbs and flavouring vegetables neatly tied up with twine to give strength and flavour to soups and stocks.

Perhaps if Hamburg parsley were considered more of a delicacy, more people would be encouraged to try it. Gardeners who have written about it all agree on its virtues. If it has a fault, it is its size. This will not deter the appreciative cook, who is always grateful for vegetables which cannot be bought, but may well dampen the enthusiasm of the gardener, especially when space is limited.

It is grown in the same way as parsnip, sowing the seeds when the soil is warm. Dig as required, saving the best of the greenery to use as parsley, preparing as for other root vegetables.

However small your crop, Hamburg parsley is best appreciated on its own: cut into strips, blanch and serve plain or dressed with a little hazelnut or walnut oil, scattered over a green salad for a first course. Alternatively, cook in a little butter, or grate it finely and serve raw to accompany smoked fish as an hors d'oeuvre. Hoard any bits too small to be useful to add to soup or stock.

Hamburg parsley soup

A delightfully delicate soup, the colour of pale buttermilk.

8oz (225g) Hamburg parsley, peeled
  and chopped
white part of 1 small leek, sliced

knob of butter for frying
1 pt (600ml) water
a little single or double cream to finish

Sweat the Hamburg parsley and the leek in a knob of butter in a covered pan. Don't let them colour, but merely soften. Add the water, cover, and simmer until soft. Blend to a purée and finish with extra water if necessary, adding a little cream to taste – do not make it too cloying. Alternatively, use more cream and serve chilled as a vichyssoise.

Grilled Hamburg parsley

Hamburg parsley, peeled and cut into thick chips, is delicious grilled the same way as parsnip. For details, see p. 236.

Leeks

References to leeks as food or medicine date back to the first Egyptian dynasty in 3200BC. It was they, we believe, who first domesticated the leek from its wild form, *Allium ampeloprasum*, a common plant of southern Europe, North Africa, the Middle East and parts of Russia, with a much thinner stem and a bulbous base, often divided into cloves like garlic. Two forms of leek eventually evolved, the fat European leek and a Middle Eastern leek, the kurrat, which is slimmer and retains its distinct bulbous base.

A modest kitchen garden can easily provide more variety and better, fresher vegetables than a greengrocer, but it can rarely provide enough leeks to see the winter through. I have to content myself with half a bed, some each of autumn and the extra-hardy winter varieties that stand well into March; if you have room, grow some for summer to pull young for soups and salads.

The battle for a decent garden leek is won or lost in the first five months. Their cultivation is not difficult but it requires skill and dedication to achieve a plant as thick as a pencil for planting out in late May in rich soil in as deep a trench as you can manage. These will then go on to form leeks of respectable size and stature. When we lived in the northeast, we would buy leek plants from a grower in Durham who owned a fruiterer's and small garden centre near the cathedral. They were his own strain, and you had to be quick for everybody knew that Mr Storey's leeks were something special. Unless you are fortunate enough to know someone similar, you will have to raise them from seed sown in trays in early February under gentle heat, planting them out in late March/early April 6in (15cm) apart.

Leeks with a good length of white stem need to be blanched diligently. The normal practice is to dib the young plants into deep v-shaped holes and water them in, the soil back-filling naturally as the plants grow. Every year our trenches get a little deeper. Recently we have adopted the northern habit of putting a plastic tube or drainpipe over the leeks, and filling it with peat in an effort to get a longer stem. This works, but even your best efforts are conditioned by the variety you choose. Many English varieties tend to produce thick short-set leeks with too much green and too little white for my liking. In part, this is a function of climate, for short set leeks tend to be hardier, but is reinforced by the fact that officially a top-grade leek is required to have only as much white as green. See what we are up against – do growers ever cook I wonder? Autumn varieties sometimes fare better. The French variety Genvilliers, a long slim autumn leek with a delicious sweet flavour, is one to try.

Leeks are left in the ground until they are needed and survive all except the most extreme weather conditions. How well they stand depends very much on the season. Sometimes they remain in good condition until March, but if they begin to deteriorate, dig them up.

It is easy to damage leeks, and nothing is more infuriating. Dig deep, and prise them out carefully with a fork. Bang off the excess soil and do the preliminary trimming in the garden before you bring them inside. Do not be tempted to pull them when the ground is icy or very hard. More often than not they will break apart, leaving the best parts in the soil. Cut off the flags and trim the root, leaving ¼in (6mm) fibres unless you are going to use them straight away. Stored somewhere cool, they keep for a couple of weeks.

Generally speaking once the outside has been cleaned up, garden leeks are cleaner than you might imagine. If very dirty, slice down the middle, flipping them as you would a pack of cards under running water. It's extravagant, but if you are serving leeks whole, it also pays to peel away the first two or three layers of white as the inside layers are more tender. The wastage on leeks is quite considerable. For a decent serving, you need to allow 6oz (180g) prepared weight, or 2 medium leeks per person.

British cooking is severely limited where leeks are concerned. The 18th-century seedsman Benjamin Townsend described them in his catalogue as 'mightily used in broths and sauces'; their fate, I imagine, since the dawn of civilisation. Leeks can be shredded, steamed, stuffed, made into pies, salads, frittatas and creamy delicate sauces. It is worth considering, also, that many dishes which have onion as a base take on a gentler and more delicate nature when leek is used instead.

Cooking times for leeks are generally too long. Depending on their size, 5–8 minutes gentle cooking in a covered pan is usually enough, especially if they are sliced or halved lengthways first. Keep testing with the point of a knife until they are just soft in the centre. Add very little water – leeks give out ample moisture. Shredded leeks take only 2–3 minutes to cook. If you are fond of steaming leeks and want to keep them whole, a good idea is to arrange two chopsticks crosswise in a large frying pan with one end resting on the bottom of the pan and the other resting on the rim. The leeks can then be arranged astride the chopsticks and the lid put over. Depending on their size, they take 10–12 minutes to cook through.

The best leeks are medium sized. Large leeks are far more satisfying for the gardener, but often have a tough woody core and a duller flavour.

Leek and anchovy savoury

Choose slim tender leeks, cut off all the green and slice the white into ¼-½ (6mm-1.25cm) rounds. Simmer until soft in a little water. Drain well and squeeze lightly. Pile onto fingers of dry brown toast, spread with cream cheese and top with a strip of anchovy. Serve warm or cool, on their own or as part of a mixed autumn hors d'oeuvre.

Julienne of leeks

This is the simplest way to cook leeks. Shred them thinly into julienne strips and steam or cook them in a tiny amount of water in a covered pan. They will not take long, 2–3 minutes. They look most attractive mounted up in a little pile or arranged neatly in a block in a serving dish with other green vegetables.

Leek salad

'I have kept what I think almost the best for the last and that is Leek Salad. Use the smallest leeks you can find – those no thicker than your finger. These often are to be found in the un-thinned rows of seedlings left after the crop has been planted out. Take plenty, for they shrink. Use only the white part, keeping them whole, and cook in fast boiling water; if small this takes only a short time. Arrange them carefully, dress with a sharp dressing, add herbs, if you wish and serve them really cold.'

Constance Spry, *Come into the Garden, Cook*, 1943

A modern way: stack the cooked leeks in a block and wrap in cling film. Put in a dish with a weighted plate on top. Leave in the fridge for 24 hours, draining off the liquid as it collects. Unwrap and serve in thin slices with a mustardy vinaigrette.

Leek and avocado vichyssoise

A delicate soup. After I had published it in *The Times*, a reader wrote suggesting skimmed milk rather than cream and water, a suggestion you may like to follow.

8oz (225g) white part of leeks, cleaned and sliced
1 smallish very ripe avocado

1¼pt (750ml) well flavoured chicken stock
2–4 fl oz (60–120ml) single cream

Simmer the leeks in the stock in a covered pan for 20 minutes until soft. Cool. Process or blend with the avocado until absolutely smooth. Adjust the consistency with water, adding cream to taste. Check the seasoning and serve chilled; it is equally good without the cream. Serves 6.

Butter beans with leeks and olive oil

8oz (225g) soaked butter beans
bay leaf
12oz–1lb (340–450g) prepared leeks, sliced

olive oil
seasoning

Simmer the butter beans in fresh water with a bay leaf until soft, but not mushy. Gently sweat the leeks in a little olive oil in a covered pan until cooked. Drain the beans and mix with the leeks, adding a little of the cooking liquor to form a small amount of sauce. Season and transfer to a serving dish. Dribble extra olive oil over the surface and serve hot as a vegetable dish or cool as a salad with a dusting of finely chopped parsley.

Leek and sage sauce

Vegetable sauces are very much part of modern cooking, either to accompany other vegetables or with meat or fish, the bulk in the vegetable providing the thickness for the sauce. They should not be too thin and have a tendency to separate out, so are best served and eaten immediately. Flavourings and herbs can be altered to suit.

8oz (225g) cleaned leeks, sliced finely into thin shreds
1 star anise

5 fl oz (150ml) creamy milk, or single cream and water mixed
1 tsp finely chopped fresh sage

Use mainly the white part of the leek with just a little of the tender green to give the sauce a hint of colour. Simmer the leeks with the star anise and milk or cream and water in a covered pan until very soft – give them 15 minutes or so. Remove the star anise (rinsed and dried it can be used again) and blend to a smooth purée. Return to the pan and adjust the consistency; it may either need firming up by reducing, or thinning by adding a little more liquid. Stir in the sage and serve. Use to accompany Sprout timbales (p. 224) or pork.

Cod *with red peppers, leeks and peppercorns*

8oz (225g) white of leeks cut into julienne shreds
1 large red pepper, sliced
1–2 tbsp olive oil

1 glass (4–5 fl oz/120–150ml) white wine
4 thick cod fish steaks
2 tsp green peppercorns, rinsed in hot water

Soften the leeks and red pepper in the olive oil in a largeish frying pan until limp, about 10 minutes. Add the wine, cover and continue cooking gently for another 20 minutes, or until the sauce is thick and much reduced. Arrange the fish in a single layer on top, add the peppercorns, cover and simmer gently until the fish is just cooked – look for the creamy curd on top. Serve from the same pan with couscous or brown rice.

Lamb and leek hot pot

In Saxon England a cottager's vegetable plot was called a 'leac tun' or leek enclosure, and would contain mainly leeks and coleworts. They went into the daily pottage, a thick mess of vegetables, cereals and sometimes meat, simmered in the iron pot over the open fire and eaten with a spoon. Something of the kind remains in our lamb and barley broths and cheap lamb stews. This is a modern version.

2 neck or best end chops per person, trimmed of obvious fat
2 lamb's kidneys (optional)
1½lb (675g) leeks, sliced into rounds
1–2 tomatoes, chopped
large sprig of thyme

4–5 juniper berries, crushed
2lb (900g) potatoes, peeled and thickly sliced
½pt (300ml) lamb stock
melted butter for brushing

Sear the chops on both sides in a nonstick frying pan over a high heat. Choose either a deep pot and arrange the ingredients in layers, finishing with potatoes on top, or a shallower casserole which will take the chops in a single layer, sandwiching between them the leeks and seasonings, with potatoes again on top. Deglaze the pan with the stock (use water if no stock is avilable), and pour into the casserole, adding enough hot water to come just short of the potatoes. Brush these with melted butter, cover, and cook in a low oven, 140–150°C/275–300°F/gas mark 1–2, for 1½ hours. Uncover, raising the heat a notch, and continue cooking for another hour or so. If necessary, finish by browning the potatoes under the grill.

Parsnips

The earliest gardening manuscript we have, *The Feate of Gardeninge*, written around 1440, includes 'persenepez' in the list of roots recommended for the kitchen garden. At that time, and for a long time after, they were mainly appreciated for their sweetness – early recipes were all sweet rather than savoury. By the late 19th century, however, culinary interest had diminished considerably. Perhaps if they had not been proclaimed such excellent food for horses and pigs, things might have been different.

We do not know when the parsnip was first cultivated – the wild form has hairy leaves and a thin wiry strong tasting root. An experiment in Cirencester in the 1850s produced large fleshy roots from wildstock within ten years, merely by planting the wild roots in rich soil and selecting seed from the largest. Suggesting that whenever domestication did take place, it did not take long.

Culturally, parsnips are fussier than their plebeian image would indicate. One year they do well, another they do not. Getting them away to a good start is the secret of success. We cover the soil with polythene sheeting a month before sowing, to warm up the ground and help it dry out. The seeds are sown as soon as feasible in April, in rows rather than stations, and covered over with Agryl P17 (see p. 18) for 6–8 weeks until the seedlings become well established. (Thinning the plants later to 6–9in (15–23cm) apart.) Parsnips should not be grown in soil that has been manured during the previous two years, otherwise they will fork, which is a great nuisance once you get them into the kitchen.

No further work is necessary. The plants are left in the ground all winter, unless they show appreciable damage. They last well, though less so when the weather is mild. As a precaution, cover the crowns with soil. The only complaint you are likely to encounter, especially in sandy soils where the sharp gritty particles easily bruise the skin, is canker. This is caused by fungi penetrating into the cracks, and shows as a brown disfigurement which can be so troublesome at times that it renders the parsnip useless. Resistant varieties should be grown, such as Avon Resister, a stump-rooted parsnip with an excellent flavour.

A parsnip needs to be well frosted – those in early November may well be a dull affair compared to those after Christmas. This is because the action of frost converts some of the stored starch into sugar, rendering the parsnip both sweeter and richer in flavour.

In very cold weather be sure to pull a supply before they become frozen in. The tapering root can sometimes be very long; be careful as you lift them. Twist off the tops and wipe off the worst of the soil before you bring them inside.

Parsnips will need a good scrub with a stiff brush. Cut off any thin or pronged roots and go over any stubborn bits of grit or blemishes with a sharp knife, or a ridged vegetable brush. If you intend to keep them in the fridge or somewhere cool for a week or so, wash them and leave to drain first.

Parsnips are one of our great winter vegetables. They make delicious purées and soups, and can be grilled, roasted (allow longer than you think), or sliced or quartered and simmered in a little water in a covered pan on top of the stove. Here they cook more quickly than you would imagine, 5–10 minutes maximum. If you are puréeing the parsnips afterwards, be sure to use the cooking liquid.

Unless you are wedded for whatever reason to steaming you will, I think, find little if any difference in flavour between a parsnip which has been steamed and one which has been cooked carefully in a little water. As for the cores, generally it is better to remove them, certainly the hard woody ones, if for no other reason than they take twice as long to cook. But they are neither tasteless nor necessarily that tough. For soups, casseroles and baked parsnips there is no harm in leaving them in. Peeling parsnip skins after they have been cooked is a fiddly business – the skin is pitted and does not come away cleanly. Garden parsnips are very messy, and often you may have no practical choice in the matter.

Parsnips are not an obvious contender for salads. Their flavour when raw is either too dull or too strong and the texture can be rather woolly. A small amount, however, very finely grated and served in little mounds sprinkled with a few celery seeds can be added to autumn and winter hors d'oeuvres. In *Acetaria* John Evelyn suggests having them boiled and eaten cold with oil and vinegar. The modern alternative is to cut them into thin chips or wedges and blanch for 1–2 minutes only. Instead of vinaigrette, try tossing them immediately in white wine. Leave to cool, turning often, and serve as part of a mixed hors d'oeuvre. A sprinkling of celery seeds can also be added.

Grilled parsnips

Scrub, peel, and cut the parsnips into chip size wedges. Brush with olive oil/butter and grill until soft and browned, turning them over as they brown. They won't take very long, but turn the grill down if they look like browning too quickly. A nice quick way of serving parsnips with roast or grilled meat, or as a winter lunchtime snack dunked into Seville marmalade.

Parsnip and horseradish purée

One of the best sources we have of meals eaten in the 18th century is the diaries of Parson Woodforde, Vicar of Weston Longeville in Norfolk from 1774 until his death in 1803. Occasionally in winter he would have salt fish and boiled parsnips, a dish often recorded in cookery books of the time and where the sweetness of the parsnips must have done much to improve the leathery saltiness of the fish.

Parsnip purée spiked with horseradish makes a pleasant change with poached or plainly grilled white fish such as cod, haddock or whiting. 12oz (340g) of purée for four will be ample. Just before serving mix in 1 tbsp freshly grated horseradish.

Parsnip with ginger and pine kernels

1lb (450g) prepared parsnips　　　*1 generous tbsp finely chopped or*
½oz (15g) butter　　　　　　　　　*finely grated ginger*
　　　　　　　　　　　　　　　　　2 tbsp pine kernels

Cook the parsnips in a little water in a covered pan until soft, and mash to a rough purée with a potato masher or fork. Take the smallest pan you have (I have a little cast iron one, 3in (7.5cm) across, which is ideal for frying spices). Heat the butter until it's hot, add the ginger and pine kernels and frizzle for about 30 seconds, shaking the pan until the nuts are brown. Mix into the purée, pile into a serving dish and serve. One of my favourite ways to serve parsnips.

Mushrooms stuffed with parsnips

Should you have a little plain parsnip purée left over, use it for this dish to serve as a first course or to accompany pork chops.

approximately 4oz (120g) parsnip purée
Worcestershire or soy sauce
4 large open-capped mushrooms, wiped or peeled

thin slices of hard cheddar or gruyère cheese
olive oil

The parsnip purée should be very thick. If it is at all sloppy, dry it out first in a pan over a gentle heat. Season vigorously with Worcestershire or soy sauce and divide between the upturned mushrooms, smoothing over the tops. Lightly cover with very thin shavings of cheese and brush all over with olive oil. Place the prepared mushrooms in a baking dish, pour in a little extra oil and bake in a moderate oven for 20–30 minutes until the mushrooms are done and the cheese is bubbling.

Parsnip bread

The idea of using parsnip in bread dough will seem bizarre to modern cooks. This would not have been the case in the early 18th century. As the price of corn went up and down with alarming consequences, great efforts were made by the Royal Society for the Encouragement of Arts to get agriculturists to grow substitute crops such as carrots and parsnips, and for the general public to utilise them as best they could. Earlier still, Gerard had observed there was a good and pleasant bread to be made from parsnips.

Do not expect the bread to have a pronounced taste of parsnip. As with potato bread the main function of the vegetable is to contribute texture and springiness.

Parsnip and cinnamon rolls

8oz (225g) strong white unbleached bread flour, or half wholewheat, half white flour
1 tsp cinnamon

½ tsp salt
¼oz (7g) fresh yeast or 1 tsp dried yeast
about 3 fl oz (90ml) warm milk
4oz (120g) smooth dry parsnip purée
½oz (15g) melted butter

Sift the flour with the cinnamon and salt into a warm bowl and cream the yeast with a little of the warm milk in the usual way. Beat the warm purée into the flour, add the yeast, milk and melted butter and knead thoroughly – you may need a little extra flour. Cover with a plate, or wrap in a plastic bag and leave to rise. Knock back and leave to rise again if there's time, otherwise shape into 8 rolls. Prove in a warm place for about 20 minutes and then bake in a hot oven, 210°C/425°F/gas mark 7, for 20 minutes. Serve warm, for dinner, with soup or the first course.

St Clementine's parsnips

A recipe which highlights parsnip's sweetness, adapted from an early Jane Grigson recipe, for when Seville oranges are in season and parsnips are at their best.

Peel sufficient parsnips for your needs; I allow a generous 6oz (180g) per person. Quarter or cut into lengthy chunks as appropriate, cutting out any obvious woody bits. Spread out over the base of a shallow pan. Pour in a mixture of half fresh Seville orange juice and half sweet orange juice to come halfway up, cover, and poach gently until the parsnips are just cooked, adding a little more juice if the liquid looks like drying up too much. Off the heat, baste with the juice, sprinkle sparingly with soft brown sugar, dot with shavings of butter and glaze under a preheated grill until the surfaces are nicely browned and the sauce bubbling. Serve from the same pan.

A simple Seville marmalade glaze over grilled or roast parsnips is also very satisfactory.

Parsnip and apple bake

Parsnips and apples are another excellent combination. This dish is adapted from *Cooking Apples*, published by Ampleforth Abbey, who maintain one of the best collections of apple varieties in the country.

1½lb (675g) prepared parsnips	juice of half a lemon
1 large cooking apple, peeled, cored and very thinly sliced	2–4 tsp soft brown sugar

Cook the parsnip and blend to a stiffish purée in the food processor or blender. Spread half over a shallow gratin dish and cover with apple slices. Repeat this once more, arranging the apple slices neatly as you would in an apple flan. Sprinkle the lemon juice over the top, followed by the sugar. Bake in a moderate hot oven, 180–190°C/350–375°F/gas mark 4–5, for 30–40 minutes, or until the apples have softened and are just beginning to catch.

Salsify and scorzonera

Salsify and scorzonera are almost twin sisters. Both belong to the daisy family, along with chicories, lettuce and dandelion. Both are natives of central and southern Europe and were developed from wild forms sometime during the late 16th/early 17th centuries. They are grown for their long thong-like tap roots, and are almost identical in flavour.

The immediate difference is the colour. Scorzonera is the one with a dark brown skin – hence it is often referred to as black salsify. To tell them apart in the garden you need to look at the leaves. Both resemble young leek flags (the latin name for salsify, *Tragopogon porrifolius*, hints at this), but scorzonera leaves are broader, deeper green in colour, and covered in a thin furry down when very young. Scorzonera has buttercup yellow flowers, while those of salsify are pinky-purple.

Historically, scorzonera is the more interesting. In the Middle Ages, and for some time after, it was used as a medicinal plant. It was best known as a cure for snake bites, which gives us its strange sounding name, derived from the Catalan *escorzo*, viper.

By the late 17th century, both vegetables were being grown by eminent gardeners of the day, and are listed in the earliest seed catalogue in our possession, a small pamphlet printed for a London seedsman, William Lucas, around 1677. Their popularity seems to have survived among gardeners until early this century.

In theory, both plants are easy to grow, free from pests or disease. To do well, however, they need a light, well drained soil which should not have been freshly manured. Salsify in particular is prone to forking, and for this reason alone, if you need to choose between the two, scorzonera is better. The seed is sown in spring, when the soil is warm enough, thinning the plants to 4in (10cm) apart. No further work is necessary. Scorzonera is perennial; salsify biennial. If left in the ground they will produce edible shoots and flowers which can be used in salads.

The ones you grow for yourself will fall well short of the standard of those occasionally found in the shops imported from Holland and Belgium. A Dutch book I have describes improved giant varieties of scorzonera – Long John, Maxima, Torpedo and others. Perhaps as they become more popular, some enterprising seedsman could be persuaded to import these seeds to Britain.

Both plants are extremely hardy and the roots are dug as required. Take care, as they can be very long and tapering, especially those of scorzonera. They are brittle and may snap: ease the fork in gently, working rhythmically to and fro to get deep down into the soil. Cut off the tops and clean off the soil. Stored somewhere cool, loosely wrapped in paper, they keep extremely well.

Bought scorzonera has a skin like thin bark, whereas that freshly dug from the garden is much thinner and not tough. It is the same with salsify. Most of it will scrub off as you clean them. A vegetable brush with ridges on the top will make short work of all the whiskery roots, a particular feature of salsify. However, as both vegetables discolour rapidly on peeling, you may prefer to leave the skins on for cooking. Alternatively, rub with a lemon or drop into acidulated water after peeling. Both exude a sticky milky fluid when cut. The best way to cook them is in a little water in a covered pan. If possible choose a pan which will take them whole. The cooked vegetable has a waxy bite and is better soft than al dente. Timings can vary, thick specimens sometimes cooking faster than thin woody ones. Test with the point of a knife until softly firm, 10–15 minutes, then run under cold water. This makes peeling the skin easier – and finish according to the recipe.

Opinions vary as to which of the two is the better flavoured. There is very little in it, though scorzonera is naturally sweeter. The comparison with oysters which led to salsify being known as the 'oyster plant' has long been forgotten. To my taste their flavour is that of a mild and rather superior Jerusalem artichoke, with a pleasant but not obvious sweetness. The flavour of the home-grown kind is more sharply defined, and the texture less woolly. Neither is palatable raw. The pretty flowers can be eaten both cooked and uncooked, when buds have fattened and are just about to open usually in an omelette. They are said to have a flavour almost like asparagus, another exaggeration. Both vegetables are a rich source of minerals, notably iron and calcium.

The obvious way to enjoy them is on their own, either plain, made into fritters or rolled in egg and breadcrumbs and fried. They are good gratinéed with cheese, in pies, or eaten as a cooked salad in the Italian style with olive oil, lemon juice and a dash of sugar. But don't be afraid to experiment. Theirs is not the finely-tuned delicacy of asparagus, and robust flavourings often suit them well.

Salsify or scorzonera in the 18th-century style

Cook your salsify or scorzoneera in a little boiling water until soft, peel and cut into short lengths. Put them in a pan with a good knob of butter, the juice of 1–2 Seville oranges and enough sugar to alleviate the tartness without making it in any way sweet, about 1–2 tsp. Toss until the vegetables are coated with an orangey slightly sticky glaze and serve. A few toasted almond flakes can be scattered on top.

Salsify or scorzonera and mushroom cocotte

This is a useful recipe for eking out small quantities of either vegetable. As a rough guide, allow 1oz (30g) each of salsify or scorzonera, mushrooms and cream per person. Peel salsify or scorzonera, slice into thin rounds, and sweat in a little butter in a covered pan until soft. Add some finely chopped mushrooms and chopped tender salsify or scorzonera shoots should you have them. Add cream or cream and water to moisten and simmer until the juices have reduced to a coating consistency. Pile into ramekins and serve with fingers of hot brown toasted bread. The same mixture makes an excellent filling for omelettes.

Scorzonera with lemon and tarragon

Prepare scorzonera in the usual way, chopping into slices and rubbing the cut surfaces with lemon juice. Cook gently in a covered pan with butter and lemon juice, adding a little water if necessary to stop the vegetables catching. Squeeze over a few extra drops of lemon juice, add some coarsely chopped tarragon and serve.

Veal braised with garlic, almonds and salsify or scorzonera

Both salsify and scorzonera stand up well to lengthy cooking. This is one of those flavoursome braised dishes which can be prepared in stages and left to cook itself. The large amount of garlic used completely transforms during the cooking, imparting no more than a gentle savouriness to the sauce.

2½–3lb (1.13–1.35kg) silverside of
   veal, tied in a piece
1 tsp salt
1 tsp sugar
lemon juice
For the braise
12 large cloves of garlic
3in (7.5cm) piece of carrot and celery
1 shallot or half small onion

1 tbsp olive oil for frying
12oz (340g) peeled salsify or
   scorzonera, cut into 3–4in (7.5-
   10cm) slices
1oz (30g) peeled and freshly ground
   almonds
5 fl oz (150ml) medium sweet sherry
1 tsp potato flour slaked in a little
   water

Start in the morning for the evening's meal. Rub the veal with the salt and sugar, sprinkle with lemon juice and leave in a cool place for 4–6 hours. Turn the meat occasionally. When the time comes to cook the meat, wash off the marinade under the tap and pat dry.

   Blanch the garlic cloves for 5 minutes in boiling water. Cool under the tap and remove the skins. Chop the carrot, celery and onion to a hash. A food processor is excellent for this and does the job in a few seconds. Choose a heavy casserole dish which will just take the meat comfortably. Gently soften the carrots, celery, onion and garlic in oil – do not let them brown. Arrange the salsify/scorzonera on top and scatter over the ground almonds. Sit the meat on top of the vegetables. Pour over the sherry. Cover with a sheet of greaseproof paper, then the lid, ensuring a tight seal. Transfer to the oven, and cook at 325°F/160°C/gas mark 3. After an hour, check the pot. If the contents are cooking vigorously, lower the temperature to 140°C/275°F/gas mark 1. Continue cooking for another 1–1½ hours. Leave the meat to relax for up to an hour in the turned-off oven.

To finish, drain off the liquid – there should be a fair amount – and taste; reduce to concentrate the flavour if necessary, otherwise bring back to the boil and thicken with potato flour in the usual way. Remove the meat to a hot serving dish and carve into thick slices. Reheat the vegetables in the sauce, and arrange around the meat. If there is too much sauce, do not swamp the plate but serve the rest in a sauceboat. Serve with rice and a plainly cooked green leaf vegetable such as spinach or kale.

Bibliography

Gardening: history

Acetaria, A Discourse of Sallets, 1699, John Evelyn, fascimile edition, Prospect Books, 1982

Adam's Luxury and Eve's Cookery, 1744, Anon, facsimile edition, Prospect Books, 1983

British Botanical and Horticultural Literature before 1800 (3 vols), Blanche Henrey, Oxford University Press, 1975

A Compendious Method for the Raising of the Italian Brocoli, Spanish cardoon, Celeriac, Fenochi, and other foreign Kitchen Vegetables, Stephen Switzer, 2nd edition, 1728

The Country Housewife and Lady's Director, 1736, Richard Bradley, facsimile edition, Prospect Books, 1980

The Country House-wife's Garden, William Lawson, 1617, facsimile edition, Country Classics, 1983

Directions for Cultivating the Crambe Maritima, or *Seakale, for the use of the table,* William Curtis, 1799

Directions for the Gardener at Sayes Court, 1687, John Evelyn, facsimile edition, ed. Geoffrey Keynes Nonesuch Press, 1932

Early Gardening Catalogues, John Harvey, Phillimore & Co., 1972

Early Nurserymen, John Harvey, Phillimore & Co., 1974

The Economic Rhubarbs, Dorothy M. Turner, Journal of Royal Horticultural Society, Vol LX 111, 1938

Encyclopedia of Gardening, J. C. Loudon, Longman, 1834 edition

The English Gardener, William Cobbett, facsimile of 1833 edition, Oxford University Press, 1980

Five Hundred Points of Good Husbandry, 1573, Thomas Tusser, facsimile edition, Oxford University Press, 1984

The Gardener's Dictionary, Philip Miller, facsimile of abridged 1754 edition, Wheldon & Wesley, 1969

Garden Kalendar, 1751–73, Gilbert White, facsimile edition, Scholar Press, 1975

The Gardener's Labyrinth, Thomas Hill, 1577, new edition, ed. Richard Mabey, Oxford University Press, 1987

The Herbal, John Gerard, 1633, facsimile edition, Dover Books, 1975

A History of British Gardening, Miles Hadfield, Penguin Books, 1985

A History of Gardening in England, Alicia Amherst, Bernard Quaritch, 1895

The History and Social Influence of the Potato, Redcliffe Salaman, Cambridge University Press, 1985

Medieval Gardens, John Harvey, B. T. Batsford, 1981

Natural History, Vol 6, Books 20–23, Pliny, Loeb Classical Library, ed. T. E. Page et al, 1967

Old English Gardening Books, E. Sinclair Rohde, Minerva Press, 1972

The Origin of the Cultivated Tomato, J. A. Jenkins, Journal of Economic Botany, Vol 2, 1948

Paradisi in Sole: Paradisus Terrestris, 1629, John Parkinson, facsimile edition, Dover Books, 1966

Plants in the Service of Man, Edward Hyams, J. M. Dent & Sons, 1971

Sturtevant's Notes on Edible Plants, ed. U. P. Hedrick, State of New York Department of Agriculture, 1919

Thomas Jefferson's Garden Book 1766–1824, The American Philosophical Society, 1944

The Vegetable Garden, M. M. Vilmorin-Andrieux, facsimile of English edition, 1885, John Murray, 1977

Gardening: general

The Complete Book of Vegetables, ed. T. Buishand, H. P. Houwing, K. Jansen, Gallery Books, 1986

The Cottage Garden, Anne Scott–James, Penguin Books, 1987

Cottesbrooke, An English Kitchen Garden, Susan Campbell, Century, 1987

Evolution of Crop Plants, ed. N. W. Simmonds, Longman, 1986

Food for Free, Richard Mabey, Fontana, 1975

Grow Your Own Fruit and Vegetables, Lawrence Hills, Faber, 1974

Gourds, John Organ, Faber, 1963

A Guide to Chinese Market Vegetables, Martha Dahlen and Karen Phillips, South China Morning Post, 1980

Harvests & Harvesting, John Hargreaves, Victor Gollancz, 1987

The Illustrated Book of Food Plants, Peerage Books, 1985

The Kitchen Garden, Charles Lyte, Oxford Illustrated Press, 1984

Know and Grow Vegetables, Vols 1 and 2, ed. P. J. Salter, J. K. A. Bleasdale and others, Oxford University Press, 1979

The Organic Garden, Sue Stickland, Hamlyn, 1989

Raised Bed Gardening the Organic Way, Pauline Pears, HDRA Publications, 1983

Rare Vegetables, John Organ, Faber, 1960

The Salad Garden, Joy Larkcom, Windward, 1987

Successful Organic Gardening, Geoff Hamilton, Dorling Kindersley, 1987

The Sweet Orange Carrot, essay in the Art of Eating, no 11, Summer 89, Edward Behr

Uncommon Vegetables and Fruits, E. Sinclair Rohde, Country Life, revised edition, 1951

Vegetable Cultivation & Cookery, E. Sinclair Rohde, The Garden Book Club, 1938

Vegetables from Small Gardens, Joy Larkcom, Faber, 1976

Vegetables in S.E. Asia, G. A. C. Herklots, George Allen & Unwin Ltd, 1972

The Well Tempered Garden, Christopher Lloyd, Collins, 1973

Herbs

The Complete Book of Herbs, Lesley Bremness, Dorling Kindersley, 1988
Culinary and Salad Herbs, E. Sinclair Rohde, Country Life, 1942
The Herb Book, Arabella Boxer and Philippa Back, Octopus, 1981
Herb Gardening, Claire Loewenfield, Faber, 1970
The Herb Society - In Celebration of Chives
                    - A Multitude of Mints
                    - In Praise of Parsley
                    - The Romance of Rosemary

  compiled by Guy Cooper and Gordon Taylor, published in association with Juniper Press, 1981
Herbs, Spices and Flavourings, Tom Stobart, Penguin Books, 1979
A Modern Herbal, Mrs M. Grieve, Jonathan Cape, 1931, reprinted Savvas Publishing, 1985
The Penguin Book of Herbs and Spices, Rosemary Hemphill, Penguin Books, 1966

Cookery

Afghan Food & Cookery, Helen Saberi, Prospect Books, 1986
The Art of Cookery made Plain and Easy, Hannah Glasse, 1747, facsimile edition, Prospect Books, 1983
The Baghdad Kitchen, Nina Jamil-Garbutt, The Kingswood Press, 1985
A Book of Middle Eastern Food, Claudia Roden, Penguin Books, 1981
The Book of Vegetable Cookery, Errol Sherson, Frederick Warne & Co., 1931
Cantaloup to Cabbage, Mrs Philip Martineau, Cobden-Sanderson, 1929
Cheese and Cheese Cookery, T. A. Layton, The Cookery Book Club, 1971
Classic Indian Cooking, Julie Sahni, Dorling Kindersley, 1988
Classic Indian Vegetarian Cooking, Julie Sahni, Doubleday, 1987
Cooking in the Country, Tom Jaine, Chatto & Windus, 1986
The Cooking of Southwest France, Paula Wolfert, Dorling Kindersley, 1987
Cooking with Pomaine, Edouard de Pomaine, Bruno Cassirer, 1962
The Cook's Oracle, Dr William Kitchener, Houlston & Stoneman, 1831 edition
The Complete Encyclopaedia of Chinese Cooking, ed. Kenneth Lo, Octopus Books, 1982
The Complete Meze Table, Rosamond Man, Ebury Press, 1986
The Constance Spry Cookery Book, Constance Spry and Rosemary Hume, J. M. Dent & Sons, 1960
Cooking Apples, Ampleforth Abbey, 1982
Come into the Garden, Cook, Constance Spry, Dent, 1943
The Covent Garden Cookery Book, Diana Troy, Sidgwick & Jackson, 1987
Cuisine Naturelle, Anton Mosimann, Macmillan, 1985
Curye on Inglysch, ed. Constance B. Hieatt and Sharon Butler, Oxford University Press, 1985
Eastern Vegetarian Cooking, Madhur Jaffrey, Jonathan Cape, 1984
Elinor Fettiplace's Receipe Book, Hilary Spurling, Penguin Books, 1987
European Peasant Cookery, Elisabeth Luard, Bantam Press, 1986
Far Eastern Cooking, Madhur Jaffrey, BBC Publications, 1989
The Food and Cooking of Russia, Lesley Chamberlain, Allen Lane, 1982
Food in England, Dorothy Hartley, Macdonald, 1962
The Food of Love, Guislane Morland, Chatto & Windus, 1987
Food with the Famous, Jane Grigson, Michael Joseph, 1979

Forbidden Fruits and Forgotten Vegetables, George and Nancy Marcus, Sphere Books Ltd, 1983

Four Seasons Cookery Book, Margaret Costa, The Cookery Book Club, 1970

French Provincial Cooking, Elizabeth David, Penguin Books, 1979

Fresh Thoughts on Food, Lynda Brown, Dorling Kindersley, 1988

Fresh Ways with Vegetables, Healthy Home Cooking Series, Time-Life Books, 1987

From Garden to Kitchen, C. H. Middleton and Ambrose Heath, Cassell, 1937

Game for All, Nichola Fletcher, Victor Gollancz, 1987

Gastronomy of Italy, Anna Del Conte, Bantam Press, 1987

Gifts from Your Garden, Celia Haddon, Michael Joseph, 1985

Good Things, Jane Grigson, Penguin Books, 1977

Good Things in England, Florence White, Jonathan Cape, 1932

Grain Gastronomy, Janet Fletcher, Aris Books, 1988

Honey from a Weed, Patience Gray, Prospect Books, 1986

Italian Vegetarian Cookery, Paola Gavin, Optima, 1987

Italy, The Beautiful Cookbook, Lorenza De'Medici, Merehurst Press, 1988

Jane Grigson's Vegetable Book, Jane Grigson, Penguin Books, 1980

Japanese Vegetarian Cookery, Lesley Downer, Jonathan Cape, 1986

A Kipper with My Tea, Alan Davidson, Macmillan, 1988

A Kitchen in Corfu, James Chatto and W. L. Martin, Weidenfeld and Nicolson, 1987

Leaves from our Tuscan Kitchen, Janet Ross and Michael Waterfield, Penguin Books, 1979

The Light Eaters' Cookbook, British Iceberg Growers' Association, ND

Marcella's Italian Kitchen, Marcella Hazan, Alfred A. Knopf, 1986

May Byron's Vegetable Book, Hodder & Stoughton, 1923

Modern Cookery for Private Families, Eliza Acton, 1845, facsimile of 1855 edition, Elek, 1966

Mrs Beeton's Book of Household Management, 1861, facsimile edition, Chancellor Press, 1986

National Mark Cookbooks, Ambrose Heath and D. D. Cottington Taylor, Ministry of Agriculture and Fisheries, revised edition, 1935

The New English Cookery, Richard Cawley, Octopus Books, 1986

The New Vegetarian, Colin Spencer, Elm Tree Books, 1986

North Atlantic Seafood, Alan Davidson, Penguin Books, 1980

The Official Garlic Lover's Handbook, Lloyd John Harris, Aris Books, 1986

The Omelette Book, Narcissa Chamberlain, The Cookery Book Club, 1967

Pestos!, Dorothy Ranking, The Crossing Press, 1985

Pickles and Relishes, Andrea Chesman, Garden Way Publishing, 1983

The Princess and the Pheasant, Elisabeth Luard, Bantam Press, 1986

The Queen-Like Closet, Hannah Wooley, fifth edition, 1684

The Roman Cookery Book, Apicius, translated by Barbara Flower and Elisabeth Rosenbaum, Harrap, 1980

Salads & Cold Hors-de'Oeuvre, The Good Cook Series, Time-Life Books, 1980

Salads and Salads, A. H. Adair, Chapman & Hall, N. D.

Seasonal Salads, David Scott and Paddy Byrne, Ebury Press, 1985

Secrets from an Italian Kitchen, Anna Del Conte, Bantam Press, 1989

Simple Cooking, John Thorne, Viking Penguin Inc, 1987

Simple French Cooking for English Homes, X. M. Boulestin, William Heinemann, 1936

Spanish Cooking, Elizabeth Cass, The Cookery Book Club, 1968

Summer Cooking, Elizabeth David, Penguin Books, 1977

A Table in Provence, Leslie Forbes, Webb & Bower, 1987

A Table in Tuscany, Leslie Forbes, Webb & Bower, 1985

Vegetable Dishes and Salads, Ambrose Heath, Faber & Faber, 1938
The Vegetable, Fruit and Nut Cook Book, Winifred Grahan, Thorsons, 1980
Vegetables, The Good Cook Series, Time-Life Books, 1979
What Shall We Have Today?, X. M. Boulestin, William Heinemann, 193.
Yan-Kit's Classic Chinese Cookbook, Yan-Kit So, Dorling Kindersley, 1987

Cookery: general

A Concise Encyclopedia of Gastronomy, Andre L. Simon, Penguin edition, 1983
Culinary Botany: The Essential Handbook, Brant Rogers and Bev Powers-Rogers, PRP-Powers, Rogers & Plants, 1988
Experimental Cookery, Belle Lowe, John Wiley & Sons, New York, 1933
Food and Drink in Britain, C. Anne Wilson, Constable, 1973
On Food and Cooking, Harold McGee, Allen and Unwin, 1986
Vegetarian Encylopedia, Kitty Campion, Century, 1986
Woodforde, Passages from the Diary of a Country Parson, Rev James Woodforde, 1758–1802, selected and edited by John Beresford, Oxford University Press, 1935

Journals and Newsletters

Petit Propos Culinaires, published quarterly, Prospect Books Ltd, 45 Lamont Rd, London SW10 OHU
The Art of Eating, Edward Behr, published quarterly, HCR 30, Box 3, Peacham, Vermont, 05862, USA
Simple Cooking, John Thorne, published quarterly, Jackdaw Press, P.O. Box 622, Castine ME 04421, USA

Addresses

HDRA, National Centre for Organic Gardening, Ryton-on-Dunsmore, Coventry CV8 3LG
Suffolk Herbs (specialist seedsman), Sawyers Farm, Little Cornard, Sudbury, Suffolk CO10 ONY
Chris Bowers, Whispering Trees Nursery, Wimbotsham, Norfolk (specialist rhubarb supplier)
A. R. Paske, Regal Lodge, Kentford, Newmarket, Suffolk CB8 7QB (suppliers of asparagus, globe artichoke and seakale)

Index

Agryl, 17, 18
aïoli: French bean and aïoli salad, 114
    kale, steak and aïoli, 56–7
allspice dressing, 166
almonds: cauliflower and almond soup, 176
    spicy almond dressing, 115
    tomato and almond sauce, 145
anchovies: basil, tomato and anchovy relish, 73
    chicken in vinegar with, 158–9
    kale with, 56
    leek and anchovy savoury, 233
    mint and anchovy dressing, 32
apples: apple and dill borscht, 78
    apple and garlic sauce, 109
    avocado with apple, prawns and horseradish dressing, 195
    cod steaks with beetroot and, 168
    cucumber, apple and melon soup, 103
    fennel, apple and walnut salad, 191
    forced chicory, apple and fennel salad, 187
    hake with fennel and apple purée, 192
    horseradish and apple sauce, 195–6
    parsnip and apple bake, 240
    stir-fried brussels sprouts with apple and ginger, 223
apricots: dried apricot, rice and fresh coriander stuffed vine
    leaves, 150
asparagus, 82–4
    asparagus, new boiled eggs and savoury breadcrumbs, 84
avocado: avocado with apple, prawns and horseradish
    dressing, 195
    leek and avocado vichyssoise, 234

bacon: broad bean, bacon and mushroom salad, 88
    brussels sprouts with, 224
    endive with hot bacon and pumpkin seed dressing, 186
bananas: beetroot and banana salad, 166
    brussels sprout and banana omelette, 224
basil, 27, 71–2
    basil custards, 73
    basil mayonnaise sauce, 74

basil, tomato and anchovy relish, 73
    buttery basil purée, 73
    chicken breasts stuffed with, 75
    melon and basil soup, 74
bay, 75–6
    Mrs Beeton's cheap blanc-mange, 76
beans: bean and rocket salad, 68
    bean salad à la basquaise, 207
    kale with beans, tomato and garlic, 56
    see also individual types of bean
beef: braised with new peas, 126–7
    braised shin, 162–3
    kale, steak and aïoli, 56–7
beetroot, 84, 163–5
    apple and dill borscht, 78
    beetroot and banana salad, 166
    blackcurrant beetroot, 85
    butter bean and beetroot salad, 166
    cod steaks with beetroot and apple, 168
    in cream, 167
    with ginger and cumin, 167
    Harvard beetroot, 85
    lamb's lettuce and beetroot salad, 64–5
    with lemon juice and capers, 167
    misticanza, beetroot and quail's egg salad, 67
    with orange juice and caraway seeds, 166
    raw beetroot, potato and horseradish salad, 166
    raw beetroot salad, 165
    red and yellow spiced rice, 167–8
    sugared beetroot, 167
    summer beetroot and carrot salad, 85
    tomato, beetroot and tarragon salad, 166
blackcurrant beetroot, 85
blanching, 21
    endives and chicories, 185–6
blanc-mange, Mrs Beeton's, 76
braising, 23
bread: bruschetta, 147–8
    parsnip and cinnamon rolls, 239

potato bread, 134
  sage and olive bread, 161
Breton salad, 64
brill with saffron and cucumber, 104
broad beans, 85–7
  braised with ham, 89–90
  broad bean, bacon and mushroom salad, 88
  broad bean, orange and rice salad, 88
  broad bean, potato and fennel salad, 88
  broad beans the Apulian way, 89
  cauliflower and broad bean salad, 175
  with pasta, 89
  rabbit with, 90
  salads, 87
broccoli, 26, 35–7
  broccoli and pasta salad, 39
  broccoli and roasted red pepper salad, 38
  broccoli carbonara, 39
  broccoli, pine kernels and raisins, 37
  broccoli, potatoes and eggs, 37
  with golden sauce, 37–8
  salads, 38
  with walnuts and black olives, 38
bruschetta, 147–8
brussels sprouts, 221–2
  with bacon and vinegar, 224
  brussels sprout and banana omelette, 224
  with coconut cream, 224
  with cumin and mustard seed, 223
  stir-fried with apple and ginger, 223
  timbale of, 224
bulgur (cracked wheat): fresh pea and coriander tabbouleh, 127
  lamb, bulgur and cumin stuffed vine leaves, 151
butter beans: butter bean and beetroot salad, 166
  with leeks and olive oil, 234

cabbage, 18, 225–7
  cabbage, olive and olive oil salad, 227
  chicken and cabbage pie, 228–9
  crackle cabbage, 228
  pickled cabbage, 227–8
  salads, 227
  stuffed cabbage leaves, 229–30
calabrese, 91–2
  stewed calabrese, 92
cannellini beans, *fagioli all' uccelletto*, 160–1
cannelloni, summer, 120
Caribbean salad, 188–9
carrots, 92–3, 168–70
  carrot and hazelnut roulade, 171
  celeriac and carrot rémoulade, 180
  with coriander, 171
  daikon, carrot and ginger salad, 204
  French beans and summer carrots, 115
  Gujerati carrot salad, 170
  lemon and sherry carrots, 171–2
  oxtail braised in Guinness with orange and carrots, 172
  salad with honey and orange flower dressing, 94
  salad with olive oil, 93
  summer beetroot and carrot salad, 85
  summer carrots with creamy garlic sauce, 94
cauliflower, 173–4
  cauliflower and almond soup, 176
  cauliflower and broad bean salad, 175
  cauliflower and green pepper salad, 175
  cauliflower and potato pie, 177
  florets with roasted peanuts, 176
  fragrant cauliflower purée, 176
  with peaches and tarragon, 176–7
  salads, 175
  in spicy tomato sauce, 177
celeriac, 177–9
  braised with orange, 181
  celeriac and red pepper salad, 180
  celeriac and carrot rémoulade, 180
  celeriac and chive soup, 30, 181
  celeriac niçoise, 181
  celeriac polonaise, 180
  guacamole, 180
  pork with prunes and, 182
  salads, 179–81
  winter salad, 209
cheese: cheese of the seven herbs, 28–9
  courgette, feta cheese and mint stuffed vine leaves, 151
  croûtes with horseradish, 196
  cucumber and feta cheese salad, 102
  fennel braised with tomato and mozzarella, 191
  grilled goat's cheese in vine leaves, 152
  Gruyère and rocket omelette, 68
  Swiss chard and mint filo pastry, 214
  Swiss chard and parmesan crumble, 213
chervil, 26, 27, 28, 155
  cheese of the seven herbs, 28–9
  chiffonade, 29
  pancakes, 29
chicken: breasts en persillade, 157
  breasts with garlic and sweet wine sauce, 111
  breasts stuffed with basil, 75
  chicken and cabbage pie, 228–9
  with fennel, tomatoes and potatoes, 193
  French bean and chicken salad, 116
  pot roast with garlic and oregano, 80
  poulet à la basquaise, 207
  roast with lemon and rosemary, 159
  in vinegar, 158–9
chickpeas: lamb, chickpeas, spinach beet and tomato stew, 146–7
  spinach, chickpeas and pasta, 141
chicories, 26, 182–6
  blanching, 185–6
  Caribbean salad, 188–9
  chicory and turkey salad, 188
  forced chicory, apple and fennel salad, 187
  grilled chicory salad with toasted nuts, 189
  pyramid salad, 188
Chinese cabbage, 197–8
  basic stir-fried Chinese vegetables, 199–200
  Chinese leaf, pomegranate and mustard seed salad, 199
  Chinese leaf salad, 198
  Chinese leaf, walnut and Sharon fruit salad, 198–9
Chinese chives, 29
Chinese winter radish, 203–4
chives, 26, 27, 29
  celeriac and chive soup, 30, 181
  courgette and cucumber salad with, 30
  mint and chive omelette, 30
  stir-fried chives, 31
  trout baked with vermouth and cream, 30
claytonia, 26, 65
coconut dressing, spicy, 175
cod: baked with olive oil, garlic and potatoes, 109–10
  with red peppers, leeks and peppercorns, 235
  steaks with beetroot and apple, 168
collards, 51
conservative cooking methods, 22–3
cooking methods, 19–24
corn salad *see* lamb's lettuce
courgettes, 94–6

courgette and cucumber salad, 30
courgette and onion pizza, 98
courgette, feta cheese and mint stuffed vine leaves, 151
courgette flower fritters, 96
courgettes and caraway seeds, 97
courgettes, tomatoes and tarragon, 97
crab and courgette ramekins, 74
with mint vinaigrette, 97
pasta with fried breadcrumbs and, 100
salads, 97
scarpaccia, 99
skate with orange, caper and courgette sauce, 99
crab and courgette ramekins, 74
cracked wheat *see* bulgur
cresses, 63
cropping plans, 219–20
cucumber, 100–2
brill with saffron and, 104
chilled cucumber and mint pesto soup, 32
courgette and cucumber salad, 30
cucumber and feta cheese salad, 102
cucumber, apple and melon soup, 103
cucumber, rice and mustard seed salad, 103
freezer dill pickles, 105
omelette Czarina, 103–4
omelette Montenegro, 104
quick salted dill cucumbers, 104–5
salads, 102
with strawberry vinaigrette, 102
summer endive, cucumbers and hazelnut salad, 71
tomato and cucumber salad, 102
custards, basil, 73

daikon, carrot and ginger salad, 204
dandelions, 62
deep bed cultivation, 16–18, 219–20
digging, 17
dill, 27, 77
apple and dill borscht, 78
freezer dill pickles, 105
quick salted dill cucumbers, 104–5
turnip and dill salad, 149
double digging, 17
dressings, 61–2
allspice, 166
ginger and walnut oil, 186
honey and garlic, 165
honey and orange flower, 94
horseradish, 195
hot bacon and pumpkin seed, 186
lemon and garlic, 139
lemon cream, 140
mustard, 139
sesame seed, 114, 140
spicy almond, 115
spicy coconut, 175
yoghurt, 140
drying herbs, 27
duck, autumn salad with, 155
dumplings, horseradish, 196–7

eggs: asparagus, new boiled eggs and savoury breadcrumbs, 84
broccoli, potatoes and eggs, 37
hard-boiled egg and spinach salad, 139
misticanza, beetroot and quail's egg salad, 67
piperade, 207
see also omelettes
endive, 71, 182–3
blanching, 185–6

Caribbean salad, 188–9
with ginger and walnut oil dressing, 186
grilled endive salad with toasted nuts, 189
with hot bacon and pumpkin seed dressing, 186
pigeon and endive salad, 186–7
Pomaine's curled endive and black olive salad, 186
summer endive, cucumber and hazelnut salad, 71

fagioli all' uccelletto, 160–1
fat, cooking methods, 22–3
fennel, 189–90
braised with cider, 194
braised with tomato and mozzarella, 191
chicken with fennel, tomatoes and potatoes, 193
fennel and saffron risotto, 191–2
fennel, apple and walnut salad, 191
grilled fish with, 193
hake with, 192
potato and fennel salad, 191
fertilisers, 17
fine herbs, 28
fish: grilled fish with fennel, chilli and garlic, 193
rhubarb and cream sauce for, 45
see also individual types of fish
freezing: herbs, 27
spinach, 137
French beans, 112–14
French bean and aïoli salad, 114
French bean and chicken salad, 116
French bean and red pepper salad, 115
French beans and summer carrots, 115
French beans niçoise, 114
green beans and potatoes with coriander, 116
green beans and potatoes à la Extremadura, 116
salads, 114
in sesame seed dressing, 114
fritters: courgette flower, 96
Hannah Glasse's vine leaf, 151–2

garden minestra, 212
garlic, 106–8
apple and garlic sauce, 109
cod baked with, 109–10
garlic and sweet wine sauce, 111
garlic purée, 108
lemon and garlic dressing, 139
new potatoes and, 110
sauce, 90, 94
sweet and sour vinegared, 110
tourin blanchi à l'ail et à l'oseille, 109
garlic chives, 29
germination, 25–6
ginger: ginger and walnut oil dressing, 186
ginger, pepper and sweetcorn stir-fry, 208
rhubarb and ginger sauce, 44
gooseberry and tarragon sauce, 82
grapefruit and rhubarb compote, 43
green beans *see* French beans
green sauce, 35
growing vegetables, 16–19
guacamole, celeriac, 180
Gujerati carrot salad, 170

hake: with fennel and apple purée, 192
peppers stuffed with, 208
ham: broad beans braised with ham, in the Spanish style, 89–90
omelette Montenegro, 104
Hamburg parsley, 230–1
grilled, 231

soup, 231
haricot beans: Tuscan bean soup, 52
Harvard beetroot, 85
harvesting, 18–19, 153
herbs: autumn and winter, 155–63
    drying, 27
    freezing, 27
    pestos, 31
    spring, 26–35
    storage, 27
    summer, 71–82
herring stuffed with rhubarb, 45
horseradish, 194–5
    cheese croûtes with, 196
    dressing, 195
    dumplings, 196–7
    horseradish and apple sauce, 195–6
    mashed potatoes with, 196
    parsnip and horseradish purée, 238

insalata di rucola, 68

Japanese bunching onions, 202–3
    fragrant noodles, 203
Japanese winter radish, 203–4

kale, 26, 55–6
    with anchovies, 56
    with beans, tomato and garlic, 56
    kale steak and aïoli, 56–7
kebabs, Greek-style lamb, 76–7

laban with thyme, 162
lamb: Greek-style kebabs, 76–7
    lamb and leek hot pot, 236
    lamb, chickpeas, spinach beet and tomato stew, 146–7
    lamb stuffed vine leaves, 151
lamb's lettuce, 26, 64
    Breton salad, 64
    lamb's lettuce and beetroot salad, 64–5
land cress, 63
leeks, 231–3
    butter beans with, 234
    cod with red peppers and, 235
    julienne of, 233
    lamb and leek hot pot, 236
    leek and anchovy savoury, 233
    leek and avocado vichyssoise, 234
    leek and sage sauce, 235
    salad, 234
    tomato, leek and potato soup, 132
lemon: cream dressing, 140
    lemon and garlic dressing, 139
    lemon and sherry carrots, 171–2
lentils: lentil, root vegetable and game broth, 217
    with mint and tarragon, 82
lettuces, 26, 65–6, 70–1, 117–19
    lettuce and red pepper summer gazpacho, 117
    lettuce cakes, 120
    summer cannelloni, 120

mackerel stuffed with rhubarb, 45
mangetout, 127
manuring, 17
marjoram, 155
marrows, 95
mayonnaise, 61–2
    basil mayonnaise sauce, 74
    saffron and vermouth, 188
melon: cucumber, apple and melon soup, 103
    melon and basil soup, 74

mint, 26, 27, 31, 155
    mint and anchovy dressing, 32
    mint and chive omelette, 30
    mint and currant jelly sauce, 32
    Moroccan mint tea, 32
    vinaigrette, 97
misticanza, 66–7, 71
    misticanza, beetroot and quail's egg salad, 67
    misticanza, tarragon, caper and orange salad, 67
Mrs Beeton's cheap blanc-mange, 76
mizuna, 201–2
    spicy fried, 202
Moroccan mint tea, 32
mulching, 25
mushrooms: broad bean, bacon and mushroom salad, 88
    with mint and anchovy dressing, 32
    pak choi braised with, 201
    salmon trout in a filo case, 34
    salsify and mushroom cocotte, 242
    stuffed with parsnips, 239
mussel and tomato chowder, 147
mustard dressing and radishes, 139

nettles, 57–8
    nettle and potato purée, 58–9
    nettle and sorrel purée, 58
    nettle and Welsh onion soup, 59
    patina of, 58
noodles, fragrant, 203

olives: sage and olive bread, 161
    Swiss chard and black olive tart, 213
omelettes: brussels sprout and banana, 224
    Gruyère and rocket, 68
    mint and chive, 30
    omelette Czarina, 103–4
    omelette Montenegro, 104
onions, 120–2
    courgette and onion pizza, 98
    see also Japanese bunching onions; spring onions
orange: broad bean, orange and rice salad, 88
    celeriac braised with, 183
    misticanza, tarragon, caper and orange salad, 67
    oxtail braised in Guinness with, 172
    raw beetroot with, 166
    rosemary and honey oranges, 159
    St Clementine's parsnips, 240
    skate with orange, caper and courgette sauce, 99
oregano, 27, 79
    pot roast chicken with, 80
    rolo, 79
organic vegetables, 16
Oriental vegetables, 197–204
oxtail braised in Guinness, 172

pak choi, 200
    braised with mushrooms, 201
pancakes, chervil, 29
parsley, 27, 28, 155, 156
    chicken breasts en persillade, 157
    fried parsley, 157
    risotto verde, 158
    soup, 156–7
    tomato and frizzled parsley sauce, 146
parsnips, 236–8
    bread, 239
    with ginger and pine kernels, 238
    grilled, 238
    mushrooms stuffed with, 239
    parsnip and apple bake, 240

parsnip and cinnamon rolls, 239
parsnip and horseradish purée, 238
St Clementine's parsnips, 240
pasta: broad beans with, 89
  broccoli and pasta salad, 39
  broccoli carbonara, 39
  with courgettes and fried breadcrumbs, 100
  with fresh peas, 126
  spinach, chickpeas and, 141
peaches, cauliflower with, 176–7
peanuts: cauliflower florets with
  roasted peanuts, 176
peas, 18, 122–5
  beef braised with new peas, 126–7
  fresh pea and coriander tabbouleh, 127
  pasta with fresh peas, 126
  pea pod purée, 125
  pea pod soups, 126
  summer pea and purslane soup, 125
peeling vegetables, 20
pennyroyal, 31
peppers, 204–5
  bean salad à la basquaise, 207
  broccoli and roasted red red pepper salad, 38
  cauliflower and green pepper salad, 175
  celeriac and red pepper salad, 180
  cod with red peppers, 235
  French bean and red pepper salad, 115
  ginger, pepper and sweetcorn stir-fry, 208
  lettuce and red pepper summer gazpacho, 117
  piperade, 207
  poulet à la basquaise, 207
  prawn, pepper and coconut gazpacho, 206
  preserved green peppers, 208–9
  roasting peppers, 206
  stuffed with hake and saffron rice, 208
  winter salad with celeriac and preserved green peppers,
    209
pesto: herb, 31
  stuffed cabbage leaves with, 229
pie, chicken and cabbage, 228–9
pigeon and endive salad, 186–7
piperade, 207
pissaladière, 98
pizza, courgette and onion, 98
Pomaine's curled endive and black olive salad, 186
pork: braised with rhubarb and honey, 44
  with celeriac and prunes, 182
  chard, pork and sorrel terrine, 215
  rolo, 79
potatoes, 128–30
  broad bean, potato and fennel salad, 88
  broccoli, potatoes and eggs, 37
  cauliflower and potato pie, 177
  chicken with fennel and, 193
  cod baked with, 109–10
  cooked in a devil, 131
  fast-boiled, 131
  green beans and potatoes, 116
  mashed with horseradish, 196
  nettle and potato purée, 58–9
  new potatoes and garlic pearls, 110
  potato and fennel salad, 191
  potato bread, 134
  potato, tomato and mint gratin, 132–3
  raw beetroot, potato and horseradish salad, 166
  soup with Swiss chard, 214
  spiced and savoury potato cakes, 133
  spring green and potato cake, 53

tomato, leek and potato soup, 132
prawns: avocado with apple, prawns and horseradish
    dressing, 195
  prawn, pepper and coconut gazpacho, 206
  prawns, ginger and dill canapés, 78
preparing vegetables, 20–1
prunes, pork with celeriac and, 182
purslane and summer pea soup, 125
pyramid salad, 188

quail with sage, 161

rabbit with broad beans, basil and garlic sauce, 90
radishes, 39–41
  Chinese and Japanese winter radish, 203–4
  mustard dressing and, 139
raw vegetables, 20
redcurrants, salmon with, 81
relish: basil, tomato and anchovy, 73
rhubarb, 26, 41–3
  braised pork with honey and, 44
  herring stuffed with, 45
  julienne of, 44
  poached, 43
  rhubarb and cream sauce, 45
  rhubarb and ginger sauce, 44
  rhubarb and grapefruit compote, 43
  rhubarb, hazelnut and cinnamon sponge, 46
rice: broad beans, orange and rice salad, 88
  with butter and sage leaves, 160
  cucumber, rice and mustard seed salad, 103
  fennel and saffron risotto, 191–2
  peppers stuffed with hake and saffron rice, 208
  red and yellow spiced rice, 167–8
  risotto verde, 158
  spring green risotto, 54–5
  Swiss chard and rice torta, 215
rocket, 67–8
  bean and rocket salad, 68
  Gruyère and rocket omelette, 68
  insalata di rucola, 68
rolo, 79
root vegetables, 153–4
rosemary, 27, 155, 158
  chicken in vinegar with, 158–9
  roast chicken with, 159
  rosemary and honey oranges, 159

sage, 27, 155, 160
  fagioli all' uccelletto, 160–1
  leek and sage sauce, 235
  quail with, 161
  rice with butter and, 160
  sage and olive bread, 161
St Clementine's parsnips, 240
salad rape, 63
salads: autumn, 154–5
  bean, 68, 207
  beetroot, 85, 165–6
  Breton, 64
  broad bean, 87–8
  broccoli, 38–9
  butter bean, 166
  cabbage, 227
  Caribbean, 188–9
  carrot, 85, 93–4, 170
  cauliflower, 175
  celeriac, 179–81, 209
  chicory, 187–9
  Chinese leaf, 198–9

courgette, 30, 97
cucumber, 30, 102–3
daikon, 204
endive, 71, 186–7
fennel, 191
French bean, 114–16
lamb's lettuce, 64–5
leek, 234
misticanza, 67
rocket, 68
seakale, 48–9
spinach, 138–40
spring, 59–68
summer, 70–1
tomato, 102, 144, 166
turnip, 149
winter, 220–1
salmon: barbecued with tarragon, 81
   with red wine, tarragon and redcurrants, 81
salmon trout with mushroom and sorrel purée in a filo case,
   34
salsify, 240–2
   in the 18th-century style, 242
   salsify and mushroom cocotte, 242
   veal braised with, 243–4
sauces: apple and garlic, 109
   chervil chiffonade, 29
   garlic, 90, 94
   gooseberry and tarragon, 82
   green, 35
   herb pestos, 31
   horseradish and apple, 195–6
   leek and sage, 235
   mint and currant jelly, 32
   quick sorrel, 35
   rhubarb and cream, 45
   rhubarb and ginger, 44
   spinach beet and saffron, 50–1
   spring green and walnut, 54
   tomato, 145–6, 177
sautéing, 23
scarpaccia, 99
scorzonera, 240–2
   in the 18th-century style, 242
   with lemon and tarragon, 243
   scorzonera and mushroom cocotte, 242
   veal braised with, 243–4
seakale, 26, 46–8
   with cream sauce, 49
   seakale and hazelnut salad, 48–9
seeds: catalogues, 219
   sowing, 25–6
shallots, 122
Sharon fruit, Chinese leaf and walnut salad, 198–9
skate with orange, caper and courgette sauce, 99
slugs, 16
sorrel, 26, 27, 33
   chard, pork and sorrel terrine, 215
   green sauce, 35
   nettle and sorrel purée, 58
   purée, 34
   quick sorrel sauce, 35
   salmon trout with, 34
   sorrel and yoghurt soup, 33
   tourin blanchi à l'ail et à l'oseille, 109
soups: apple and dill borscht, 78
   cauliflower and almond, 176
   celeriac and chive, 30, 181
   chilled cucumber and mint pesto, 32
   cucumber, apple and melon, 103

garden minestra, 212
Hamburg parsley, 231
leek and avocado vichyssoise, 234
lentil, root vegetable and game broth, 217
lettuce and red pepper summer gazpacho, 117
melon and basil, 74
nettle and Welsh onion, 59
parsley, 156–7
pea pod, 126
potato soup with Swiss chard, 214
prawn pepper and coconut gazpacho, 206
sorrel and yoghurt, 33
summer pea and purslane, 125
tomato and mussel chowder, 147
tomato, leek and potato, 132
tourin blanchi à l'ail et à l'oseille, 109
Tuscan bean soup with cabbage, 52
sowing seeds, 25–6
spinach, 21, 135–6, 137
   braised young turnips with, 148–9
   purées, 140
   salads, 138, 139–40
   spinach and strawberry salad, 138
   spinach au jus, 140
   spinach, chickpeas and pasta, 141
   spinach parcels, 138
spinach beet, 21, 26, 49–50
   pot-roasted veal with, 50–1
spring greens, 26, 51–2
   crispy fried, 53–4
   risotto, 54–5
   spring green and potato cake, 53
   spring green and walnut sauce for pasta, 54
   Tuscan bean soup with cabbage, 52
spring onions: mustard and spring onion vinaigrette, 102
   nettle and Welsh onion soup, 59
steaming, 22
stir-frying, 23–4
strawberries: spinach and strawberry salad, 138
   vinaigrette, 102
sugar loaf chicory, 184–5
sugar snap peas, 127–8
summer cannelloni, 120
swedes, 216–17
   lentil, root vegetable and game broth, 217
   with sesame seeds and soy, 217–18
   swede pot, 218
   swede shoots, 217
sweetcorn, 18
   ginger, pepper and sweetcorn stir-fry, 208
Swiss chard, 21, 49, 210–11
   chard, pork and sorrel terrine, 215
   garden minestra, 212
   midribs persillade, 213–14
   potato soup with, 214
   Swiss chard and black olive tart, 213
   Swiss chard and mint filo pastry, 214
   Swiss chard and parmesan crumble, 213
   Swiss chard and rice torta, 215
   Swiss chard, olive oil and sun-dried tomatoes, 216

tarragon, 27, 80
   barbecued salmon steaks with, 81
   gooseberry and tarragon sauce, 82
   lentils with mint and, 82
   salmon with red wine and, 81
   tarragon cocottes, 81
tart, Swiss chard and black olive, 213
   tea, Moroccan mint, 32
terrine: chard, pork and sorrel, 215

thyme, 27, 155, 161–2
  braised shin of beef, 162–3
  laban with, 162
tomatoes, 141–3
  basil, tomato and anchovy relish, 73
  bruschetta, 147–8
  chicken with fennel and, 193
  courgettes, tarragon and, 97
  fennel, braised with, 191
  green tomato salad, 144
  lamb, chickpeas, spinach beet and tomato stew, 146–7
  potato, tomato and mint gratin, 132–3
  salads, 144
  sauces, 145–6, 177
  skinning, 144
  Swiss chard, olive oil and sun-dried tomatoes, 216
  tomato and cucumber salad, 102
  tomato and mussel chowder, 147
  tomato and yoghurt drink, 145
  tomato, beetroot and tarragon salad, 166
  tomato juice, 144–5
  tomato, leek and potato soup, 132
tourin blanchi à l'ail et à l'oseille, 109
trout baked with vermouth and cream, 30
turkey and chicory salad, 188
turnips, 148
  braised with spinach, 148–9
  roast summer turnips, 149
  turnip and dill salad, 149
Tuscan bean soup with cabbage, 52

veal: braised with garlic, almonds and salsify, 243–4
  pot-roasted, 50–1
vinaigrettes: mustard and spring onion, 102
  mint, 97
  strawberry, 102
vine leaves, 149–50
  grilled goat's cheese in, 152
  Hannah Glasse's fritters, 151–2
  stuffed, 150–1
vitamin C, 20

walnut and spring green sauce, 54
water, cooking methods, 22
weeding, 17, 69–70
Witloof chicory, 184
woks, 24

yoghurt: dressing, 140
  laban with thyme, 162
  sorrel and yoghurt soup, 33
  tomato and yoghurt drink, 145